This study is dedicated to the memory of William H. Gleysteen, Jr.

To whom we all owe a debt.

Table of Contents

Foreword

It is with great pleasure that I present *Rein In at the Brink of the Precipice*, the latest monograph in the Henry L. Stimson Center's regional security series. This study was undertaken out of concern that, in recent decades, too many U.S. leaders have been either inattentive to—or unaware of—the commitments undertaken with the People's Republic of China regarding Taiwan, and have therefore made occasionally unwise decisions. This study provides rich insight into the diplomacy and domestic deliberations that shaped a dramatic phase of U.S.-China relations. The story is an unusually dramatic case of changing geopolitical imperatives and, at the same time, a potent reminder of the enduring importance of notions of sovereignty and identity in Asia, which remain strong despite changing views elsewhere in an age of increasing globalization.

Senior Associate Alan D. Romberg, a former senior State Department official, was a participant in and an observer of many of these events, and draws on his extensive knowledge and direct access to many of the other players in weaving this fascinating tale. This study recounts how normalization was delayed and nearly derailed before a delicate balance was reached with Beijing over the Taiwan issue. It also serves as a sober warning to current and future policymakers that history does matter and that new presidents cannot make Taiwan policy in a vacuum. Too much is resting on the peaceful evolution of U.S.-China relations: the stability of China, the well-being of the people of Taiwan, as well as broader U.S. interests in East Asia.

The Stimson Center is committed to innovative thinking on ways to achieve regional stability and reduce security threats to the United States. This study, with generous support from the Smith Richardson Foundation, will be a lasting contribution to improving understanding of—and policy toward—China, and hopefully will help readers in the PRC, Taiwan and elsewhere gain greater appreciation of the complex and occasionally confounding ways the U.S. makes policy.

Ellen Laipson
President and CEO
The Henry L. Stimson Center

Acknowledgements

Countless debts of gratitude have accrued over the many months of research that have culminated in this study. I was tremendously fortunate to have friends, colleagues and so many others who were willing to share liberally of their time, recollections, experience and insight.

In particular, a number of former (and current) government officials involved in U.S. China policy over the years since Nixon were willing to dig deep into their memories and share their knowledge. Some are still serving in relevant government positions and probably should not be named. Among those who can be, I am especially grateful to Richard V. Allen, Donald M. Anderson, Samuel R. Berger, David Dean, Chas. W. Freeman, Jr., Alexander M. Haig, Scott S. Hallford, Herbert J. Hansell, Charles Hill, James R. Lilley, Winston Lord, Mark E. Mohr, Davis R. Robinson, William F. Rope, Stanley O. Roth, J. Stapleton Roy, Robert L. Suettinger, Roger W. Sullivan and Harry E. T. Thayer, who responded to various persistent inquiries with good humor and wisdom. Special appreciation goes to Steven M. Goldstein, who slogged through two versions of this and provided extensive invaluable comments.

As will be obvious from a quick glance through the study, much of the archival content would not have been possible without the tenacity of the National Security Archive and especially Dr. William Burr and his colleagues. Thanks are also due to Patrick Tyler, James Mann, the staff of the National Archive and Records Administration in College Park, Maryland, the historians and staff of the Richard Nixon Library & Birthplace and the Jimmy Carter Library, and the staff of the FOIA office at the State Department—all of whom generously shared documents. Appreciation, too, goes to K. Lorraine Graham and Zhen Sun, and especially to Kim Dorazio, all of whom helped with numerous research tasks. Most of all, deep thanks are owed to Adam J. Hantman, without whose able, creative and multifaceted partnership, completion of this project would simply not have been possible.

Finally, my appreciation goes both to the Smith Richardson Foundation and the leadership of the Henry L. Stimson Center, for whose support and patience I am most grateful.

The responsibility for what I have done with all that this army of supporters has provided is, of course, mine alone.

Explanatory Note:
"Rein In at the Brink of the Precipice"

Following his brilliant flanking move in the Inchon Landing of mid-September 1950 and the recapture of Seoul ten days later, General Douglas MacArthur drove the North Korean army back across the 38th Parallel, captured Pyongyang in late October, and continued to press the UN counterattack up toward the Yalu River and the border with the People's Republic of China (PRC). China sought to signal to the United States that further advances toward China would precipitate its intervention. It did so in part by sending a message to Washington through a diplomatic intermediary to "rein in at the brink of the precipice." The United States ignored the warning and, on November 25th, China entered the fray in massive numbers, greatly altering the course of the conflict and of history.

Ever since then, China watchers have carefully scoured PRC statements at times of crisis in an effort to detect similarly serious warnings. During the Vietnam War, in particular, while the United States was careful not to take actions that would seem to threaten the existence of the Democratic Republic of Vietnam (DRV)—and thus draw China into the conflict—Washington kept a weather eye on Chinese pronouncements. China made clear not just through words but through its military support to Hanoi, including the stationing of People's Liberation Army forces in North Vietnam, that PRC national security interests were at stake. But Beijing apparently credited the limits that the U.S. was observing in its military operations against the DRV; the admonition to "rein in at the brink of the precipice" did not reappear.

Over the past decade or so, the warning has made a comeback, largely in connection with what Beijing sees as pro-independence activities in either Taiwan or Tibet, and alleged U.S. support for them. Although not conveying the same sense of urgency as in the Korean War, its core message remains clear: sovereignty is a fundamental issue for the PRC and its violation could trigger the severest consequences.

— 1 —

Introduction

As the Chinese frequently say, the Taiwan question is the most important and sensitive issue in relations between the United States and the People's Republic of China (PRC). At times, Chairman Mao Zedong would brush it aside almost dismissively: "The small issue is Taiwan, the big issue is the world."[1] This reflected both the difficulty of resolving the Taiwan issue and the overriding importance of the strategic factors that drove the U.S. and the PRC together, particularly common concern with Soviet expansionism. But Mao's seeming nonchalance was not a serious reflection of the Taiwan issue's paramount place on the list of obstacles to the establishment of full diplomatic—"normalized"—relations. Nor did it reflect the important impact that disputes over the Taiwan question have had on overall U.S.-PRC relations over the years. While the United States would have preferred to set the Taiwan question aside—and to some extent that is what normalization was all about—achieving that was a challenge of extreme complexity for the United States, just as it was for China.

U.S. policy toward Taiwan has been a controversial issue for American policy—and American politics—since even before Chiang Kai-shek's forces took control of the island after World War II and the Nationalists—the Republic of China (ROC)—moved the government there in the wake of their defeat by the Communists. Taiwan had been ceded to Japan by China in 1895 under the terms of the Treaty of Shimonoseki, following Japan's victory in the Sino-Japanese War that year. Along with British Prime Minister Winston Churchill, Presidents Franklin D. Roosevelt—in the Cairo Declaration of December 1, 1943—and Harry S. Truman—in the Potsdam Proclamation of July 26, 1945—had committed to returning Taiwan to China at the conclusion of World War II. But neither Washington nor London viewed the official Japanese surrender on September 2, 1945 or the surrender of Japanese forces on Taiwan on October 25, 1945 as a "formal" action effecting such a

---

[1] Memorandum of Conversation, October 21, 1975, cited in William Burr, ed., *The Kissinger Transcripts* (New York: The New Press, 1998), p. 391.

transfer of sovereignty.[2]   That, the Allies maintained, had to await the conclusion of a formal peace settlement with Japan.

Although President Truman did not abandon this view of the legal situation, he set it aside after the establishment of the People's Republic of China on October 1, 1949, when it appeared that the Communists were destined for victory over the island within a year.   On January 5, 1950, he issued a statement saying that:

> The United States Government will not pursue a course which will lead to involvement in the civil conflict in China. Similarly, the United States Government will not provide military aid or advice to Chinese forces on Formosa.[3]

Less than six months later, however, with the start of the Korean War, Truman reversed course:

> The attack upon Korea makes it plain beyond all doubt that Communism has passed beyond the use of subversion to conquer independent nations and will now use armed invasion and war…In these circumstances the occupation of Formosa by Communist forces would be a direct threat to the security of the Pacific area and to United States forces performing their lawful and necessary functions in that area.

Ordering the Seventh Fleet to prevent any attack on—or from—Taiwan, Truman set new conditions for settling the island's status:

---

[2] Robert I. Starr, Memorandum to Charles T. Sylvester, "Legal Status of Taiwan," July 13, 1971, p. 2, declassified and released by the State Department pursuant to the Freedom of Information Act. Starr, the State Department's Legal Adviser wrote: "Pursuant to Japanese Imperial General Headquarters General Order No. 1, issued at the direction of the Supreme Commander for the Allied Powers (SCAP), Japanese commanders in Formosa surrendered to Generalissimo Chiang Kai-shek 'acting on behalf of the United States, the Republic of China, the United Kingdom and the British Empire, and the Union of Soviet Socialist Republics.'"

[3] "President Truman's Statement on U.S. Policy Respecting the Status of Formosa (Taiwan), January 5, 1950," published in Hungdah Chiu, ed., *China and the Question of Taiwan* (New York: Praeger Publishers, 1973), p. 221.

The determination of the future status of Formosa must await the restoration of security in the Pacific, a peace settlement with Japan, or consideration by the United Nations.[4]

But when Japan signed the San Francisco Peace Treaty with the Allies in September 1951, while the U.S. and UK agreed that Taiwan should not be turned over to the PRC, they differed over whether the Nationalist regime should take sovereign control as "China."[5] Moreover, not only did the United States want to avoid creating an irredentist conflict with Beijing, if possible, but Washington also had deep concerns over the nature—even the legitimacy—of Nationalist rule on the island. Thus, despite Truman's identification of a peace agreement with Japan as one vehicle for settling the issue, the Allies adopted the common position that the status of Taiwan had not yet been—indeed, should not yet be—determined. As a result, while under the treaty Japan ceded sovereignty over the island, Tokyo did not specify to whom it ceded it. Tokyo followed the same pattern in the separate peace treaty it signed with the Republic of China in April 1952.

In the 1950s, 1960s and even the 1970s, Taipei and Beijing equally rejected this position, both insisting that there was only "one China" and that Taiwan was part of it, having been "returned" to China in 1945.[6] Their "only" difference was over which of them was the legitimate government of that China.

Even in these early years, while not representing the mainstream by any means, a small but determined group of Taiwan independence advocates was active in Japan and the United States, and at times they seized on the American position on Taiwan's "undetermined" status as substantiating their cause. In fact, however, wherever the American heart may have been on this subject, its head, with rare exception, has been firmly rooted in avoiding entanglement in the substance of any eventual cross-Strait arrangement, insisting instead only on a peaceful process.

---

[4] "Statement Issued by the President," June 27, 1950, in Department of State, *Foreign Relations of the United States, 1950, Volume VII* (Washington, DC: Government Printing Office, 1976), pp. 202-203.

[5] The UK had recognized the PRC in January 1950; the U.S. continued to recognize the ROC.

[6] An interesting historical footnote is that neither the Nationalists nor the Communists pressed their claim that Taiwan was part of China until the early 1940s.

And even though Beijing rejected the U.S. policy in many other respects, some analysts judged that it welcomed continued U.S. support of "one China." As the "Conlon Report" of 1959 put it:

> The Chinese Communists are certainly not interested in bidding for recognition by accepting...the 'two Chinas' solution [in the UN]. Indeed, it might be said...that the Communists prefer the present American policy because it does not alter a basic situation which they hope eventually to manipulate—namely, the identification of Taiwan as a part of China. Communist China is confident that within a decade her power and influence will demand acknowledgement, and that the basic issues involving China can then be settled on her terms, probably without war. Consequently, she sees no reason to make any basic concessions involving her national interests at this time.[7]

Nonetheless, Beijing has long suspected U.S. complicity with the Taiwan Independence Movement, and it became enough of an issue that the PRC's mantra in dealing with the United States on Taiwan came to encompass the unacceptability not only of "one China, two governments" or "two Chinas," but also of "one China, one Taiwan," an "independent Taiwan," and "the status of Taiwan remains to be determined."

Over time, while still formally holding that Taiwan's status was "undetermined," the U.S. position increasingly focused on the need, not for an international event as Truman had prescribed, but for some sort of peaceful resolution to be worked out by the two sides of the Strait. Because of the life-and-death competition between Beijing and Taipei, this policy was never destined for easy success, but it was not nearly as complicated early on as it has become in the years since.

As Taiwan's political system has opened up since the late 1980s, and advocacy of Taiwan self-determination or even outright independence has become an increasingly accepted position within the ambit of debate on the island, the thin fiction of common dedication by "all Chinese on

---

[7] Conlon Associates, Ltd., *United States Foreign Policy: Asia*, a study prepared at the request of the Senate Committee on Foreign Relations (Washington, DC: Government Printing Office, 1959). One might note that it was almost exactly a decade later that U.S. Ambassador to Poland, Walter Stoessel, chased after a Chinese diplomat following a Yugoslav fashion show with the message that President Nixon wanted to resume diplomatic dialogue.

either side of the Taiwan Strait"[8] to "one China" has become less and less credible to Americans. The importance of workable—and, if possible, cooperative—relations with the PRC, and of avoiding confrontation over Taiwan, is broadly accepted by Americans. But solicitousness to Beijing's views on Taiwan issues—especially in a post-Tiananmen, post-Cold War world—has become harder and harder to justify. Moreover, those who worry about the rise of an economically—and eventually militarily—strong China as a challenge to U.S. power and influence in the region have been quite content to follow policies that preserve Taiwan's separate status from the Mainland, even while avoiding the PRC's "redline" of supporting Taiwan independence.

Where the U.S. has occasionally gotten into trouble is in not truly understanding—or at least not respecting—the fundamental nature of the PRC's position on Taiwan's place within "China" and the price Beijing is willing to pay to prevent unacceptable outcomes. Even Henry Kissinger reportedly had doubts about the intensity of Beijing's attitude toward this question as late as fall 1971—months after his secret trip in July—when he questioned whether the PRC really would insist on delaying normalization until the United States broke relations with Taiwan.[9]

And since then, American leaders have also occasionally allowed their empathy for the people of Taiwan and their enmity toward PRC policies and practices—as well as their sensitivity to U.S. domestic politics—to take the United States along paths that were harmful, even dangerous, to American national interests. This has sometimes resulted in U.S. policy toward Taiwan sliding out of joint with broader China policy, damaging both. At times this has largely been the result of overwhelming, if narrowly focused, domestic political or economic

---

[8] Language used by the U.S. side in the Shanghai Communiqué of February 27, 1972, excerpts from which can be found in the appendix; the full text is in Department of State, *United States Foreign Policy 1972: A Report of the Secretary of State* (Washington, DC: Government Printing Office, 1973), p. 640.

[9] Oral History of John S. Service, excerpted in Nancy Bernkopf Tucker, ed., *China Confidential: American Diplomats and Sino-American Relations, 1945-1996* (New York: Columbia University Press, 2001), p. 254. As we shall see, Kissinger, seeking to lock in the U.S.-PRC relationship while Mao and Zhou could still give it their imprimatur, continued to work with the thought that, if only the U.S. and PRC could find the right formula, Beijing would establish diplomatic relations with Washington even while the United States still had official ties to Taipei.

interests. But as often as not, it has been due to a failure to perceive the core political motivations of both sides of the Strait and to properly assess how they meshed with America's own interests—or did not.

It is important to recall that the cross-Strait competition started as a feature of the unfinished Chinese civil war. To Beijing it is, in the most basic sense, still that. But to the authorities in Taiwan, who no longer harbor ambition to "retake" the Mainland, and to Taiwan's people, most of whom never did, it is an issue of managing the future so as to maximize their control over their own lives. To the extent possible, this includes establishing and maintaining a separate national and international identity. Except for the small number of people in Taiwan at either extreme—favoring either near-term political reunification or outright independence "no matter what"—the debate is largely over the degree to which Taiwan can tolerate any association with the Mainland and with the concept of "one China." It is hard to find anyone who wants to come under Beijing's sovereign control, but there is a substantial body of opinion within Taiwan on either side of the debate about whether it is acceptable to adhere to a loosely defined "principle" of "one China."

These differences—and the extreme gap between the PRC's insistence on an undivided sovereignty and Taiwan's insistence on the opposite—frame the dilemma for American policy.

THE CORE ISSUE: SOVEREIGNTY AND THE "ONE CHINA PRINCIPLE"

Despite occasional spikes of impatience on Beijing's part, the core of the Taiwan issue has centered not on realizing actual reunification, but rather on the question of establishing sovereignty. In Beijing's view, reunification is something to be handled as an "internal" matter, on a timetable and via methods to be determined by them alone. As the PRC sees it, sovereignty, however, is a matter of fundamental principle— observed generally in the breach by the United States and an unresolved question underlying American policies that obstruct peaceful reunification. If the U.S. would only get the sovereignty issue right, all else would follow as a matter of natural course.

As already noted, in formal terms, both the PRC and the ROC claim sovereignty over the entire territory of "China."[10] However, in 1991, the

---

[10] Although there have been occasional adjustments in both places that have not entirely meshed—for example, the PRC early on recognized the independence

ROC adjusted its constitution and, while it never abandoned its claim to "all of China," in effect it recognized the "legitimacy" of PRC rule over the Mainland, limiting the area covered by ROC rule to Taiwan and the Pescadores (Penghus), as well as Jinmen (Quemoy) and Matsu—the so-called "offshore islands" that are within sight of the Mainland. The PRC has made no such "adjustment," and, though recognizing that it currently has no effective jurisdiction over "local" affairs within Taiwan, Beijing still claims sovereignty over the island and insists that the PRC is the representative in the international community of "the entire Chinese people"—including those in Taiwan.

So, from the beginning of the Sino-American political minuet on normalization, the core issue for Beijing has been its claim that Taiwan "belongs" to China. By the time the interaction began in earnest, the United States had backed away from any direct involvement in the legal niceties—and complexities—of determining Taiwan's status. And in fact, many Americans did not care whether there *was* a settlement at all. Some favored keeping Taiwan separate in perpetuity, among other reasons because they believed that in PRC hands it would be a strategic liability for the United States. Others felt that any sort of unification between "Free China" and "Communist China" would be unthinkable for both political and moral reasons. Still others thought that reunification was an historical inevitability, and while the terms were important, Taiwan's future well-being depended on its intimate association with the Mainland. Those divided attitudes continue until today.

But official U.S. policy, as it has evolved, takes the position that this is not "our issue." "Our issue"—and, as often expressed, the U.S. "abiding interest"—is the maintenance of peace and stability in the Taiwan Strait. Clearly, "interest" here means strategic national interest, not idle curiosity, and the U.S. stance not only has implications for contacts with Taiwan, arms sales to the island, and formal public positions, but it leaves open the possibility of direct American involvement in the event of a cross-Strait military confrontation. Moreover, all of these actions implicitly challenge PRC claims to sovereignty and reveal the limits on the degree to which the United States can subscribe to those claims. As we shall see, therefore, one

---

of Mongolia (the former "Mongolian People's Republic" or "Outer Mongolia"), whereas, at least until recently, Taipei did not—the territory claimed "in principle" is essentially the same.

persistent conundrum for U.S. policy makers has been how to preserve a legal basis for American involvement in the island's security while, at the same time, not explicitly contradicting the PRC over the question of sovereignty.

This dilemma was summed up well in a memorandum from the State Department Legal Adviser's office to the East Asia Bureau on the eve of the normalization effort, written, ironically, just after Kissinger's secret trip to Beijing in July 1971 but before it had been publicly announced:

> The future relationship of Taiwan to mainland China and the resolution of disputes dividing the governments in Taipei and Peking involve issues that the United States cannot resolve. We have made clear that our primary concern is that these issues should be resolved by peaceful means, without resort to the use of force. Until such a resolution is achieved we may continue to deal respectively with the Government of the People's Republic of China and the Government of the Republic of China on matters affecting our mutual interests, accepting the practical situation as we find it.[11]

Beijing, of course, not only rejected the long-standing U.S. position on the island's "undetermined" status, but it rejected, and still rejects, the idea that the United States has any right to *have* a role in—or even a view on—that question. The PRC believes that President Truman's 1950 intervention order to the Seventh Fleet, and the later creation of a U.S. military alliance with Taipei, were solely responsible for blocking reunification, and that the United States thus owes China a debt.

DEFINING THE TAIWAN ISSUE

When Henry Kissinger arrived in Beijing on his secret mission in July 1971, he was taken off guard by his hosts' focus on gaining U.S. agreement to establish full diplomatic relations—"normalization" in the lexicon of U.S.-PRC diplomacy—and not simply on removing U.S. forces from Taiwan and the Taiwan Strait. In one sense, the American National Security Adviser had a right to be surprised. All of the prior communications from the Chinese leadership about his visit had concentrated on the issue of the U.S. military presence, the most obvious symbol of U.S. "interference" in China's unfinished civil war. An oral message from Beijing in December 1970, for example, stated:

---

[11] Starr, "Legal Status of Taiwan," p. 11.

Taiwan and the Straits of Taiwan are an inalienable part of China which have now been occupied by foreign troops of the United States for the last fifteen years. Negotiations and talks have been going on with no results whatsoever. *In order to discuss this subject of the vacation of Chinese territories called Taiwan*, a special envoy of President Nixon's will be most welcome in Peking.[12]

But it was not just the troops, it was the larger dimensions of the Taiwan issue that had been the principal point of contention since the mid-1950s and the key focus of Chinese statements at ambassadorial talks in Warsaw during January and February 1970. Indeed, Kissinger's opening presentation in Beijing showed a recognition of the need to get past this hurdle in his early, explicit rejection of a "two Chinas" or "one China, one Taiwan" policy.

Especially in light of the strategic urgency that impelled both sides away from two decades of enmity and toward cooperation, it was not surprising that the Chinese wanted to transform the entire relationship. But what caught the American envoy unawares was Beijing's insistence that making common cause against the Soviet Union was not enough. To China, what was also required was resolution of the underlying issue of principle that had divided the two countries since 1949: sovereignty over Taiwan.

---

[12] Oral message from Zhou Enlai—also on behalf of Mao Zedong and Lin Biao—conveyed verbatim to Henry Kissinger in Washington on December 9, 1970 by Pakistan Ambassador Agha Hilaly; emphasis added. The full message is found in Henry Kissinger, Memorandum for the President, "Chinese Communist Initiative," c. December 10, 1970, in William Burr, ed., *The Beijing-Washington Back-Channel and Henry Kissinger's Secret Trip to China: September 1970-July 1971*, National Security Archive Electronic Briefing Book No. 66, online at http://www.gwu.edu/~nsarchiv/NSAEBB/NSAEBB66/ (hereafter *The Beijing-Washington Back-Channel*). In a practically identical communication delivered through the Romanians in early January 1971, Zhou declared: "There is only one outstanding issue between us—the U.S. occupation of Taiwan. The PRC has attempted to negotiate on this issue in good faith for 15 years. If the U.S. has a desire to settle the issue and a proposal for its solution, the PRC will be prepared to receive a U.S. special envoy in Peking." Zhou went on to say that President Nixon would also be welcome; see Henry Kissinger, Memorandum for the President, "Conversation with Ambassador Bogdan, Map Room, January 11, 1971," January 12, 1971, in Burr, ed., *The Beijing-Washington Back-Channel*.

As this study will show, the history of the thirty-plus years ever since Kissinger's first trip is replete with examples of ploy and counter-ploy, manipulation and counter-manipulation—sometimes nuanced, sometimes heavy-handed—as both sides worked to move the Taiwan issue in directions that suited their priorities. The PRC sought to maneuver Washington into at least acknowledging—and hopefully endorsing—Beijing's claim to the island; the United States sought to avoid an explicit endorsement while extracting from the PRC a commitment to resolve cross-Strait issues only through peaceful means. That history is also, unsurprisingly, replete with misunderstandings, miscalculations and cross-purposes, sometimes leading to crossed swords.

Even today, when U.S.-PRC relations are touted as "the best ever"—or at least the best since the Tiananmen tragedy of 1989, the "Taiwan question" sits as a potential time bomb that could have grave consequences not just for that relationship and for the twenty-three million people of Taiwan, but also for the future strategic and economic prospects of the PRC, the United States, Japan and the entire East Asian region. Indeed, the reverberations would be felt around the world as the global political and economic fallout overwhelmed even the disastrous, but geographically more concentrated, military consequences.

Because the problems and relationships involved are not only fascinating but also profoundly consequential for American national interests and the national interests and lives of countless millions of people, this writer, like many others, has devoted a great deal of his professional life to "the Taiwan question." I have approached these matters with a certainty about the critical importance of positive and productive U.S.-PRC relations, a belief in the centrality of maintaining peace and stability in the Pacific, and a strong sense of empathy for the people in Taiwan and their right to live under a system of their own choosing—along with a firm conviction about U.S. responsibility to help assure all of that. Managing it is a tall order, but I believe it is achievable with creativity and common sense on the part of those most centrally concerned, and with a focus on basic principles and strategic interests rather than on tactics and rigid adherence to form.

For better or for worse, the policy of the United States will be a crucial determinant in whether movement is in a positive direction or down a path fraught with danger. And that is the focus of this study.

An examination of the record suggests that senior American leaders have often conveyed mixed signals about U.S. policy toward Taiwan, voicing ideas or taking concrete steps in the service of immediate needs without adequately considering the broader, longer-term implications. In some cases, a lack of precision has been purposeful. In October 1971, for example, when negotiating language about Taiwan for the communiqué to be issued at the conclusion of President Richard M. Nixon's historic trip to China four months later, Kissinger was direct with PRC Premier Zhou Enlai:

> The trouble is that we disagree, not that we don't understand each other. We understand each other very well. The Prime Minister seeks clarity, and I am trying to achieve ambiguity.[13]

So, ambiguity has its obvious and important uses, at least when you know what you are being ambiguous about, and why. But over the years since the Nixon opening, a lack of precision in American thinking, speaking, and acting on Taiwan issues has often been due not to purposeful deliberation, but to inattention to the meaning of words, to the relevant history, and to the seriousness of the issues to both Taiwan and the PRC. Domestic opinion, of course, has been an important factor shaping U.S. policy, where "selling out" an old ally in Taipei was unacceptable across the American political spectrum just as, in Mainland China, "losing Taiwan" could have been—and still could be—politically fatal. Even those Americans who sought in the late 1950s and early 1960s to promote a sensible policy of dealing with the PRC did so on the premise that the United States would not abandon Taiwan to Beijing's whims, not simply because of political expediency but because it would have been morally reprehensible and, as an example of American inconstancy, strategically unwise.[14]

---

[13] Memorandum of Conversation, October 26, 1971 (10:12 am–11:00 am), p. 10, in William Burr, ed., *Negotiating U.S.-Chinese Rapprochement: New American and Chinese Documentation Leading Up to Nixon's 1972 Trip*, National Security Archive Electronic Briefing Book No. 70, online at http://www.gwu.edu/~nsarchiv/NSAEBB/NSAEBB70/ (hereafter *Negotiating U.S.-Chinese Rapprochement*). Zhou responded: "But the Chinese people will be dissatisfied with something that is ambiguous"; Kissinger cautioned: "And we have got trouble if it is too clear."

[14] See, for instance, the testimony of A. Doak Barnett before the U.S. House Committee on Foreign Affairs in *United States Policy Toward Asia: Hearings Before the Subcommittee on the Far East and the Pacific*, 89th Cong., 2nd sess., 26 January 1966, pp. 63-64.

And although the rationale and nature of U.S. involvement in Taiwan have evolved over the years, the fact remains that, except for a brief period in early 1950—when, as we have already noted, policymakers decided that contesting a near-term Communist victory over Taiwan was simply not worth a war with China—the maintenance of peace and stability in the Taiwan area and the prevention of forceful takeover of the island have been consistent goals of American policy ever since World War II. So, too, concern for the well-being of the people in Taiwan has remained an American priority. U.S. consideration in the late 1940s of "third options" involving neither acquiescence in a Communist takeover nor continued support for the Nationalist rule on the island reflected that concern, and it remains a key element of U.S. policy up until the present moment.

The U.S. support for—and commitment to—the government in Taipei has had its ups and downs, twists and turns, as the Chinese might say. When Generalissimo Chiang Kai-shek and the Nationalists imposed a repressive authoritarian regime on the island 1940s, many American were uncomfortable with the U.S. ties to that regime. Still, they offered it support as part of the fight against Communism.

But the United States was not satisfied to limit its role to "fighting Communism" and over time played a significant part in helping to bring Taiwan out of that dark period. The U.S. was the driving force in creating a benign international security environment and contributing large amounts of economic and technical assistance as well as political "advice" that were instrumental in promoting the remarkable prosperity and political evolution on the island in recent decades.

It did not take decades, however, to realize that treating the ROC government, sitting in Taipei with no realistic prospect of returning to the Mainland, as the legitimate government of all of China was ludicrous and inconsistent with American national interests. As already suggested, many Americans, including China specialists, would have been delighted to see the evolution of a "two Chinas" or "one China, one Taiwan" policy that reflected the reality of the situation, even while taking care not to oppose future reconciliation across the Strait.

However, since neither Taipei nor Beijing would countenance such an approach, each insisting there was but "one China" and that *it* was the legitimate government of that nation, this was not a feasible option.

Despite the evolution of politics in Taiwan toward outspoken separate identity, despite the fact that Taipei now claims effective jurisdiction only over Taiwan itself and related islands, and despite the reality that there is virtually unanimous support on the island for the position that "the Republic of China on Taiwan" is a sovereign, independent state politically unconnected to the People's Republic of China, *constitutionally* the Republic of China still adheres to the concept of a single China. Even the vast majority of people in Taiwan, who would, in this writer's opinion, instantly opt for "independence" if they did not fear the negative consequences, show themselves today as in the past to be extremely pragmatic about not provoking their brethren across the Strait. So preserving the "status quo" is their overwhelming preference for now. That said, the increasingly outspoken sense of separateness from the Mainland, and the sympathy it has evoked among Americans as well as the angst it has generated in Beijing, have vastly complicated the formulation and conduct of American policy.

Fundamental to the complexity is the fact that the PRC, while recognizing the obvious reality that China is not "unified," insists that even today, not just potentially in the future, there *is* only one China in the world, that Taiwan and the Mainland both belong to that one China, and that the sovereignty and territory of China are indivisible.[15] In establishing diplomatic relations with other countries over the years, Beijing has insisted that its partner somehow give a nod to this position and recognize the government of the PRC as the "sole legal government" of China. On this basis, Beijing asserts that in the international community it represents the entire Chinese people, including those on Taiwan.

In fact, while all countries that have established diplomatic relations with Beijing recognize the government of the PRC as the "sole legal government of China," many—and certainly all the major countries— have bobbed and weaved in stating their position on "one China" and Taiwan's role in it. Like the United States, they have said they "acknowledge" or "understand and respect" Beijing's claims. But they have generally avoided a direct endorsement.

Some aspects of U.S. Taiwan policy have been politically problematic because they run against the grain of American traditional values, and so it takes considerable time and thought to absorb why it is in the U.S. national interest to embrace the "one China" policy. A principal example is in the area of self-determination.

---

[15] See, for example, "Full Text of Jiang Zemin's Report at 16th Party Congress," November 8, 2002, sec. VIII, online at http://www.chinadaily.com.cn/ highlights/party16/news/1118full.htm

The international definition of "self-determination" has evolved over the years so that it no longer automatically equates to "independence."[16] But the basic concept that individuals should have the right to control their own lives retains great importance for Americans. For most, it is counter-intuitive to argue that the twenty-three million people living in a democracy and ruling themselves with great—indeed, increasing— success for over half a century cannot choose their own future. But the reality is that to support "Taiwan independence" would be to guarantee perpetual crisis, and perhaps conflict, with the People's Republic of China, in which all would be losers, most especially the people in Taiwan. And the impact on U.S.-PRC relations would be fundamentally contrary to U.S. national interests.

This is discussed in greater detail later. But the point here is simply to illustrate not just the complexity of these issues but their serious consequences. Indeed, it is my contention that the Taiwan question is the only issue in the world today that could realistically lead to war between two major powers. So, this is serious stuff, and those making policy had better know what they are doing.

LEARNING FROM THE PAST

This study seeks to illuminate the complex and interrelated set of issues involved in U.S. relations with the PRC over the Taiwan question, to point out how they have evolved and how they have (or have not) been addressed over the years, with what expectations—and with what results. It tries to point to how a combination of a failure to adhere to the basic principles of normalization and a lack of real understanding of some of those principles have sometimes led to serious crises in U.S.-PRC relations that have threatened not only the overall strategic environment in East Asia but Taiwan's security. Beijing and Taipei both bear heavy responsibility for those events, as well, and that will be discussed. But the focus here is on American interests and American policy.

Any U.S. president has the right to change policy. But he has a responsibility to do so with a full appreciation of the implications of what he is doing. For that, he needs to know what has gone before. A basic aim of this study is to provide some help in understanding these issues so that future leaders can make policy toward Taiwan from a more informed base of knowledge, in particular with an understanding of the

---

[16] See, for example, Ralph Gustav Steinhardt. *International Law and Self-Determination* (Washington, DC: Atlantic Council of the United States, 1994).

relationship of Taiwan policy to overall China policy and the difference between "pushing the envelope" and "crossing redlines."

This study does not seek to be comprehensive, detailing all domestic and international political influences, as crucial as they were in the course of normalizing U.S.-PRC relations—and since. That larger story been told, and told well.[17] Here we focus on the single issue that not only was but remains the most difficult in Sino-American relations: Taiwan and the question of sovereignty. In approaching that issue, we

---

[17] For a sampling of some of the relatively recent scholarly, documentary and reportorial works, see: Robert Suettinger, *Beyond Tiananmen: The Politics of U.S.-China Relations, 1989-2000* (Washington, DC: Brookings Institution Press, 2003); David M. Lampton, *Same Bed, Different Dreams* (Berkeley: University of California Press, 2001); Patrick Tyler, *A Great Wall* (New York: PublicAffairs, 1999); Robert S. Ross, *Negotiating Cooperation: The United States and China, 1969-1989* (Stanford: Stanford University Press, 1995); James Mann, *About Face: A History of America's Curious Relationship With China From Nixon to Clinton* (New York: Alfred A. Knopf, 1999); Harry Harding, *A Fragile Relationship: The United States and China Since 1972* (Washington, DC: The Brookings Institution, 1992); and John Garver, *Face Off: China, the United States and Taiwan's Democratization* (Seattle: University of Washington Press, 1997). A rich canon of memoirs by senior U.S. policymakers also provides a good perspective on the story from a more personal angle; see, for example: Richard Nixon, *RN: The Memoirs of Richard Nixon* (New York: Grosset & Dunlap, 1978); Richard Nixon, *In the Arena* (New York: Simon and Schuster, 1990); Henry Kissinger, *White House Years* (Boston: Little, Brown & Company, 1979); Henry Kissinger, *Years of Upheaval* (Boston: Little, Brown & Company, 1982); Henry Kissinger, *Diplomacy* (New York: Simon and Schuster, 1994); Henry Kissinger, *Years of Renewal* (New York: Simon and Schuster, 1999); John Holdridge, *Crossing the Divide: An Insider's Account of the Normalization of U.S.-China Relations* (Lanham, Maryland: Rowman and Littlefield, 1997); Jimmy Carter, *Keeping Faith: Memoirs of a President* (New York: Bantam Books, 1982); Cyrus Vance, *Hard Choices: Critical Years in America's Foreign Policy* (New York: Simon and Schuster, 1983); Zbigniew Brzezinski, *Power and Principle: Memoirs of the National Security Adviser, 1977-1981* (New York: Farrar, Straus, Giroux, 1983); George Shultz, *Turmoil and Triumph: My Years as Secretary of State* (New York: Charles Scribner's Sons, 1993); Alexander Haig, Jr., *Caveat: Realism, Reagan and Foreign Policy* (New York: Macmillan, 1984); Alexander Haig, Jr. with Charles McCarry, *Inner Circles: How America Changed the World* (New York: Warner Books, 1992); James Baker III with Thomas M. Defrank, *The Politics of Diplomacy* (New York: G.P. Putnam's Sons, 1995); George Bush and Brent Scowcroft, *A World Transformed* (New York: Vintage Books, 1998); and Warren Christopher, *Chances of a Lifetime* (New York: Scribner, 2001).

have drawn as much as possible on the actual negotiations or on first-hand accounts. We have done so in many cases by using extensive quotes from the record, letting the words of the original actors convey their positions in as direct and clear a manner as possible.

To say that the United States cannot control everything, and especially that it cannot control political developments on either side of the Strait, is an obvious understatement. And in writing from the perspective of American policy, as I have suggested, I do not by any means intend to absolve the central players in Beijing and Taipei of their fundamental responsibility to manage their relationship well. At heart, the future of peace and stability across the Taiwan Strait rests in their hands. But the United States can influence the policies and actions of both sides on even some of the most sensitive questions, and to dodge that reality would be irresponsible. The issue is not whether we can do so but how to do so in a way that best serves American national interests. It is in pursuit of answering that question that this study is written.

ACHIEVING NORMALIZATION

"There's no question that if the Korean War hadn't occurred, a war which we did not seek and you did not seek, Taiwan would probably today be part of the PRC. For reasons which are now worthless to recapitulate, a previous Administration linked the future of Korea to the future of Taiwan, partly because of U.S. domestic opinion at the time. Whatever the reason, a certain history has now developed which involves some principles of foreign policy for us."

—Henry Kissinger to Zhou Enlai, Beijing, July 1971

— 2 —

The Road to the Summit

"Mr. Sainteny said that he frequently saw the Communist Chinese Ambassador in Paris, Huang Chen. Dr. Kissinger said that we had tried to have conversations with the Chinese, but they seemed to get nowhere, even though we have no basic problems with the Chinese."

—Memorandum of a Kissinger conversation with Jean Sainteny
Paris, September 1970

A starting point for any examination of the role the Taiwan issue has played—and continues to play—in U.S.-PRC relations must be the actual bargain of normalization, fashioned over the course of nearly the entire decade of the 1970s. Without that foundation, one cannot understand the course of Sino-American relations since normalization in 1979, or hope to manage this relationship well in the future.

The history of Beijing-Washington ties over the past quarter-century contains many missteps, miscalculations and misunderstandings over Taiwan, most of relatively minor consequence, but some that have produced significant crises. To understand why these crises occurred, and to avoid similar episodes in the future, one must begin with the past and, in particular, with the benchmark of normalization itself.

EDGING TOWARD HIGH-LEVEL TALKS: DEFINING THE AGENDA

Whatever the strains and animosities in their own relationship as the 1960s drew to a close, the United States and China both viewed their respective relations with the Soviet Union as far more threatening. Each saw strategic benefit to be derived from making common cause, and sensed an opportunity to do so. Leaders on both sides believed their almost total estrangement was harmful and, although rectifying this situation would predictably arouse strong opposition from certain domestic political forces in both countries, they both determined that it was worth the effort. At one level, the result was a grand enterprise of earthshaking proportion; at another, it was a tedious, laborious, and frustrating slog through the minutiae of the preceding two decades of their mutual animosity. But it began, however tentatively, with purpose and hope on both sides.

Thus, a civil and constructive tone prevailed in the Warsaw talks[1] of early 1970 as, in these first formal rounds in over two years, each side was groping toward a new relationship based on common strategic purposes. Still, the Chinese and American representatives were talking at cross-purposes about their main topic, Taiwan. The American, U.S. Ambassador to Poland Walter Stoessel, asserted that, while the United States would maintain friendly relations with the government in Taipei and honor its commitment to assist in defending Taiwan and the Pescadores from attack, this did not represent "interference" in China's internal affairs and was "without prejudice to any future peaceful settlement" between the two sides.[2] Moreover, Taiwan was but one issue of a broader agenda that the United States and China should address.

To his Chinese counterpart, PRC Chargé d'Affaires Lei Yang, however, there was a deep "contradiction" in the U.S. position.[3] On the one hand, the United States said it was willing to discuss the "five principles of peaceful coexistence" (including non-interference in each other's internal affairs), yet, the U.S. intended to maintain "friendly" relations with, and continue to honor its "commitment" to, the "Chiang Kai-shek clique." Saying that the United States position was "without prejudice" to a settlement between the two sides was totally inconsistent with maintaining such relations and such a commitment, for it was precisely the U.S. role, especially its military role, which, in China's eyes, prevented a settlement. From Beijing's perspective, the "five principles," which applied to international relations, meant not that the

---

[1] Ambassadorial-level bilateral U.S.-PRC talks first convened in Geneva in 1955 and then moved to Warsaw in 1958, hence the term commonly applied: "Warsaw talks."

[2] Warsaw A-25, "Stoessel-Lei Talks: Report of 135th Meeting, January 20, 1970," January 24, 1970, document 00124 in National Security Archive, *China and the United States: From Hostility to Engagement, 1960-1998*, a collection of declassified China-related U.S. Government documents released under the Freedom of Information Act, available on-site at the National Security Archive, George Washington University, Washington, DC (hereafter *NSA*, followed directly by document number).

[3] Warsaw 376, "Sino-US Talks: February 20 Meeting," February 20, 1970, *NSA* 00140; Warsaw A-84, "Stoessel-Lei Talks: Report of 136th Meeting, February 20, 1970," February 21, 1970, *NSA* 00143.

Taiwan issue should be settled peacefully[4] but that the U.S. should not involve itself in this "internal" Chinese matter.

We now know Beijing had decided that no progress on Taiwan was possible at the ambassadorial level and that higher-level talks were necessary for progress. Deliberately foregoing any preconditions,[5] at the 136th—and, as it turned out, last—session of the Warsaw talks in February 1970, Lei Yang therefore proposed:

> If the U.S. Government wishes to send a representative of ministerial [i.e., cabinet] rank or a special envoy of the United States President to Peking for further exploration of questions of fundamental principle between China and the United States, the Chinese Government will be willing to receive him.[6]

In contrast to the American position that Taiwan was but one of a number of issues needing review, Beijing was intensely focused on that core issue. Indeed, dealing with this issue was the purpose of inviting a U.S. presidential envoy to Beijing.[7]

---

[4] As a former State Department China expert points out, a principal American goal at Warsaw from the beginning had been to obtain a PRC commitment not to use force against Taiwan (David Dean, interview by author).

[5] For an insight into the decision to eschew preconditions see Xiong Xianghui, "Prelude to the Opening of Sino-U.S. Relations: The Study of the International Situation by Four Chinese Marshals in 1969 and Their Suggestions," in *Zhonggong Dangshi Ziliao*, no. 42 (1992), translated in Chen Jian, ed., *Chinese Materials on the Sino-American Rapprochement (1969-1972)*, a compilation prepared for the George Washington University Cold War Group Conference on the Sino-American Opening and the Cold War, held February 8-9, 2002, p. 79 (hereafter *Chinese Materials*).

[6] Warsaw A-84, "Stoessel-Lei Talks: Report of 136th Meeting, February 20, 1970." It should be noted that this was not the first time China had proposed discussion of the Taiwan question at a higher level. In 1956, albeit in very different circumstances, Beijing had made a proposal for foreign minister talks; see Steven M. Goldstein, "Dialogue of the Deaf?: The Sino-American Ambassadorial Level Talks, 1955-1970," in Robert S. Ross and Jiang Changbin, eds., *Re-Examining the Cold War: U.S.-China Diplomacy, 1954-1973* (Cambridge: Harvard University Asia Center, 2001).

[7] See again, for example, Zhou Enlai's verbal message to Kissinger of December 9th, delivered by Ambassador Hilaly (p. 9).

Even though both sides had the previous month raised the possibility of elevating the level of the talks,[8] the U.S. objective in February was to "deflect" a proposal for a higher-level meeting until further progress was made at the ambassadorial level.[9] The U.S. did not reject the idea of higher-level talks, but a key American aim was to find a way to put Taiwan "on the back burner." If there was no progress at the ambassadorial level, and no sign that Beijing would agree to a formula that set the Taiwan issue aside, then the U.S. felt that a higher-level meeting was too risky in terms of U.S-Soviet relations, dealings with the ROC, and the fight to hold Taipei's seat in the United Nations, which was coming under increasing challenge.

As a result, when Lei tabled his proposal, Stoessel avoided a direct response. The plan to probe the prospects of further progress at Warsaw was aborted when China cancelled the next session, set for May 20, 1970, after the U.S. incursion into Cambodia. They were not to resume.

WRESTLING WITH TAIWAN POLICY

In preparing for the February session in Warsaw, the U.S. had noted internally that "[a]t some point in our current series of discussions…we may have to decide…Are we prepared to accept that Taiwan and the mainland are parts of 'one China'?"[10] The first attempt to address this question was made in a National Security Study Memorandum (NSSM) on U.S. China policy written in early 1971. NSSM-106 summed up much of Washington's thinking on Taiwan policy at the time:

> We are largely responsible for the very existence of the GRC [Government of the Republic of China]; we have a defense treaty commitment to it (though we would not stand in the way of a peaceful resolution of the "Taiwan problem"), and we have a degree of responsibility for the people of Taiwan. We therefore have a moral obligation as well as political, economic and

---

[8] Warsaw A-25, "Stoessel-Lei Talks: Report of 135th Meeting, January 20, 1970," p. 4.

[9] Marshall Green, Action Memorandum to Secretary of State, "Sino-U.S. Ambassadorial Talks on January 20, 1970," February 4, 1970, *NSA* 00127.

[10] "U.S. Strategy in Current Sino-U.S. Talks: Summary," undated (though drafted some time after the 135th meeting on January 20, 1970 in preparation for the 136th on February 20, 1970), *NSA* 00120.

military interests arising from our long association with the GRC.[11]

The NSSM observed that reductions of U.S. forces elsewhere in the region under the Nixon Doctrine without concomitant reductions in Taiwan "could well be regarded by Peking as an indication of US interest in keeping Taiwan permanently separate from the mainland, as a US base directed against the PRC."[12] And as, over the months of maneuver leading ultimately to Kissinger's July 1971 trip the U.S. indicated to Beijing that it would reduce its military presence in East Asia and the Pacific "as tensions in this region diminish,"[13] that was related by the White House directly to the issue of the U.S. troop presence in Taiwan. This formulation was eventually enshrined in the Shanghai Communiqué at the end of Nixon's visit.

Because of the centrality of the sovereignty issue, and the non-communication, miscommunication and simple disagreement over this issue—then and now—it is worth relating in somewhat fuller fashion the NSSM's view of the Taiwan issue and the question of sovereignty:

> For more than a decade Peking has maintained that there can be no significant improvement in Sino-US relations until the US ends its "occupation" of Taiwan. Peking has made clear that this means, at a minimum, removal of the US military presence from the Strait area and Taiwan. Although not explicitly demanded by the Chinese, it could also mean termination of our defense commitment to the GRC and perhaps even cessation of our support for the GRC internationally or breaking of US relations with Taipei. Beyond that, Peking probably seeks US acceptance, at least in principle, that Taiwan is an integral part of the PRC.

---

[11] "United States China Policy," first SRG [Senior Review Group] draft of National Security Study Memorandum 106, February 16, 1971, pp. 3-4, *NSA* 00202 (hereafter NSSM-106.)

[12] Ibid., p. 6.

[13] *Note verbale* passed to Zhou Enlai via Pakistan President Yahya Khan, the text of which is attached to Col. Richard T. Kennedy, Memorandum of Record, December 16, 1970, in Burr, ed., *The Beijing-Washington Back-Channel.* In passing this message to the Pakistan Ambassador, Kissinger indicated that it would not be difficult to comply with the Chinese request for withdrawal of American forces from Taiwan since only advisory and training missions were there.

For our part, we have taken the position since the Korean War that sovereignty over Taiwan is an unsettled question subject to future international solution. We have therefore avoided stating that we regard Taiwan as a part of China, while similarly avoiding statements implying separate sovereignty for the island. We recognize the GRC as legitimately occupying and exercising jurisdiction over Taiwan, with a provisional capital at Taipei. In practice, however, we have dealt with the GRC as the de facto government of the territory which it controls. For at least the past five years, we have avoided public statements recognizing the GRC as the legal government of all China, but we have also avoided challenging the GRC claim to that status.

Without departing from our position that sovereignty remains to be determined, we have tried to set aside the Taiwan issue by making clear to Peking that we would accept any peaceful resolution by the parties directly concerned, and that we will not interfere in such a settlement. Although not made explicit, this position implies that we would not oppose the peaceful incorporation of Taiwan into the mainland. However, we have also made clear to Peking that until a peaceful settlement is reached we intend to maintain our defense commitment to, and continue our diplomatic relations with, the GRC.

While Peking is not now prepared on this basis to discuss other issues standing in the way of an improvement of US-PRC relations, it did so in the late 1950's and may again in the future.[14]

On the issue of Taiwan's future status, the study made several points of note:

Whatever attitudes may be toward sovereignty over Taiwan, it seems clear that for the foreseeable future the vast majority of Taiwanese, as well as many mainlanders on Taiwan, would oppose any settlement placing Taiwan under PRC control. In addition, among influential, better-educated and politically concerned Taiwanese there is a strong sentiment in favor of eventual independence. Although there is no organized independence movement on Taiwan, such sentiment could

---

[14] NSSM-106, pp. 23-24.

become politically significant in the event actions either by the GRC or the US should appear to foreclose this possibility…

…[Peking] is apprehensive that the US seeks to separate Taiwan permanently from the mainland and ensure its long-term availability as a military base. Hence Peking may make any real improvement in our relations contingent on our willingness to acknowledge, at least in principle, that Taiwan is a part of China.[15]

In May 1971, another NSSM laid out a broad spectrum of options for carrying out China policy, ranging from some very modest initiatives to ones as far-reaching as offering some form of official U.S. presence in Beijing, an indication of U.S. willingness to regard Taiwan as part of China, and removal of U.S. forces from the Taiwan area provided there were some assurance against Beijing provoking a crisis.[16] Most of these more robust options were described not only as extremely upsetting to Taipei (as well as to Tokyo and Moscow), but also as potentially harmful to domestic and international support for continued close U.S. relations—including the security commitment—with the ROC. Still, none was seen as jeopardizing basic American objectives with respect to Taiwan, which included safeguarding the island from external attack, preserving necessary U.S. military access there, and maintaining the general U.S. policy of recognition and diplomatic support for Taiwan in the international arena.[17] Trying to project China's likely reaction, the NSSM's authors noted that, despite Beijing's expressed patience on resolving the Taiwan question, time was not necessarily on its side:

The drift of events, notably Taiwan's progressively greater viability, increases the possibility of a one China/one Taiwan solution. These considerations must be evident to the PRC also, and Peking may fear that unless it succeeds in obtaining a change of U.S. policy Japan and the United States will ultimately join in ratifying (and defending) this solution.[18]

---

[15] Ibid., pp. 38-39.

[16] Winthrop G. Brown, Memorandum for the Chairman, NSC Senior Review Group, "NSSM 124: Next Steps Toward the People's Republic of China," c. May 1971, p. 2, *NSA* 00210.

[17] Ibid., p. 5.

[18] Ibid., p. 4.

Beyond that, the NSSM equated the U.S. "tactical dilemma" to that of Beijing, i.e., "to improve relations—without making crucial concessions on the Taiwan issue."[19] Still, it noted, the U.S. should be careful "not to convey to Peking by words, acts or even nuance that our objective is to obtain PRC agreement to 'put the Taiwan issue aside.'"[20]

A week later, President Nixon sent a message to the Chinese leadership via Pakistan accepting an invitation for Kissinger to travel to China in July to arrange Nixon's own trip.

PREPARING FOR KISSINGER'S SECRET TRIP

...in Beijing

In May 1971, during the lead-up to Kissinger's visit in July, the Chinese Communist Party (CCP) Politburo adopted a set of eight principles,[21] which are interesting for several reasons. They tell us a great deal about Chinese objectives not just with Kissinger but for the entire normalization process. They reinforce the sense of priority given to removing the U.S. military presence from Taiwan (if not agreed in principle, then Nixon's trip might even be postponed) and also from the region. But they reveal, as well, the underlying intention from the beginning to move toward diplomatic relations.

The eight principles were:

1. All U.S. armed forces and military installations should be withdrawn from Taiwan and the Taiwan Strait area in a given period. This is the key to restoring relations between China and the United States. If no agreement can be reached on this principle in advance, it is possible that Nixon's visit would be deferred.

---

[19] "Next Steps Toward the People's Republic of China – NSSM 124," May 27, 1971, p. 6, enclosed in Jeanne W. Davis, Memorandum for John Irwin, David Packard, Admiral Thomas Moore and Richard Helms, "Response to NSSM 124: Next Steps Toward the People's Republic of China," June 1, 1971, *NSA* 00211.

[20] Ibid., p. 7.

[21] "Politburo Meeting's Decisions on the Principles of Improving Relations with the United States, May 26, 1971," in *Zhonghua Renmin Gongheguo Shilu*, vol. 3 (Changchun: Jili Renmin, 1994), pp. 713-714, translated in Chen, ed., *Chinese Materials*, pp. 22-23.

2. Taiwan is China's territory, and the liberation of Taiwan is China's internal affairs [sic]. No foreign intervention should be allowed. Japanese militarism in Taiwan should be strictly prevented.

3. We will strive to liberate Taiwan in peaceful ways, and will carefully work on the Taiwan issue.

4. The activities aimed at making "two Chinas" or "one China and one Taiwan" should be firmly opposed. If the United States is willing to establish diplomatic relations with China, it must recognize the People's Republic of China as the sole legal government representing China.

5. If the previous three [sic] conditions have not been fully realized, it is not suitable for China and the United States to establish diplomatic relations, and a liaison office can be established in each other's capital.[22]

6. We will not initiate the question concerning [China's seat in] the UN. If the Americans touch upon this question, we will make it clear that no arrangement involving "two Chinas" or "one China and one Taiwan" is acceptable to us.

7. We will not initiate the question concerning Sino-American trade. If the Americans touch upon this question, we will discuss it with them after the principle of American troops withdrawing from Taiwan has been accepted.

8. The Chinese government stands for the withdrawal of U.S. armed forces from the three countries in Indochina, Korea, Japan and Southeast Asia, so that peace in the Far East will be maintained.

---

[22] Some of the U.S. officials most involved with normalization issues over the course of the 1970s are puzzled by this reference to liaison offices, the creation of which we discuss later. They find highly improbable the apparent coincidence in thinking, with both sides seizing on this previously nonexistent form of representation at the same time (Roger W. Sullivan and J. Stapleton Roy, correspondence with author). However, at this point, we have no evidence to suggest that this provision was a later addition to the original account of the Politburo decision.

...and in Washington

Meeting with Kissinger and his deputy, Alexander Haig, in a strategy session on July 1, just days before the National Security Adviser left on his secret mission, President Nixon addressed—in detail—how he wanted Taiwan handled. Kissinger was "not to indicate a willingness to abandon much of our support for Taiwan *until it was necessary to do so.*" Moreover, the issue of "one China vs two Chinas"[23] was to be mentioned only once in the conversation rather than "threaded throughout" as in Kissinger's proposed talking points. For Nixon, the critical point was that "the discussions with the Chinese cannot look like a sellout of Taiwan" or like we were "dumping our friends." Indeed, he directed, the overall statement with respect to Taiwan should be "somewhat more enigmatic," "somewhat more mysterious" than in Kissinger's current draft about the Administration's overall willingness to make concessions "in this area."[24]

So, on the eve of Kissinger's secret trip, the United States understood with considerable nuance the PRC positions on Taiwan and the direction the U.S. would have to move to improve relations. But there was no sense about how far Beijing wanted to take this process in the short run or what it would demand of Washington for improvement short of full normalization. Nor was there a refined sense of how far the Administration might be willing to go down that path. Perhaps, especially given China's obvious strategic motivations—which Nixon also played up in his instructions—there might have been some expectation of at least tactical PRC flexibility on Taiwan in order to serve "larger" purposes.

Given that both sides viewed this trip as preliminary to a visit to China by Nixon, himself, it is fair to assume that both saw its purposes in a very broad framework. Still, Nixon was approaching this encounter cautiously, reining in Kissinger on more sensitive topics such as the overall U.S. relationship to Taiwan, but revving him up where the President thought he could obtain leverage, such as in painting a picture of Japan's possible ambitions.

---

[23] Presumably referring to the statement Kissinger was to make in Beijing that the U.S. would not support a "two Chinas" or "one China, one Taiwan" policy.

[24] Memorandum for the President's Files, "Meeting Between President, Dr. Kissinger and General Haig, Thursday, July 1, Oval Office," July 1, 1971, in Burr, ed., *The Beijing-Washington Back-Channel.* Emphasis added.

Other than the fact that the National Security Adviser was to disavow any intention to pursue a "one China, one Taiwan" or "two Chinas" policy and that he was to promise to reduce U.S. forces on Taiwan, there was no indication of how far the United States would go in embracing Beijing's view of sovereignty over Taiwan, what was required from China in return, or at what pace improved relations might proceed. There were hints in Nixon's instruction "not to indicate a willingness to abandon much of our support for Taiwan *until it was necessary to do so*" and that this should not *"look like"* a sellout[25] that the President was willing to go some distance if he could cover his political bases in the process. Moreover, even though Kissinger initially did not arrive prepared to talk about the terms of full normalization, he showed a willingness in Beijing to commit to full normalization early in Nixon's second term, a fact that strongly suggests that this subject had been discussed in some detail with Nixon beforehand.

In any event, we are getting ahead of ourselves. Without access to the actual instruction at this point, our best option for informing ourselves is to turn to the record of what actually was said.

THE "MOST CRUCIAL ISSUE," JULY 1971: PRESSING THE CASE FOR SOVEREIGNTY

Sovereignty was a central concern raised by Zhou Enlai from the very outset of his meetings with Kissinger in July 1971. In his opening statement, after Zhou invited him to speak first, Kissinger identified the topics he felt they should cover. First was the Taiwan issue. "Mr. Premier," he said, "you have defined this as the withdrawal of U.S. forces from Taiwan and the Taiwan Straits."[26]

In his response, Zhou made clear that while the military issue was important, first and foremost the question involved the history of the Taiwan question and the American stance toward it. In 1949 and 1950, Zhou observed, the U.S. had viewed the Chinese civil war as an "internal affair of China." And, he went on, "[b]y then, Taiwan was already restored to the motherland, and China was that motherland." However, the Premier continued, with the outbreak of the Korean War, the U.S. "surrounded" Taiwan and declared its status was "still unsettled."

---

[25] Ibid. Emphasis added.

[26] Memorandum of Conversation, July 9, 1971 (4:35 pm-11:20 pm), p. 5, in ibid. Except as otherwise noted, the remaining quotes in this discussion are from the same document.

Coming to the point, Zhou said: "If this crucial question is not solved, then the whole question [of relations between the PRC and the United States] will be difficult to resolve." Citing one thousand years of history, the Cairo Declaration, the Japanese surrender and various other events, Zhou then jumped to the bottom line:

> Therefore, in recognizing China the U.S. must do so unreservedly. It must recognize the PRC as the sole legitimate government of China and not make any exceptions.

The Premier concluded by returning to the military issue, insisting on the need to withdraw all U.S. armed forces and dismantle all U.S. military installations on Taiwan and in the Taiwan Strait "within a limited period." He also denounced the U.S.-ROC Mutual Defense Treaty as "illegal."

The ensuing conversation revealed the extent of the gap between the American and Chinese approaches to the question of sovereignty. Kissinger sought to divide the issue into two parts: the military situation and "the question of political evolution between Taiwan and the PRC." Zhou interrupted to note that the Chinese view was different, that the second issue, cross-Strait relations, was "China's internal affair."

> What I was speaking of just now, that if relations are to be established between our two countries, China and the United States, the United States must recognize that the PRC is the sole legitimate government in China and that Taiwan Province is an inalienable part of Chinese territory which must be restored to the motherland. Under these circumstances, the U.S.-Chiang Kai-shek Treaty would not exist.

Kissinger sought, at least inferentially, to address Zhou's concern:

> As for the political future of Taiwan, we are not advocating a "two Chinas" solution or a "one China, one Taiwan" solution. As a student of history, one's prediction would have to be that the political evolution is likely to be in the direction which Prime Minister Chou En-lai indicated to me. But if we want to put the relations between our two countries on a genuine basis of understanding, we must recognize each other's necessities.

Pressed by Zhou to explain what "necessities" he was referring to, Kissinger replied: "We should not be forced into formal declarations in a brief period of time which by themselves have no practical effect.

However we will not stand in the way of basic evolution, once you and we have come to a basic understanding." Zhou came back forcefully to his main point. The issue was not only the withdrawal of U.S. forces "but also the basic relations between our two countries." "Taiwan must be regarded," he insisted, "as a part of China. The solution of the question must follow in order to find a way out."

Much of the conversation then turned to the pace and sequence of normalization. Zhou suggested that it might come within Nixon's first term. Kissinger parried with the notion that, while the major part of the question of the U.S. troop presence could be resolved within that time frame (assuming the war in Southeast Asia had been ended), and while political "evolution" could begin within that period, "settling" the political question (i.e. normalization) would have to wait until Nixon's second term.

When Zhou reported the conversation to Mao that night, the Chairman took a more relaxed position on the pace of normalization. "There's no hurry for Taiwan, for there's no war there. A war is being fought and lives lost in Vietnam! If we want Nixon to come, we can't merely think of ourselves."[27]

Nonetheless, on the second day of the talks,[28] Zhou returned to Taiwan, arguing that in an oral message of November 1970, Nixon had indicated a desire to move toward friendship with China. "If you are going to move towards friendship," Zhou said, "this should mean normalization of relations between our two countries." He then laid out specific requirements for such "friendship." All focused on the question of Taiwan—and the matter of sovereignty:

- It must be recognized that the Government of the People's Republic of China is the sole legitimate government representing the Chinese people.

- It must be recognized that Taiwan belongs to China; that it is an inalienable part of China which was returned to China after World War II.

---

[27] Wei Shiyan, "Kissinger's Secret Visit to China in July 1971," in *Xin Zhongguo Waijiao Fengyun*, vol. 2 (Beijing: Shijie Zhishi, 1991), translated in Chen, ed., *Chinese Materials*, p. 43.

[28] See Memorandum of Conversation, July 10, 1971 (12:10 pm-6:00pm), in Burr, ed., *The Beijing-Washington Back-Channel*.

- That...the U.S. does not support a two Chinas or a one China, one Taiwan policy and does not support the so-called Taiwan Independence Movement.

- Also, as you pointed out explicitly yesterday, the spokesman of the Department of State no longer reiterates what he said, that the status of Taiwan is undetermined.[29]

Zhou again dwelled on the issue of normalization timing, relating it directly to Taiwan's future status by suggesting that if the U.S. moved only incrementally, step-by-step, "the consequence would be that Japan would go into Taiwan and have a hand." Chiang would strive for such a relationship with Japan (or the Soviet Union) in order to "seek another way out," Zhou said, even though the Nationalist leader took the same position on "one China" that Beijing did.[30]

> Therefore, the Taiwan question is a very small matter to you. As you said, it was created by President Truman, and what use is Taiwan to you at the present moment? Taiwan is not an isolated issue, but is related to recognition of the People's Republic of China, and it is also related to the relations of all other countries to China. If your President were to come to the PRC without a clearcut attitude on this issue, then what impression would this give to the world? In my view it would be inconceivable.

---

[29] On April 28, 1971, in response to a question from the *New York Times*, State Department spokesman Charles Bray had reiterated the standard position on the undetermined status of Taiwan. He then got into a convoluted exchange with reporters that went on late into the afternoon about whether this required an "international act" (as per the Truman statement) or whether direct talks between Taipei and Beijing would suffice. (They would.) The next day, President Nixon told a press conference that settling cross-Strait differences through direct negotiations between the parties—as "speculation from various departments" suggested—was "a nice legalistic way to approach it, but I think it is completely unrealistic"; see "The President's New Conference of April 29, 1971," in *Public Papers of the Presidents of the United States: Richard Nixon, 1971* (Washington, DC: U.S. Government Printing Office, 1972), p. 154.

[30] Throughout these dialogues, Zhou revealed considerable apprehension that Japan might seek to replace the United States in Taiwan. This emerged in seemingly contradictory fashion both as an argument for rapid normalization (before Chiang had time to make an accommodation with Japan) and as an argument that the U.S. not withdraw too quickly (to avoid creating a vacuum that Japan could fill).

Kissinger argued that most of the points Zhou laid out could be accomplished "within the near future." The one that would have to wait until after the next U.S. presidential election, he reiterated, was the recognition of the government of the PRC as the sole legitimate government of China.

In making this statement, however, Kissinger slid over the "requirement" that the U.S. must recognize that Taiwan "belongs to China." He merely assured Zhou that this would "take care of itself as a result of the other three points." It is not entirely clear what Kissinger meant by this, but the implication is that, rather than merely suggesting that establishment of U.S.-PRC diplomatic relations "would take care of itself," he thought that Taiwan would face little choice other than accepting some form of unification (presumably peacefully if not happily) once the U.S. began to withdraw its military and political support.

This reading is supported by an exchange later that evening. In discussing strategic relations among the great powers, Kissinger denied any possibility of cooperation among the United States, USSR and Japan to divide up China, as Zhou had at one point suggested they intended to do. Kissinger asked how it could possibly be in the U.S. interest to destroy another country, "particularly one with which, as the Prime Minister has himself pointed out, *after the solution of the Taiwan issue, which will be in the relatively near future*, we have no conflicting interests at all." Zhou responded: "But to deal with Taiwan, we must still have [military forces] there," to which Kissinger came back: "I understand but *I consider this problem will be solved*."[31]

The question of the military face-off across the Strait surfaced again on the morning of Kissinger's departure on July 11th, when Zhou recapped Chinese positions on a number of Taiwan-related issues. In response to Kissinger's statement that the United States hoped the

---

[31] Memorandum of Conversation, July 10, 1971 (12:10 pm-6:00 pm), p. 28. The next day, Zhou acknowledged that normalization would take time, but by the end of that process, the U.S. defense treaty with Taipei "should not have any effect." "By that time," Zhou told Kissinger, "when all your armed forces have withdrawn from Taiwan *and we ourselves have solved the matter*, it should no longer be a problem." Kissinger responded with an expression of "hope" that the issue would be resolved peacefully; see Memorandum of Conversation, July 11, 1971 (10:35 am-11:55 am), in Burr, ed., *The Beijing-Washington Back-Channel* (emphasis added). This issue, of course, dominated much of the discussion over the succeeding years.

Taiwan issue would be resolved peacefully, Zhou replied: "We are doing our best to do so",[32] a position he reiterated in October[33] during Kissinger's next visit and that, as we have seen, reflected the Politburo's May 26th decision to "strive to liberate Taiwan in peaceful ways."[34]

THE "MOST CRUCIAL ISSUE," OCTOBER 1971: SEEKING COMMON GROUND

When Kissinger returned to Beijing in October he took up this critical subject again. In a discussion that was to be repeated in various ways over the entire course of normalization negotiations, he observed:

> We recognize that the People's Republic considers the subject of Taiwan an internal issue, and we will not challenge that. But to the degree that the People's Republic can on its own, in the exercise of its own sovereignty, declare its willingness to settle it by peaceful means, our actions will be easier. I am not speaking of undertaking to talk towards us as we asked in 1955, but something you do on your own. But whether you do or not, we will continue in the direction which I indicated.[35]

It is worth pausing to examine this statement for a moment, since it implicates a number of the central issues of our inquiry. First, while Kissinger had told Zhou in July that U.S. government spokesmen would no longer assert that the status of Taiwan was "undetermined," in fact that stance was never abandoned as the American formal position, even

---

[32] Memorandum of Conversation, July 11, 1971 (10:35 am-11:55 am), in Burr, ed., *The Beijing-Washington Back-Channel*, p. 10.

[33] Memorandum of Conversation, October 21, 1971 (10:30 am-1:45 pm), p. 26, in Burr, ed., *Negotiating U.S.-Chinese Rapprochement*.

[34] An interesting sidelight on the July trip is that, while Kissinger downplayed discussion of Taiwan in his memoirs (he claimed in *White House Years*, op. cit., p. 749, that "Taiwan was mentioned only briefly during the first session" with Zhou), he was far more open with ROC Ambassador James C. H. Shen when he met him two weeks after returning from Beijing. According to Shen, Kissinger reported to him that Zhou had spoken heatedly about Taiwan, as well as about the China seat in the UN. For Shen's account, see his memoir, *The U.S. & Free China: How the U.S. Sold Out Its Ally* (Washington, DC: Acropolis Books, 1983), p. 74.

[35] Memorandum of Conversation, October 21, 1971 (10:30 am-1:45 pm), p. 20.

though it was not articulated in that fashion again.[36] As observed earlier, since even before 1971, but especially after that, the U.S. has sought to downplay that legal issue, focusing instead on the political need for "the Chinese themselves" to resolve their relationship (and, by extension, the status of Taiwan). But while Washington adopted the "acknowledge/do not challenge" formula in the Shanghai Communiqué, and related formulas in later communiqués and public statements, the best that such pronouncements produced from Beijing's point of view was a U.S. foreswearing of "one China, one Taiwan" and "two Chinas" policies, or support for Taiwan independence. It did not, however, rule out the acceptance of Taiwan independence (or, for that matter, reunification), only taking a neutral stance on the outcome, so long as it was arrived at peacefully.[37]

Indeed, that was the second key issue: the stress on seeking some sort of Chinese commitment to a peaceful process. Kissinger's reference to "1955" and the U.S. search for a pledge on peaceful resolution at that time was designed to address the PRC's sensitivity on the issue of sovereignty and its insistence that, since this was an "internal" question, China would give no commitments to others about not using force.

His promise that the U.S. would "continue in the direction I indicated" was a commitment to persist even in the face of the political

---

[36] As one example of how this position continued to emerge, in a discussion of possible ways of rebutting any PRC attempts in the UN to attack the U.S. military presence in Taiwan, the ad hoc interagency working group working on another NSSM suggested: "If there are any opportunities for private conversations with the Chinese during which talking about this subject would be appropriate, we could state that public discussion could force us to reiterate our commitment to the defense of Taiwan *and our views on the status of Taiwan*" (emphasis added). The obvious implied threat was to restate the U.S. view that "the status of Taiwan" was still "undetermined." See "Implications for U.S. Policy of the Participation of the People's Republic of China in Multilateral Diplomacy," National Security Study Memorandum 141, December 1971, enclosed in Samuel De Palma, Memorandum for Henry A. Kissinger, "Submission of NSSM 141," December 3, 1971, *NSA* 00230.

[37] Although maintaining ambiguity in the U.S. position on Taiwan's status leaves open the theoretical possibility of supporting Taiwan independence at some future time, in this writer's view, that is not a serious issue for U.S. policymakers at this point. On the other hand, certain developments such as an unprovoked PRC attack against the island or a dramatic change in circumstances on the Mainland could make this a practical consideration once again in the world of U.S. politics.

sensitivity of this issue in the United States, sensitivity that eventually led, for example, to the controversial language adopted in the Taiwan Relations Act in 1979. Thus, for Nixon and Kissinger, as later for Carter and his Administration, obtaining some PRC commitment on "peaceful resolution" was a high priority in negotiating normalization, for both strategic and domestic political reasons.

Zhou once again stressed that Taiwan was the PRC's "central question of concern" and turned to the issue of Taiwan's supposedly "undetermined" status. He brought up the case of the UK.

We noted earlier that London had recognized the PRC in 1950 and had, because of that, blocked the ROC's attendance at the San Francisco Peace Conference. But relations with Beijing had been kept to the level of Offices of the Chargé d'Affaires.[38] Now, in 1971, the British were seeking to raise relations to the ambassadorial level. While the UK had "acknowledged" the PRC position on Taiwan,[39] London nonetheless took the position that the island's status remained undetermined. "It's a ludicrous state of affairs," Zhou railed. He pressed Kissinger to state the U.S. position.

Kissinger tried to address this issue by separating policy from public statements.

> We do not challenge the fact that all Chinese maintain that there's only one China and that Taiwan is part of that China. And therefore we do not maintain that the status *in that respect* is undetermined. How this can be expressed is a difficult matter, but we would certainly be prepared in a communiqué that might be issued to take note of the fact that all Chinese maintain that there is only one China. So that is the policy of this government.[40]

Unsatisfied, Zhou pushed further. Beyond not issuing statements on its own asserting Taiwan's "undetermined" status, what would the U.S. position be if others raised it? Noting that he would have to refer to the

---

[38] The UK had maintained a consulate in Taiwan at Tamshui throughout this period.

[39] Memorandum of Conversation, October 21, 1971 (10:30 am-1:45 pm), p. 23. Zhou interestingly amplified: "Not recognize but acknowledge. So for lawyers there might be a slight differentiation between acknowledge and recognize. That is a question of international law."

[40] Ibid., p. 261. Emphasis added.

President for an authoritative response to that specific question, Kissinger said that he could confirm that the U.S. policy was to "encourage" a peaceful solution within the framework of one China.[41]

Zhou then turned to the U.S.-Taiwan military relationship. He wanted to be sure that the United States understood not only that all American forces and installations had to be removed from Taiwan before normalization, but that action had to be taken to render the Mutual Defense Treaty "null and void." "Otherwise," he said, "it's not possible for us to go to Washington, to have two Chinese Ambassadors there."

According to the information we cited earlier, the Politburo had already decided the previous May that, if full normalization were not possible, Beijing would support the establishment of liaison offices in each other's capitals. So, while Zhou apparently did not want to signal this fallback position so early in the game (and it took another year and a

---

[41] That said, then-ROC Ambassador James Shen reported that, upon returning from the Nixon visit in February 1972, Kissinger suggested to him that one option for the future was to work out a peaceful cross-Strait settlement. At the same time, Kissinger reassured Shen: "We will never urge you to do anything against your will" (*The U.S. & Free China*, pp. 82-83). Shen also reported that the President said something similar: "Further on the Taiwan Question, Nixon said that it had been the U.S. Government's position that this should be settled by peaceful means. The United States had no intention of interfering, nor would it urge either side to negotiate or offer any suggestion or formula. How should the question be settled? That was something for the two parties directly concerned to study and work out by themselves. The United States, Nixon stressed, wanted no part of it." When Shen asked what sort of timeframe he had in mind for peaceful settlement, Nixon responded (quite frankly, in the circumstances): "maybe two years, three years or five years" (p. 109). Kissinger then intervened in the conversation with a theme he returned to more than once in his dialogue with Shen over time: "He said the U.S. Government wanted to give the Republic of China time. Within a matter of three to five years, both Mao and Chou would most likely pass away and the entire mainland might be thrown into chaos. The Republic of China would in the meantime be well advised to pursue a steady course and 'do nothing to rock the boat.'" Shen added perceptively: "He didn't amplify this bit of unsolicited advice, but obviously he didn't want us to do anything that might spoil the American plans" (p. 110). As time went on, although Washington tried to control Taiwan's reaction, it also gave Taipei hints of the anticipated pace of U.S.-PRC relations in order to allow Taiwan to prepare itself. When Kissinger returned from Beijing in February 1973, for example, he told Shen U.S.-ROC relations would not change "in the foreseeable future." Asked how long the "foreseeable future" was, Kissinger responded: at least until the end of 1974 (p. 134).

half to get there), the PRC in fact was willing to be "present" in Washington while the ROC was still represented there, just not in an "official" or "diplomatic" capacity. On the then-pending UN representation issue as well, Zhou stuck with principles, saying "we will certainly not give up Taiwan, or accept a so-called undetermined status for Taiwan in exchange for a seat in the UN."[42]

Beating the drums once more in case Kissinger had somehow missed the point, Zhou noted that, although the PRC's lawful rights in the UN should be restored, "what we think is more important is the future of Taiwan. And this is the most crucial issue between our two countries."[43]

When they turned to the Shanghai Communiqué draft, Zhou argued that the American side needed to say something "which would be of a decisive nature for normalization of relations between China and the United States." Specifically on Taiwan independence, Zhou explained, "the matter of crucial importance is for the U.S. to indicate it will not carry out or support any activities aimed at separating Taiwan from China." He pushed Kissinger to endorse the characterization of the Taiwan issue as an "internal [i.e., Chinese] matter."[44]

Kissinger declined to adopt the phrase "internal matter" since it was politically risky. Instead, he proposed that the U.S. could in some other way indicate it had no intention of splitting China. After the U.S. statement, which he had introduced into the communiqué draft, that the U.S. acknowledged that "all Chinese on either side of the Taiwan Strait maintain there is but one China," the U.S. could then say that it "does not challenge" that position.[45] This is the formulation that was enshrined in the Shanghai Communiqué.

---

[42] Memorandum of Conversation, October 21, 1971 (4:42 pm-7:17 pm), p. 6, in Burr, ed., *Negotiating U.S.-Chinese Rapprochement*. As it turned out, this part of the conversation was overtaken by events when, on October 25, 1971, just about the time Kissinger was leaving China, the UN General Assembly adopted Resolution 2758, admitting the PRC and expelling the ROC.

[43] Ibid., p. 8. Zhou also said, however, that among the three powder kegs in the Far East, Vietnam and Korea were more urgent than Taiwan "because we are separated by an ocean"; see Memorandum of Conversation, October 22, 1971 (4:15 pm – 8:28 pm), p. 7, in ibid.

[44] Memorandum of Conversation, October 24, 1971 (10:28 am-1:55 pm), p. 22, in ibid.

[45] On this exchange, see Memorandum of Conversation, October 24, 1971 (9:23 pm-11:20 pm), in ibid. Kissinger had already introduced that formulation three days earlier (see p. 34, note 35), but raising it again here served a particularly

Zhou then sought Kissinger's admission that Beijing was exercising "great restraint" on the Taiwan issue (which he got). The Premier then made a critical point:

> [I]n solving this crucial matter…for the sake of normalization of relations between the two countries, we are not demanding an immediate solution for [reunification] in all aspects but that it be solved step by step.[46]

Also relevant to issues of sovereignty that have continued to affect the triangular relationship to this day, the U.S. had originally expressed support for efforts to reach "an equitable and peaceful resolution" of cross-Strait relations. Zhou, however, objected to "equitable" on the grounds that it could be construed as an endorsement of a plebiscite on Taiwan for self-determination. Kissinger acquiesced.[47]

Communiqué language on Taiwan, which was to remain in dispute until the last day of Nixon's visit, came up again during Kissinger's final meeting in October. The U.S. team had drafted a proposed paragraph stating the American position. But Zhou claimed it was not sufficiently explicit, and once again he hit his theme on the centrality of this issue: "[I]f we do not make clear the future of this, how can we begin normalization?"[48] He then issued a thinly veiled threat:

> For us we are also running a risk here. That is, we are placing our reliance on your President continuing to remain in office…But we cannot speak on behalf of the American people…So even after your President comes, and even if he undertakes such an obligation, if he is not voted into office for the next term, we don't know whether it will be put into implementation…If we are to wait another six years, we may

---

useful function in deflecting a problematic formulation that Zhou was pushing.

[46] Memorandum of Conversation, October 24, 1971 (10:28 am-1:55 pm), p. 25, in ibid.

[47] Memorandum of Conversation, October 25, 1971 (9:50 pm-11:40 pm), p. 10, in ibid.

[48] Memorandum of Conversation, October 26, 1971 (5:30 am-8:10 am), p. 8, in ibid. It was during the course of this conversation that Kissinger cited the virtues of ambiguity (see p. 11).

wait another six years, but then we will liberate by another means, not this means. You understand.[49]

Kissinger's goal in handling Taiwan was to advance U.S.-PRC relations, but not to move so fast that opponents would seize on it as a vehicle for destroying the normalization process. In so doing, he encountered the reality that, although the PRC was anxious to advance bilateral ties for obvious reasons—including not just for strategic benefit vis-à-vis the Soviets but because it would create pressures on Taiwan to deal with the Mainland—Beijing adamantly refused to accept or endorse U.S. half steps on Taiwan as sufficient for full normalization. The resulting incompleteness of the situation, even after the establishment of liaison offices in early 1973, produced in Kissinger's mind a concern over the fragility of the relationship and its vulnerability to unforeseen events or simply a loss of momentum and a withering on the vine. This concern was reinforced when both the Nixon Administration and the Chinese leadership entered troubled domestic political waters after mid-1973, and Kissinger began to search for creative ways to complete the process without first meeting Beijing's full terms.

In any event, in the remaining months before Nixon arrived, there was no greater success in coming to closure. Kissinger's deputy, Alexander Haig, traveled to Beijing in early January 1972 with some new wording on the Taiwan portions of the communiqué. But, having decided ahead of time that they would not accept any new wording on that subject until Kissinger returned with the President,[50] the Chinese simply put Haig off. But not, of course, before Zhou reminded the General that this was "the crucial question" in Sino-American relations.[51]

Thus, on the eve of the President's trip, the fundamental dilemma that was to plague U.S.-PRC relations—not only through the Nixon/Ford Administrations but through normalization and up to the present time—had already emerged. Although Beijing was willing, indeed anxious, to advance bilateral relations in order to protect its strategic interests, it would hold back on full normalization until the United States met certain

---

[49] Ibid., p. 14.

[50] "Haig's Preparatory Mission for Nixon's Visit to China in January 1972," in *Xin Zhongguo Waijiao Fengyun*, vol. 3, op. cit., translated in Chen, ed., *Chinese Materials*, p. 60.

[51] Memorandum of Conversation, January 7, 1972, (11:45pm), p. 5, in Burr, ed., *Negotiating U.S.-Chinese Rapprochement*.

fundamental requirements regarding Taiwan. But the United States could not readily meet those requirements. The issue was to some extent, as the history of normalization demonstrated, a matter of form—finding creative ways to "observe" the PRC's principles while preserving the necessary substantive ties to the island. But there were clear limits on both sides to a smoke-and-mirrors approach.

One of the issues was time. What was the extent of Beijing's patience? An objective analysis left one with the sense that Zhou's veiled threat about using non-peaceful methods to "liberate" Taiwan after another six years fell largely into the category of what China has called "empty cannons." At that time, the PLA simply lacked the means to seize Taiwan by force—or coerce Taiwan into surrender—and had no realistic prospect of being able to do so in the near future. But as the NSSMs had assessed, these were issues of first order principle for Beijing, and trifling with them was risky business for the PRC leadership. That said, while at this stage Zhou's emphasis was still on reunification, he had already revealed that "for the sake of normalization," China could approach that goal step by step.

By the eve of Nixon's trip, normalization itself was squarely on the table. The U.S. was fully committed to recognizing the government of the PRC as the "sole legal government of China" in Nixon's second term, though the U.S. position on Beijing's writ over Taiwan remained murky.

In this connection, Kissinger had avoided buying into formulations that would get the President—and the opening to China—in political trouble, such as that the Taiwan issue was an "internal" Chinese matter. On the issue of "one China" of which Taiwan was a part, although he refused to publicly endorse it, by agreeing not to "challenge" the Chinese position, he showed a willingness to create an inference that the U.S. did so.

While, in private, Kissinger took the dialogue fairly far toward actually accepting the "one China principle," he declined to step across the line that affirmatively and unambiguously agreed that Taiwan was a part of China. This underscored an underlying contradiction: what the PRC meant by the "one China principle" and what the U.S. meant by it were not the same. Moreover, as time went on, and the U.S. spoke increasingly of its "one China policy," this placed the two positions at an even further remove from each other.

As we shall see presently, Nixon went quite far in Beijing's direction on these issues in private, but in public he adhered to the much more restrained positions that Kissinger had worked out in the communiqué negotiations.

One final point as we move to consider the Nixon visit itself. Kissinger left the question of U.S. activism on behalf of a "one China" solution in a rather forward-leaning posture. While he said the United States could not "bring about" a peaceful solution within a "one China" framework, the U.S. would "encourage" this. Although Kissinger said that this was something for the Chinese themselves to settle, this still raised the issue of what the United States envisaged—and wanted—for Taiwan's future.

NIXON IN CHINA

Laying Out Basic Principles

Nixon arrived in China in late February 1972 fully prepared to make the most of what he would term "the week that changed the world." He had read extensively and made copious notes on the points he wanted to make in his historic meetings with Mao and Zhou.[52] On Taiwan, while he intended to stay within the framework Kissinger had, under his direction, established, he wanted the words to come from him, and to be taken as the authoritative statement of American policy.

In his first substantive meeting with Zhou Enlai, Nixon endorsed a version of the five principles to which Kissinger had subscribed. He enumerated them for Zhou:

- Principle one. There is one China, and Taiwan is a part of China. There will be no more statements made—if I can control our bureaucracy—to the effect that the status of Taiwan is undetermined.[53]

---

[52] See Mann, *About Face*, op. cit., pp. 45-46.

[53] In the notes Nixon prepared for the meeting he wrote: "*Taiwan*: I reiterate what our policy is: 1. Status is determined—one China, Taiwan is part of China" (for this and the remainder of Nixon's original notes on the so-called "five points," see ibid., p. 46). But as we can see from the transcript, when he made his statement, he pulled back to where Kissinger had been, speaking only about what would be *said*, not what the U.S. substantive position was. And in fact, even a year later, senior State Department officials were still indicating publicly that the status of Taiwan was undetermined. Assistant Secretary for East Asian and Pacific Affairs Marshall Green, for instance, told one audience that at the

- Second, we have not and will not support any Taiwan independence movement.

- Third, we will, to the extent we are able, use our influence to discourage Japan from moving into Taiwan as our presence becomes less.

- The fourth point is that we will support any peaceful resolution of the Taiwan issue that can be worked out. And related to that point, we will not support any military attempts by the Government on Taiwan to resort to a military return to the Mainland.[54]

- Finally, we seek the normalization of relations with the People's Republic. We know that the issue of Taiwan is a barrier to complete normalization, but within the framework I have previously described we seek normalization and we will work toward that goal and will try to achieve it.[55]

Nixon went on to inform Zhou of his intention to withdraw most of the U.S. military presence on Taiwan as the Vietnam War was resolved.

Beijing summit, "we were not engaged in any plot to determine the status of Taiwan"; see "U.S.-China Relations: Progress Toward Normalization," a speech to the Sulgrave Club on February 20, 1973, in *American Foreign Relations 1973: A Documentary Record* (New York: NYU Press, 1976), p. 80.

[54] The purpose of this point, which had been made at the Warsaw talks as well as by Kissinger, is not entirely clear. Donald Anderson, who was the U.S. interpreter at Warsaw, feels it was simply a way of assuring Beijing that the U.S. forces in Taiwan had no aggressive intentions toward China (correspondence with author). But we also note that, although Taiwan's premier, Chiang Ching-kuo, had informed Washington by 1968 that raids on the Mainland were ending, there was at least one ROC raid on PRC shipping near the Min River estuary during the first year of the Nixon Administration; see Steven M. Goldstein, "The United States and the Republic of China, 1949-1978: Suspicious Allies," Stanford University, Institute for International Studies, Asia-Pacific Research Center, February 2000, pp. 28, 32.

[55] Memorandum of Conversation, February 22, 1972 (2:10 pm-6:00 pm), p. 5, in *Record of Richard Nixon-Zhou Enlai Talks, February 1972*, a National Security Archive Electronic Briefing Book, online at http://www.gwu.edu/~nsarchiv/nsa/publications/DOC_readers/kissinger/nixzhou/ (hereafter *Nixon-Zhou Talks*).

The balance, Nixon reported, would be removed "as progress is made on the peaceful resolution of the [Taiwan] problem."[56]

These remarks were the most far-reaching on the Taiwan issue Nixon would utter to a Chinese official on the trip, Mao included. Indeed, Nixon spoke to Zhou on Taiwan with great clarity and with scrupulously chosen words. He spoke to the world in the Shanghai Communiqué issued at the conclusion of his visit with words that were chosen equally as scrupulously, but that were far less specific and direct. This was not by mistake.

The Shanghai Communiqué: Shaping the Future

As Henry Kissinger has explained it, the "basic theme" of the Shanghai Communiqué, as of the entire Nixon visit, was "to put off the issue of Taiwan for the future, to enable the two nations [i.e., the U.S. and the PRC] to close the gulf of twenty years and to pursue parallel policies where their interests coincided."[57]

Finding a mutually agreeable way to express this in the communiqué, however, proved challenging. Nixon and Kissinger wanted to refer to the U.S. "interest" in peaceful resolution of the Taiwan question— implying a continuing commitment—while Zhou sought to limit the American expression to "hope." The Chinese wanted the U.S. to commit unconditionally to total withdrawal of the U.S. military (albeit without a specific timetable), while the U.S. side was unwilling to go beyond identifying withdrawal as an "objective," tying it to peaceful developments in the region and progress in resolving the Taiwan question.[58] However, in what may have seemed in Kissinger's mind to be a constructive self-fulfilling prophecy, he apparently envisioned normalization as importantly affecting Taiwan's future course:

> We recognized that on some issues the only thing negotiators can achieve is to gain time with dignity. On Taiwan it was to leave the ultimate outcome to a future *that in turn would be shaped by the relationship which would evolve from the rest of the communiqué* and by the manner in which it was negotiated.[59]

---

[56] Ibid., p. 6.

[57] Kissinger, *White House Years,* p. 1074.

[58] Ibid., p. 1075.

[59] Ibid., p. 1076. Emphasis added.

Referring to negotiations Kissinger had held that morning on the still unresolved communiqué language on Taiwan, Nixon reiterated to Zhou Kissinger's earlier caution: if too much was said publicly, that would be seized upon by Americans who opposed the opening to China from both right and left with regard to a variety of issues (including not just policy toward Taiwan, itself, but U.S. approaches toward the Soviet Union, South Asia, and Japan) as an excuse to disrupt normalization.[60]

Zhou noted that because Chiang Kai-shek still believed in "one China," the question of reunification could be resolved "comparatively easily."[61] And he reiterated the statements he had made to Kissinger that the PRC would strive for "peaceful liberation."[62] In the course of this conversation, the premier observed that John Foster Dulles had once said that, as long as China did not use force for ten, fifteen or twenty years, he would be satisfied. If China had agreed to that, Zhou noted, more than fifteen years would already have passed (and, by implication, the United States would not object to whatever solution the PRC resorted to in pressing reunification). "But if we accepted such a principle, it would be equivalent to accepting interference in our internal affairs. So we cannot accept that."[63] Still, he expressed confidence that China could resolve the problem, peacefully, as an internal matter.

Zhou returned to a familiar theme on Taiwan as "the crucial question" between the United States and the PRC, warning that the Chinese people had "feelings" about this. However, while he pressed for a more forthcoming U.S. position on communiqué language, he also revealed flexibility when he added: "But it is possible for us to persuade our people because of the prestige of the leadership of Chairman Mao."[64] The communiqué was issued on February 27, 1972.

Having instructed the U.S. delegation not to offer "interpretations" of the communiqué's meaning,[65] Kissinger would later argue that, as satisfactory as the outcome was from an American perspective, the U.S. statement on Taiwan in the Shanghai Communiqué should not be cast as

---

[60] Memorandum of Conversation, February 22, 1972 (2:10 pm-6:00 pm), p. 6.

[61] Ibid., p. 28.

[62] Memorandum of Conversation, February 24, 1972 (5:15 pm-8:05 pm), p. 6, in National Security Archive, *Nixon-Zhou Talks*.

[63] Ibid., p. 8.

[64] Ibid., p. 10.

[65] Chas. W. Freeman, Jr., interview by author.

a "victory" of one side over the other. "No constructive relationship can be built on that basis." "Rather," he continued,

> it put the Taiwan issue in abeyance, with each side maintaining its basic principles. Despite the continuing difference over Taiwan our rapprochement with China accelerated because we shared a central concern about threats to the global balance of power.[66]

In discussing the handling of Taiwan, Nixon revealed in his own memoirs the ambivalence in the U.S. position, and in his own thinking. On one page he wrote:

> Taiwan was the touchstone for both sides. We felt that we should not and could not abandon the Taiwanese; *we were committed to Taiwan's right to exist as an independent nation.*[67]

But on the facing page, while promising support against forceful takeover, he seemed to deny that "right":

> We knew that no agreement concerning Taiwan could be reached at this time. *While both sides could agree that Taiwan was a part of China*—a position supported by both Peking and Taiwan governments—we would have to oppose the use of military force by Peking to bring Taiwan under Communist control.[68]

The Chinese, as the Americans, were extremely pleased by the results of Nixon's visit, which they characterized as "a turning point in postwar international relations." Their take on what had happened, however, was somewhat different from the American view. A Chinese Communist Party Central Committee circular hailed the summit for its success in "utilizing [others'] contradictions, dividing up enemies, and

---

[66] Kissinger, *White House Years*, p. 1080.

[67] Nixon, *RN: The Memoirs of Richard Nixon,* op. cit., p. 570. Emphasis added.

[68] Ibid., p. 571. Emphasis added. The most likely explanation for this apparent contradiction is that Nixon did not see it as a contradiction at all. Taiwan's existence as an "independent nation" was quite possible, in his view, within a framework that accepted Taiwan as "a part of China." To Beijing, of course, though Taiwan could function with full autonomy, the notion that it was an "independent nation" was in direct contradiction to the notion that it was "part of China."

enhancing ourselves," and credited this to Mao's "brilliant decision" to invite the American President.[69] Yet at the same time, the Chinese seemed to clearly understand the constraints confronting Nixon in moving from paper agreements to implementation. The Central Committee thus offered instructions strikingly similar in tenor to Kissinger's:

> We should not provide any excuse for our enemy to use as means to sabotage the achievements of the Sino-American talks. We should not make excessive statements. In particular, it is inappropriate for us to claim that the joint communiqué represents our victory and America's failure.[70]

Kissinger was to later write that, in the Shanghai Communiqué, the U.S. and China agreed on "a carefully crafted formulation that *accepted* the principle of one China but left the resolution to the future."[71] In fact, however, as a State Department briefing paper for President Ford noted in 1975, the United States "accepted" the principle of one China *privately*.[72] In public, however, it was a different matter:

> In effect, the U.S. position as embodied in the Shanghai Communiqué established the basic outlines for an eventual normalization agreement, but did so in a qualified manner. We indicated indirectly our movement toward a position of accepting Peking's one China condition by saying the United States Government "does not challenge" the position of the two Chinese parties that Taiwan is a part of China.[73]

All that being said, it is not clear that the most senior Americans involved in this process fully absorbed the centrality of Taiwan to PRC interests. Obviously focusing on the larger strategic issues that drove the two countries together, Kissinger later observed: "There was, in fact, an

---

[69] "CCP Central Committee: 'Notice on the Joint Sino-American Communiqué,' March 7, 1972," in *Zhonghua Renmin Gongheguo Shilu*, vol. 3, op. cit., translated in Chen, ed., *Chinese Materials*, p. 25.

[70] Ibid.

[71] Kissinger, *Years of Upheaval*, op. cit., p. 47. Emphasis added.

[72] "Normalization," Department of State briefing paper, November 1975, p. 3, *NSA* 00381.

[73] Ibid., p. 5.

incongruity between the intensity of the discussion [of what to say about Taiwan in the U.S. portion of the Shanghai Communiqué] and its intrinsic importance."[74] For the Americans, the Taiwan question was a practical obstacle to be gotten around in order to deal with more important issues.   For the Chinese, however, it was a matter of sovereignty that did not permit compromise, at least not in principle. Zhou had conveyed an important signal about flexibility in practice when he noted that the prestige of Mao's leadership could overcome "the feelings of the people." Implicit in that pronouncement, of course, was that Mao would only exercise that leadership when he was convinced it was in China's interests. What mattered was what people could see.

Nixon adopted an almost mirror image approach: he could quietly do more than he could openly say, reflecting the very different policy "management" problem he faced.   Still, the President was careful, while making various statements of intent for the future, not to reach any "secret agreements" with Mao and Zhou, so that he could deny any such agreements existed.

The declaratory sentence Nixon used both with Zhou and in his memoirs—"there is one China and Taiwan is a part of China"—with all of its implications for the issue of sovereignty, was ahead of his own policy, even then. But it was less controversial in 1972 than any such statement would be in later years.

---

[74] Kissinger, *White House Years,* p. 1078.

3

"One China"—Squaring the Circle

"The Chinese side reiterated that the normalization of relations between China and the United States can be realized only on the basis of confirming the principle of one China."

—Joint U.S.-PRC Communiqué, November 1973

As he was embarking on his second term, in January 1973, Nixon wrote to Zhou Enlai, reviewing a number of global issues. Laying the groundwork for Kissinger's upcoming trip to Beijing in February he said:

> As far as direct U.S.-Chinese dealings are concerned, I would like to reaffirm our intention to move energetically in my second Administration toward the normalization of our relations. Everything that has been previously said on this subject is hereby reaffirmed. Dr. Kissinger will be prepared to discuss this fully when he visits Peking. [1]

During that visit, the Chinese responded positively to the U.S. proposal to establish liaison offices. [2] Although the PRC willingness to

---

[1] Richard Nixon, letter to Zhou Enlai, January 3, 1973, National Archives, Record Group 59, Department of State Records, Records of Policy Planning Staff (Director's Files), 1969-1977, box 329. (Subsequent documents from this Record Group hereafter *National Archives*, followed by box number.)

[2] In his memoirs, Kissinger describes how he had no clear-cut plan for increasing visible contacts when he went to Beijing in February 1973 and had only planned to suggest an American trade office in China. When Zhou made clear he wanted more of a political relationship, Kissinger says he raised the idea of a liaison office, a concept originally created for (but rejected by) Vietnam. Zhou embraced the U.S. "proposal," which puzzled Kissinger, since he did not think he had really made a formal "proposal." See *Years of Upheaval*, pp. 61-62, for his account of this.

Roger W. Sullivan, who later served as Deputy Assistant Secretary of State for East Asian and Pacific Affairs at the time of normalization and as Senior Staff Member on the NSC, adds important detail on the proposal's origin and establish such an office in Washington surprised the U.S. side, we have already noted the report that the Chinese leadership anticipated this arrangement two years earlier. Still, in the February talks, Zhou sought to maintain the principled fiction that, while the American office in Beijing could be official in reality, even though unofficial in name, the Chinese office in Washington would "have to be unofficial" even in practice.[3] Formal diplomatic exchanges were still to go through Paris,

---

significance. Sullivan was a senior adviser on the China desk in fall 1971. He recounts that he and William Brown, then Deputy Director on the desk, were on a special, highly compartmented assignment by the NSC to work on the Nixon trip. Among other things, they were charged with coming up with options for representation short of full diplomatic relations. They prepared a paper proposing the establishment of liaison offices. Among the arguments they advanced in support of the proposal was that this was not only a step toward diplomatic relations, but that a liaison office was a unique institution, a structure that would not be used in the case of any other entity or country. (That it might have been raised initially in the case of Vietnam was not relevant, Sullivan notes, since it had not taken hold.) Kissinger rejected the whole idea—apparently because he saw it as an attempt by the State Department to get into a process over which he wanted to maintain tight control—and he did not raise it with Beijing. But Senior NSC Staff Member John Holdridge took the paper with him when he traveled to China as part of Kissinger's entourage in October 1971 and left it with the Chinese. Before the February 1973 trip, Sullivan, then Acting Director of the China desk, raised it again, and Kissinger rejected it again. However, on his return from the trip, Holdridge—who once more accompanied Kissinger—reported to Sullivan that, while Kissinger had not raised it, the Chinese had. They cited the Sullivan/Brown 1971 memo—the "proposal" Kissinger had not made—noted its arguments in favor of liaison offices, and endorsed the idea.

The later failure to take account of the fact that the rationale on uniqueness underlay Chinese acceptance of the idea explains a great deal, Sullivan observes, about why Deng Xiaoping reacted so strongly to later efforts to switch the embassy and liaison office arrangement, as discussed below. When Kissinger proposed such a switch in 1974, he might simply have overlooked the 1973 conversation. Sullivan surmises that when Vance proposed something similar in 1977 (even though not using the label "liaison offices"), the record of earlier conversations to which the Secretary and his associates had access might not have included the details of the original U.S. proposal on liaison offices or the Chinese statements about why they eventually accepted it. Sullivan notes that, if that is correct, this experience highlights a serious problem that such strict compartmentalization created in the system (all from correspondence with author).

[3] "Bilateral Relations," included in "Taiwan/Normalization," an undated briefing

where a channel had been created in 1971, and extremely sensitive exchanges were to go through Huang Hua, China's Ambassador to the United Nations.[4]

Kissinger interpreted this PRC "eagerness to institutionalize our relationship" as stemming from political struggles in China and a desire by Mao and Zhou to consolidate the gains with the United States while they still were alive and in a position to do so.[5] The American side felt a parallel sense of need to strengthen ties "before the present dynasty passe[d] from the scene," a sense intensified both by the growing perception in Washington of "substantial opposition" to Mao's policies within the Chinese leadership and by the prospect that Nixon, too, was being weakened as the Watergate debacle gained momentum.[6]

For his own part, stretching out the normalization timetable originally presented to the Chinese of "early in the second term," Kissinger pledged that after the 1974 elections, "we want to work toward full normalization and full diplomatic relations before mid-1976," moving to "something like the Japanese solution."[7] However, in addition

---

paper prepared for President Ford's December 1975 trip to China, p. 1, *National Archives*, box 372.

[4] This complicated arrangement quickly dissolved, however, as Huang Zhen, the PRC ambassador in Paris, a senior PRC official and a frequent Kissinger interlocutor there, was assigned to head the PRC Liaison Office in Washington and became the channel for all communication. Still, the formal distinction of the PRC Liaison Office (as the USLO in Beijing) not being a diplomatic mission was maintained due to the continued U.S. relationship with Taiwan.

[5] Henry Kissinger, Memorandum for the President, "My Trip to China," March 2, 1973, cited in Burr, ed., *The Kissinger Transcripts*, p. 116.

[6] Having missed the opportunity to normalize relations by the time Mao died, Kissinger understandably took a different tack in 1976. He was asked whether he regretted not having made more progress on the Taiwan issue while Mao was alive. He responded: "The specific issues that are involved in the process of normalization of relations with the People's Republic of China cannot be tied to the lifetime of personalities." See "Excerpts from Secretary Kissinger's News Conference, September 9, 1976," in U.S. Department of State Office of Public Communication, *Selected Documents: U.S. Policy Toward China, July 15, 1971-January 15, 1979* (Washington: Bureau of Public Affairs, January 1979).

[7] Reference to the "Japanese solution" or "model" became the standard Chinese way of insisting that all official ties with Taipei had to be severed before formal diplomatic relations with Beijing could be established. When Tokyo and Beijing established diplomatic relations in 1972, Japan created a nominally totally private representation office in Taipei, cutting off all "official" as well as

to highlighting that over that time the U.S. would like to "discuss some understanding that the final solution will be a peaceful one," Kissinger implied that the United States preferred some variant of the "Japanese model," raising an issue that would plague normalization to the end:

> We would like to keep some form of representation on Taiwan but haven't figured out a formula that will be mutually acceptable.[8]

COPING…AND SEEKING CREATIVE SOLUTIONS

By November 1973, amidst the "disintegration" of the government in Washington and the President's "weakening authority" as the Watergate scandal grew,[9] Kissinger was becoming increasingly concerned to further institutionalize the relationship with Beijing—described even a year later as a "still rather personalized and fragile beginning."[10] But there was no prospect of breaking with Taipei within the coming year. On one level, as the newly-appointed Secretary of State, Kissinger sought to expand the status of the liaison offices "so that they become more and more similar to full diplomatic recognition."[11] But on another level, he began

---

"diplomatic" relations with the island. On the other hand, the Japanese office was staffed with officials on secondment to the "private" institution. (Beijing's other two requirements for U.S.-PRC normalization were severance of the U.S.-ROC Mutual Defense Treaty and the withdrawal of all U.S. forces and installations from Taiwan.)

[8] "Taiwan," undated briefing paper detailing the U.S. and Chinese positions taken in the February 1973 talks, p. 2, *NSA* 00270. Probably for a variety of reasons—e.g., there were larger issues to deal with, and nothing much could be done right away about Taiwan, anyway—Zhou's approach to Taiwan was a study in relaxation: "The PRC can leave Chiang Kai-shek as he is at the moment because this question is bound to be settled finally, because in principle the U.S. and China know each other well. So China won't be very put out about whether the U.S. withdraws its troops early or later" (p. 1). This pattern of relaxed implementation of certain aspects of Beijing's Taiwan policy was followed over the years when China wanted to achieve major goals. But this was only possible if certain "fictions"—as Roger Sullivan calls them—were maintained on issues of "principle" (Sullivan, correspondence with author).

[9] These are Kissinger's terms (*Years of Upheaval*, pp. 104-105).

[10] Memorandum for Henry Kissinger, "Normalization of Relations, and the Taiwan Issue," September 1974, p. 11, *National Archives*, box 331.

[11] Memorandum of Conversation, November 11, 1973 (3:15 pm-7:00 pm), p. 8, *National Archives*, box 372.

to search for a formula that would allow the actual establishment of full U.S.-PRC diplomatic relations even while U.S.-ROC ties were still intact. Perhaps stimulated by statements of some Chinese in early fall that progress would be easy "if only" the United States adopted a face-saving approach by "recognizing the principle of one China,"[12] Kissinger probed Zhou on this prospect on his sixth trip to Beijing during the second week of November:

> We are prepared at any point to intensify the existing relationship or to establish full diplomatic relations, but we have the difficulty of how to handle the relationship with Taiwan in the interim period. But we will be prepared to listen to any proposal that you might have in this connection and make every attempt to meet it. If at any point the Chinese thought the formulation of the Shanghai Communiqué or an adaptation would provide some way to have diplomatic relations we would be prepared to proceed on that basis.[13]

Asked by Zhou to amplify his point, Kissinger explained:

> I have in mind something like the Shanghai Communiqué which would make clear that the establishment of diplomatic relations does not mean giving up the principle that there is only one China…As I understand it, Mr. Prime Minister, your problem in having diplomatic relations while we have relations with Taiwan is that it might give rise to a two-China policy which we have agreed not to support. What we should search for is a formula for consideration that makes clear that that principle is not being abandoned; that there is only one China by either side.[14]

In meeting with Mao shortly after this exchange, Kissinger thought he detected an oblique hint of a solution. The Chairman referred to the fact that the Soviet Union had not insisted that the U.S. first break ties with the Baltic states of Estonia, Latvia and Lithuania before establishing diplomatic relations with Washington in 1933. Kissinger later said that the domestic situation in China changed too rapidly to permit an exploration of all the implications of what he believed was a Chinese

---

[12] Kissinger, *Years of Upheaval*, p. 680.

[13] Memorandum of Conversation, November 11, 1973 (3:15 pm-7:00 pm), p. 8.

[14] Memorandum of Conversation, November 12, 1973 (3:00 pm-5:30 pm), p. 5, *National Archives*, box 372.

invitation for a proposal "that combined the principle of a unified China with some practical accommodation to the status quo."[15] Nonetheless, he was to make efforts to find a workable formula along those lines for at least two more years.

In the process of doing so, he had to overlook the fact that, while Mao did muse over the Soviets' attitude toward U.S. relations with the Baltic states, when the Chairman turned to the next subject in their November 1973 conversation—Taiwan—he was quite clear:

> So long as you sever the diplomatic relations with Taiwan, then it is possible for our two countries to solve the issue of diplomatic relations. That is to say like we did with Japan.[16]

Kissinger probed:

> From our point of view we want diplomatic relations with the People's Republic. Our difficulty is that we cannot immediately sever relations with Taiwan, for various reasons, all of them having to do with our domestic situation…So the question is whether we can find some formula that enables us to have diplomatic relations, and the utility of it would be symbolic strengthening of our ties, because, on a technical level, the Liaison Offices perform very usefully.

Mao rejoined:

> That can do. [Kissinger: What can do?] It can do to continue as now, because you still need Taiwan…We have established diplomatic relations with the Soviet Union and also with India, but they are not so very good. And they are not even as good as our relations with you, which are better than our relations with them. So this issue [of establishing formal diplomatic relations] is not an important one.[17]

In the course of this exchange, Mao also said that, although Sino-U.S. normalization could come much more quickly, Beijing could wait one hundred years to resolve cross-Strait issues. However, when they

---

[15] Kissinger, *Years of Upheaval*, p. 692.

[16] Memorandum of Conversation, November 12, 1973 (5:40 pm-8:25 pm), in Burr, ed., *The Kissinger Transcripts*, p. 186.

[17] Ibid., pp. 186-187.

were resolved, the Chairman did not "believe in" a peaceful transition. Despite Mao's statement about non-peaceful resolution, because of the extended time frame he cited, Kissinger concluded that Beijing was in no hurry to resolve the cross-Strait relationship and that "the Taiwan issue would not be an obstacle to our relations."[18] At the level of strategic cooperation against the USSR, he was right. If meant also to apply to normalization, it is hard to see what lay behind the judgment that Taiwan would not stand in the way.

This is especially relevant since, as already noted, Kissinger felt under pressure to try to establish formal relations while he could. Trying to press the case, he seized on Mao's concern that the Democrats might be isolationist if they came into power.[19] "[T]his is why I believe we should use this period, when all of us are still in office and understand the situation, to so solidify it that no alternative will be possible anymore."[20] Mao was having none of it and responded only obliquely, deflecting the conversation from normalization to other subjects.

In the communiqué issued at the end of Kissinger's November 1973 visit, the Chinese inserted an intriguing "new sentence" into the standard PRC formula that Zhou suggested could "move the issue a little bit forward."[21] Taken together with his view of Mao's statement on the Baltics, Kissinger interpreted the new formulation then—and for some time after—as indicating potential flexibility toward a normalization formula of the sort he was seeking. The sentence read:

> The Chinese side reiterated that the normalization of relations between China and the United States can be realized only on the basis of confirming the principle of one China.[22]

---

[18] Kissinger, *Years of Upheaval*, p. 692.

[19] This may have been Mao's way of probing what would happen if Nixon left office as the result of Watergate, which was consuming Washington at the time.

[20] Memorandum of Conversation, November 12, 1973 (5:40 pm-8:25 pm), p. 198.

[21] Memorandum of Conversation, November 13, 1973 (4:30 pm-7:15 pm), p. 13, in *The Kissinger Transcripts and Related Material*, an online National Security Archive document reader available at http://www.gwu.edu/~nsarchiv/nsa/publications/DOC_readers/kissinger/docs/ (hereafter *Kissinger Transcripts Online.*)

[22] "Joint U.S.-PRC Communiqué," November 14, 1973, excerpts from which can be found in the appendix. The full text is in *Department of State Bulletin*

Rather than being a signal of pragmatic flexibility, there is another interpretation, however, and that is that the new sentence was intended to drive home the point, in accordance with Mao's statement to Kissinger, that the only way to move ahead was by breaking with Taiwan.[23] Kissinger, clearly hopeful that the new language suggested an opening, undertook to study the "many layers of meaning" of Mao's remarks on Taiwan and the "many possibilities" they opened, and to submit further ideas to Zhou.[24]

In his report to the President, Kissinger termed the new sentence "the most significant development of the visit" and a "breakthrough...that requires only that the 'principle' of one China be respected as we normalize relations."[25] He expanded on this:

> This suggests that we might be able to continue a substantial relationship with Taiwan when we establish diplomatic relations with Peking so long as we maintain the "principle" of one China. They may be willing to settle for considerable autonomy for Taiwan and continuing U.S. ties so long as the nominal juridical framework reflects the one China approach. Our task now is to come up with some formulas that can begin to move toward this goal.[26]

In the final negotiations on the communiqué to be issued at the end of his November 1973 visit, Kissinger told Zhou that, as part of his response to Mao's words, he was proposing to extend the U.S. statement beyond what had been said in the Shanghai Communiqué. After repeating the sentence about "all Chinese on either side of the Taiwan

---

LXIX, no. 1798 (December 10, 1973), p. 716.

[23] This latter interpretation is reflected in Charles W. Freeman, Jr., "The Process of Rapprochement: Achievements and Problems," in Gene T. Hsiao and Michael Witunski, eds., *Sino-American Normalization and its Policy Implications* (New York: Praeger, 1983). See also Tyler, *A Great Wall,* op. cit., pp. 167-177.

[24] Memorandum of Conversation, November 13, 1973 (4:30 pm-7:15 pm), p. 13.

[25] Henry A. Kissinger, Memorandum for the President, "My Visit to China," November 19, 1973, p. 1, in Department of State, *FOIA Released Documents Collection*, online at http://foia.state.gov/documents/foiadocs/51c5.PDF (hereafter *FRDC*).

[26] Ibid., pp. 4-5. Winston Lord, one of Kissinger's top aides, confirms that Kissinger's enthusiasm about the potential contained in the new language was genuine (interview by author).

Strait" maintaining there is one China and Taiwan is part of it, Kissinger proposed to add:

> The United States Government does not challenge that position *and will not create obstacles to the peaceful settlement of that issue.*[27]

Without explanation, Zhou asked that the new language be dropped, perhaps because it inferentially conditioned U.S. non-interference on "peaceful settlement," which was both unacceptable in principle and especially problematic in light of Mao's statement to Kissinger only two days earlier that he did not "believe in" peaceful resolution.

Kissinger conducted a press backgrounder in Tokyo on November 14th on his way home, and out of that came stories that the U.S. considered Zhou's new sentence to be a "softening" or "subtle advance" of the PRC position on diplomatic normalization.   According to then-ROC Ambassador James Shen, Kissinger personally downplayed to him Washington's interest in diplomatic relations with Beijing, telling Shen that "the idea that we are compulsively seeking diplomatic relations is nonsense." However, Shen noted, a widely-distributed U.S. Information Agency (USIA) report based in part on the Tokyo press conference included an assessment by U.S. officials that "[t]here is a major evolution represented in the latest document because it contains a nuance in the Chinese statement about what normalization depends upon."[28]

CONFIRMING THE PRINCIPLE OF "ONE CHINA"

Throughout the early months of 1974, Kissinger and his staff continued to wrestle with the possible implications of Zhou's "new sentence" and Mao's Baltics reference, searching for any opening those statements might have suggested for establishment of U.S.-PRC diplomatic relations without immediately breaking with Taipei.   In January, National Security Council (NSC) Senior Staff Member Richard Solomon drafted a memo examining the issue. Solomon argued that Beijing's more "relaxed" mood regarding Taiwan stemmed from the PRC's concern to ensure that, as the U.S. lowered its profile in Asia, Moscow did not fill in behind it as the guarantor of ROC security. He

---

[27] Memorandum of Conversation, November 14, 1973 (1:00 am-2:20 am), p. 5, *National Archives*, box 372. Emphasis added.

[28] Shen, *The U.S. & Free China*, pp. 162-170.

judged that Beijing might have grown disinclined to hasten any severing of the United States from Taiwan's future either out of an exaggerated concern about Taipei choosing such a "Soviet option" or for fear that economic chaos on the island in the wake of a U.S. break could undermine KMT (Kuomintang—i.e., Nationalist) rule and generate greater pressures for independence.

This view included discussion of the possibility that Beijing favored an American "bridge" between the two sides of the Strait, and that this, in turn, potentially implied greater PRC toleration of substantial American political, economic "and perhaps even military ties to Taiwan, *as long as we meet certain requirements of form and legal precedent which will 'confirm the principle of one China.'*"[29]

In this document, for the first time we can find recorded, U.S. officials began to address in a serious way the question of the residual U.S. relationship with Taiwan in a post-normalization world. Solomon's preferred option was to transform the American embassy in Taipei into a consulate general, with personnel holding diplomatic privileges and immunities, but leaving ambiguous the precise status of the island entity (and the authorities) with which the U.S. was maintaining such relations. He would have tried to persuade Beijing to accept this by tying it to a statement endorsing U.S. acceptance of "one China."

On the assumption that the Mutual Defense Treaty with Taiwan would lapse with normalization, the question of how to maintain a legal foundation to come to Taiwan's aid was raised. The State Department Legal Adviser argued that, although establishing diplomatic relations with Beijing and breaking with Taipei would not, in itself, destroy that legal foundation, any public statement by the United States recognizing the "principle of one China" could be "fatal" to the maintenance of a defense commitment to the island unless very carefully handled. As the Legal Adviser put it:

> Unlike the severance of diplomatic relations, withdrawal of U.S. recognition of the Republic of China as a state would unavoidably terminate the Mutual Defense Treaty and would, in the absence of the establishment of some other international status for Taiwan and the Pescadores, render unlawful any threat

---

[29] Richard Solomon, Memorandum for Henry Kissinger (draft), "'Confirming the Principle of One China': Next Steps in the Evolution of U.S.-PRC-ROC Relations," p. 5, conveyed from Solomon to Winston Lord on January 9, 1974, *NSA* 00286. Emphasis added.

or use of force by the United States to defend these areas from attack by the PRC.[30]

Solomon sought to deal with this legal dilemma in his memo by suggesting some combination of a PRC commitment to "peaceful liberation," a U.S.-PRC understanding on continued U.S. cash arms sales to Taiwan, a congressional resolution "sustaining our commitment to the defense of Taiwan even in the absence of a formal security treaty," and a small residual military/intelligence liaison cadre that could stand as a "visible symbol" of the continuing U.S. involvement in the island's security. Because these "residual expressions" of the U.S. defense relationship with Taiwan would both assist in maintaining stability on Taiwan as well as help block inroads of Soviet influence, they were seen as potentially acceptable to Beijing. On the other hand, they would leave the United States involved in a lingering defense relationship that future American administrations might not wish, and that could lead to complications with those in Beijing who wanted to attack such arrangements as sustaining "two Chinas."[31]

What we can see here are not only elements of the normalization package as it evolved over the years, but also a recognition that establishment of full diplomatic relations with Beijing required breaking such relations with Taipei, whatever de facto relationships were able to be maintained. Based at least on the record, it does not appear that Kissinger was willing to accept this approach, since it meant breaking with Taipei at a time when that was politically impossible. If that was the only workable approach, U.S.-PRC relations seemed consigned to an institutional limbo. A key aspect of this, the desire to maintain some level of official presence on the island, was to remain a feature of the U.S. position—and a stumbling block to normalization—all the way through the first talks between the Carter Administration and China in August 1977 and until serious normalization talks began in spring 1978.

In any event, several months passed at the start of 1974 as domestic political tensions continued to build in both countries, and the U.S. still did not go back to China with any further thoughts about how to

---

[30] George H. Aldrich, Memorandum for Winston Lord and Arthur W. Hummel, Jr., "Normalization of Relations with the People's Republic of China—Legal Implications for the Defense of Taiwan," January 7, 1974, p. 2, *National Archives*, box 330.

[31] Solomon, "'Confirming the Principle of One China': Next Steps in the Evolution of U.S.-PRC-ROC Relations," p. 5.

"confirm the principle of one China." When Kissinger met with Deng Xiaoping in New York in April, however, Deng conveyed a sense of calm: "We are going along the track of the Shanghai communiqué."[32]

At that meeting, Kissinger volunteered to Deng that he had been thinking about how to "give effect to the principle of one China" as raised by China in the November 1973 communiqué, when Vice Foreign Minister Qiao Guanhua intervened to say that he had been involved in the drafting of that language: "The essential meaning is as Chairman Mao told you. The normalization of our relations can only be on the basis of the Japanese pattern. No other pattern is possible." Deng added that China hoped this question could be solved relatively quickly, but, on the other hand, that the Chinese side was in no hurry.[33]

Whatever Deng's expressions of calm, signs of PRC impatience with U.S. Taiwan policy in the course of a domestic Chinese political struggle emerged throughout the first half of 1974. Various visitors were treated to one or another version of the Chinese view that the U.S. had lost interest.[34] U.S. policy planners, too, shared this sense of U.S. policy drift, seeing a lack of vision in Washington about the shape of any future normalized relationship with the PRC ("particularly as it affects Taiwan") or a strategy for getting there.[35] Once more Kissinger's assistants seemed to have in mind that full normalization could only come in the context of a break with Taipei, something that remained politically impossible in the short run. Thus, while tacitly accepting the full normalization was unattainable in the immediate future, they looked for other steps that could "confirm the principle of one China" and "that could be taken over the coming two years which would move us in that

---

[32] Memorandum of Conversation, April 14, 1974 (8:05 pm-11:00 pm), in Burr, ed., *The Kissinger Transcripts,* p. 283.

[33] In a note reporting on this dinner to Winston Lord, then-Deputy Assistant Secretary Hummel commented that the "Japanese pattern" clearly meant the complete de-recognition of Taiwan and severance of all but "nominally" private ties; see Arthur Hummel, Memorandum for Winston Lord, "Random Notes on HAK-PRC Dinner April 14," April 15, 1974, *NSA* 00296.

[34] See, for example, Memorandum for Secretary Kissinger, "Indicators of PRC Internal Debate and Desire for Movement on the Taiwan Issue," May 23, 1974, *NSA* 00299.

[35] See Arthur Hummel, Winston Lord and Richard Solomon, Memorandum to the Secretary, "Imperatives for Planning and Action on the China Issue," May 24, 1974, *NSA* 00300.

direction."[36] They stressed that, without an overall strategy, problems would arise. For example, coordination of individual agencies' relationships with Taiwan was difficult and, unless such ties were controlled, options for further movement toward normalization might be foreclosed. On the other hand, they were increasingly concerned that the United States might get locked into an "irreversible position" with a "potentially unstable Chinese leadership whose future political orientation may not be so inclined to dealings with the U.S."[37]

The advisers reviewed various Chinese rebuffs of Kissinger's efforts to move ahead in order to see if they could discern anything further about the meaning of the phrase about normalizing relations on the basis of "confirming the principle of one China." They were puzzled about the Chinese stance, but in any event concluded that the Chinese had little bargaining room in what was clearly a turbulent period in PRC leadership politics. Still, they held out the possibility that Mao, himself, was more flexible than lower-level officials—and more patient. Nonetheless, they concluded, a clean break with Taipei would be required, and while that might not be possible in the short run, they saw the relationship with Beijing as fragile on the Taiwan front and in need of some near-term bolstering.

So here, on the eve of the Watergate-induced presidential transition in the United States, the Taiwan issue—and, with it, normalization—was stuck, caught in the gears of the domestic political turmoil in both countries. Relations had actually taken a significant step forward with the establishment of Liaison Offices in spring 1973, especially as the complicated arrangements about using the Paris channel for some things and the New York channel for others quickly fell away when Ambassador Huang Zhen moved from Paris to Washington.

Kissinger was still struggling to find a way to consolidate the relationship in the form of diplomatic relations while Mao and Zhou could give it their imprimatur, but he was running up against strong resistance in China to anything that smelled of compromise on the core issue of sovereignty and the requirement that the U.S. maintain only unofficial relations with Taiwan.

Not that he would live to see it through, but Mao's statements about the near-certainty of a non-peaceful resolution of the Taiwan question were not especially helpful. They were cast in a time frame of one

---

[36] Ibid., p. 2.

[37] Ibid., p. 3.

hundred years that Kissinger was able to describe as taking the issue out of the picture, but this still did not provide the political offset that Nixon needed to justify pulling the plug on defense relationships with Taiwan. At the end of the day, of course, he was too weak to pull off normalization in any event.

Finally, Zhou Enlai's "new sentence" seemed almost designed to torture Kissinger and his staff, who kept looking for flexibility that apparently was not there. Even if it had not been a time of such great political turmoil at the top in Beijing, Mao himself had dismissed the idea of violating the principle of "one China" through word games. The Chairman seemed quite content to focus on the substance of U.S.-PRC relations and he positioned himself not to be railroaded into making compromises on "one China" because Beijing "needed" the United States.

TRANSITIONS: TAKING STOCK

Richard Nixon resigned as President of the United States effective noon, August 9, 1974; Gerald R. Ford was sworn in shortly thereafter. As one of his "first acts," President Ford sent a message to Mao Zedong affirming the continuing U.S. commitment to all previous undertakings, including those reflected in the Shanghai Communiqué. He said that there would be "no higher priority" during his tenure than "accelerating the normalization process," a sentiment echoed by Kissinger in a message to Zhou.[38] That same afternoon, PRC Liaison Office (PRCLO) Chief Huang Zhen went to the White House where Kissinger—later joined by President Ford—reconfirmed to him "all discussions, understandings, and commitments made with President Nixon, as well as by me on behalf of President Nixon."[39]

In briefing the new President, Kissinger described U.S. relations with the PRC as "essentially on course," but he cautioned that the U.S. could not afford to be complacent. On the handling of Taiwan he reported:

> Our basic approach has been to move our relations forward by using the Chinese geopolitical concerns about the USSR as leverage; at the same time we have managed the difficult

---

[38] WH 42541, "Voyager Channel" message to U.S. Liaison Office Peking, August 9, 1974, *National Archives*, box 380.

[39] Memorandum of Conversation, August 9, 1974 (4:50 pm-5:20 pm), p. 2, *National Archives*, box 376.

bilateral issues of Taiwan/diplomatic relations through private agreement in principle on our final destination but proceeding in gradual public steps to accustom our various audiences.[40]

Noting that, for geopolitical reasons, Beijing had been willing to adopt rounded formulations in the Shanghai Communiqué rather than insisting on denouncing the U.S.-ROC Mutual Defense Treaty or demanding a timetable for recognition, he went on:

Privately we have done the following to give their leaders the long-term assurance that they must have: we said we would complete the normalization process by 1976; we have assured them that we would not foster any two-Chinas policy or Taiwan independence or third country influence in Taiwan; and we have gradually withdrawn our forces from Taiwan as unilateral acts in the wake of the Vietnam peace settlement.[41]

Describing the ROC's attitude toward the evolving U.S. policy, Kissinger told the President:

Taiwan sees the language of the Shanghai Communiqué—that the Taiwan problem is up to the Chinese on both sides of the Strait to settle—as preserving Taiwan's options either to integrate with the Mainland or to decide to become a separate nation. The government in Taiwan clearly understands that the U.S. Government strongly opposes any declaration of separate status, but they feel that this is still an option for the future."[42]

Kissinger identified the chief unresolved substantive issue regarding post-normalization relations with Taiwan as achievement of a level of security for Taiwan "that is acceptable, or tolerable" to the U.S., PRC and ROC. Although, he said, government lawyers asserted that the defense treaty could not survive after the U.S. recognized Beijing and acknowledged "one China." He noted:

...we do not wish to be seen as forcing Taiwan into an integration with Peking that it does not want, nor abandoning

---

[40] "People's Republic of China," briefing paper for the President, August 14, 1974, p. 2, *NSA* 00307.

[41] Ibid., p. 3.

[42] Ibid., p. 7.

Taiwan to possible later subjugation by invasion from the PRC. Moreover, it is certainly not in our interests or those of the PRC to have the ROC conclude that it is in such dire straits that it decides to take unilateral action.[43]

In what strikes one, at this late stage in the process, more as a statement of hope than hard-headed analysis of the PRC's position on sovereignty or China's reading of history, Kissinger argued that the United States could announce that the Mutual Defense Treaty with Taipei was "moot" rather than formally abrogating it.

MORE CREATIVE THINKING: RECONFIGURING "ONE CHINA"

In early October 1974, as Kissinger prepared for a trip to China the next month, he met with Vice Foreign Minister Qiao Guanhua in New York, where they again engaged on the subject of normalization. And as Kissinger once more probed on possible flexibility that he had detected in Mao's comments the year before and in the "new sentence," Qiao once more said there was only one model: "the Japanese model."[44]

Nonetheless, in the weeks immediately prior to his departure, Kissinger's staff wrote several memos on the subject. They argued that the PRC saw continued U.S. ties with Taiwan as a moderating factor on Taiwan's policies and actions that could otherwise damage the prospects for realizing "one China" and that this provided leverage in working out post-normalization arrangements.[45] In this connection, although they gave a nod to the possibility that the U.S. would have to go all the way to the strictly private Japanese model,[46] they saw China under "substantial pressure" to consolidate the U.S. relationship[47] and said they would "be surprised" if Beijing did not accept "some fairly reassuring remnant U.S.

---

[43] Ibid., p. 9.

[44] Memorandum of Conversation, October 2, 1974 (8:15 pm-11:35 pm), p. 13, in *Kissinger Transcripts Online.*

[45] Winston Lord, Arthur Hummel and Richard Solomon, Memorandum for Secretary Kissinger, "Briefing the President on Your Forthcoming Trip to Peking," November 9, 1974, p. 4, *NSA* 00317.

[46] "The Operational Issues Associated with a Normalization Agreement," undated, p. 9, *National Archives*, box 331.

[47] "Normalization of U.S.-PRC Relations and the Future of Taiwan," undated briefing paper for Kissinger's November 1974 trip to Beijing, p. 5, *National Archives*, box 375.

presence in Taipei—as long as that presence did not give formal legitimacy to the ROC as a separate state or government."[48] They went so far as to raise the issue of "what price" the United States should expect to collect from Beijing for helping restrain Taiwan from opting for independence or inviting in a third country presence.

In the event, in their talks with Kissinger in November 1974, the Chinese showed no such haste or sense of obligation. Rather, they took the opposite perspective. For the first time, Vice Premier Deng Xiaoping, now the chief PRC interlocutor in place of the hospitalized Zhou Enlai, insisted that the U.S. "owed" China "a debt," a theme that was invoked many times over the succeeding years.[49] Kissinger nevertheless went on to lay out his normalization proposal.

On the political side, the U.S. plan included breaking diplomatic relations with Taipei, recognizing the PRC as the "legal government of all China," and transforming the Taipei embassy into a Liaison Office. On the security side, it provided for the removal of all U.S. forces and installations by the end of 1977.

At the same time, however, despite what Kissinger called the "absurdity" of maintaining a defense arrangement with part of a country that one recognizes, it included preserving the form of a defense treaty with Taipei in order for Washington to be able to say, "at least for some period of time," that there were assurances of peaceful integration which "[could] be reviewed after some interval." After all of the other steps, Kissinger said, "[a]ll that would remain is that we would have some relation to peaceful reintegration."[50] What Washington wanted, Kissinger maintained, was "for at least a reasonable period of time" that the two sides "avoid a situation where the United States signs a document which leads to a military solution shortly after normalization." But, he assured Deng, President Ford was not seeking "a commitment that maintains separation" of Taiwan and the Mainland.[51]

Deng flatly rejected this overall approach. He termed the switching of liaison offices and embassies "still a variation of one China and one

---

[48] Ibid., p. 8.

[49] Memorandum of Conversation, November 26, 1974 (10:30 am-11:02 am), in Burr, ed., *The Kissinger Transcripts,* p. 288.

[50] Memorandum of Conversation, November 26, 1974 (3:45 pm-5:00 pm), pp. 3-6, *NSA* 00322.

[51] Ibid., p. 10.

Taiwan." He insisted that if they were to achieve normalization and abide by the course set by the Shanghai Communiqué, then the defense treaty with Taiwan had to be done away with. "It still looks as if you need Taiwan," he concluded.[52]

In the subsequent back and forth, Deng articulated what he identified as three immutable principles:

- We insist on the Shanghai Communiqué. That is, we refuse any method which will lead to the solution of "two Chinas," or "one China, one Taiwan," or any variation of these two.

- The solution of the Taiwan question is an internal issue of the Chinese people, and it can only be left to the Chinese people themselves to resolve. As to what means we will use to finally solve the Taiwan question—whether peaceful methods or non-peaceful methods—it is a matter, an internal affair, which should be left to the Chinese people to decide.

- We do not admit that there can be another country which will take part in the solution of the Taiwan question, including the United States.[53]

The proposal for switching U.S. liaison offices and embassies between Beijing and Taipei, or even establishing a consulate in Taiwan, violated the first principle, Deng argued, and the handling of the defense relationship violated the others. Kissinger's rejoinder—that the three principles were all accepted and that the only practical problem was how to implement them—was to no avail. Deng's response was short: sever diplomatic relations, withdraw the troops, abolish the treaty. As to how the issue was resolved between Beijing and Taipei, that was China's internal affair. Again, Kissinger sought to argue, as he had since 1971, China could make a unilateral statement of intentions, not to the United States but merely as a "general statement." The discussion closed inconclusively, with each agreeing to return to it at a later date.[54] Nonetheless, it was agreed—and announced—that President Ford would visit China in 1975.

---

[52] Ibid., pp. 7-9.

[53] Ibid., p. 11.

[54] Memorandum of Conversation, November 28, 1974 (4:00 pm-6:15 pm), pp. 11-16, *NSA* 00329.

Whatever flexibility had existed in Beijing's approach to normalization—and this writer does not detect that there ever was much, if any—it was decisively rejected early on in the year stretching between November 1973, when these issues first arose, and November 1974, when Deng dismissed them. Kissinger's hopes to persuade China that its sovereign claims to Taiwan would not be compromised by a form of residual U.S. representation on the island somewhat more official—or less unofficial—than the Japanese model, and that a symbolic security "tail" was in the long-term interest of Beijing's quest for reunification, fell on deaf ears. The priority that the two sides assigned to normalization simply did not mesh. Whether primarily due to leadership politics in Beijing, to a sense that it was not strategically so critical to institutionalize the relationship in short order, or perhaps a belief that a weakened administration in Washington was now incapable of following through on prior commitments and was simply trying to manipulate them, or some combination of these and perhaps other factors, the net result was that the PRC raised high the sovereignty banner, the wind went out of the sails of this endeavor, and expectations fell flat.

MARKING TIME

Over the next several months into early 1975, while U.S. spokesmen sought to reaffirm that the new relationship with China was a "durable feature" of the world scene,[55] the effort to use the announced Ford trip to China as the occasion to complete normalization was complicated by both the fall of Saigon, which raised questions about the validity of U.S. commitments, and domestic American politics. Chiang Kai-shek died in early April, and Senator Barry Goldwater (R-AZ) seized the occasion to turn the screws on an unelected American President who was not beloved by his party's conservative wing, threatening "a hell of a fight" if Ford sought to change the relationship with Taiwan.[56] It was not by happenstance that President Ford, answering press questions on April 16th, said that "we consider our relationship, our cooperation with the Republic of China a matter of very, very great importance to us"[57] and it

---

[55] "Secretary Kissinger's June 23 Speech in Atlanta," excerpted in Oscar V. Armstrong, Memorandum to various recipients, "Official U.S. Statements on China," June 23, 1975, *National Archives*, box 380.

[56] These events are laid out well in Tyler, *A Great Wall*, pp. 202-203.

[57] "President Ford's Question and Answer Session on April 16," excerpted in "Official U.S. Statements on China."

was not a coincidence that at a press conference in early May he proclaimed that, just as he was strengthening other alliance relationships in the region, he wanted to "reaffirm our commitments to Taiwan."[58]

As a result, although the President had as recently as April 10th declared publicly that he was "firmly fixed" on the course set forth in the Shanghai Communiqué and laid out his plan to visit China later in the year "to accelerate the improvement in our relations,"[59] within a few weeks Kissinger was telling interviewers that, while Ford would of course have to discuss Taiwan when in the PRC, he could go "without bringing that situation to a conclusion."[60]

Policy papers also quickly reflected the general retreat from the more ambitious normalization goal. A memorandum to Kissinger in early July offered the judgment,

> not that there should be 'normalization at any price,' but that long-term American foreign policy interests will be served by a consolidation of our present, if limited, relationship with Peking, and that we can avoid future problems with the PRC at a relatively low price as well as posture ourselves in Asia favorably for the future if an acceptable normalization deal can be worked out now.[61]

The authors saw the Chinese leadership as "more anxious than ever" to have a visible relationship with the United States for security reasons and thus probably "as likely as they may ever be" to accommodate American political needs. That said, they acknowledged that the only way to determine the exact degree of flexibility on the most sensitive issue, Taiwan's security, was through negotiations. Given the risks of sustaining the relationship at only its current level for some years to come, the memorandum argued that it was in the U.S. interest to see whether substantial assurances on Taiwan's security could be obtained as well as to probe for other terms that would allow near-term

---

[58] "President Ford's Press Conference on May 6," excerpted in ibid.

[59] "President Ford's State of the World Speech on April 10," excerpted in ibid.

[60] "Interview with Secretary Kissinger by U.S. News & World Report, June 16, 1975," excerpted in ibid.

[61] Philip Habib/William Gleysteen, Winston Lord and Richard H. Solomon, Memorandum for Secretary Kissinger, "U.S.-PRC Relations and Approaches to the President's Peking Trip: Tasks for the Rest of 1975," July 3, 1975, p. 3, *NSA* 00357.

normalization. Those terms were still seen to include some official or "semi-official" U.S. presence in Taiwan that was less "formally unofficial" than the Japanese model. The security arrangements envisaged closely paralleled what actually emerged four years later: a Chinese statement of peaceful intent, a congressional expression of concern for the future of Taiwan's security and expectation that the Taiwan issue would be resolved peacefully, and a residual program of arms sales to the island.

The area where later developments notably outpaced American policy assumptions involved attitudes on Taiwan toward cross-Strait relations. The July memorandum argued that self-determination "has never been an element at issue in America's China policy and...those Taiwanese intellectuals who have advocated independence (primarily as residents of the U.S. or Japan) have been unable to evoke a substantial response from the people or authorities on the island."[62] The reality, of course, is that the subsequent change in Taiwan's domestic political dynamic in just that direction has been rapid and has seriously complicated the picture for all concerned.

Despite his advisers' argument in favor of testing PRC flexibility, in a meeting between Kissinger and his Asia team a week later, the Secretary rejected any attempt to reach normalization before the 1976 elections. Arguing that there was no "legal basis for defending part of one country," Kissinger said the President could not afford to have Taiwan as an issue in the campaign because of the risk of a conservative reaction. Moreover, despite some indicators of flexibility on Beijing's part that permitted the President to go to China without any prospect for a normalization agreement, he saw no sign of Chinese flexibility on the Taiwan issue, itself. Still, Kissinger was willing to look for "intermediate steps" short of normalization to consolidate the relationship (e.g., a further U.S. statement on "one China").[63] He so informed Foreign Minister Qiao Guanhua in their meeting in New York in September, thus preparing Beijing for his approach later on.[64]

---

[62] Ibid., p. 16.

[63] Memorandum of Conversation, July 6, 1975 in Burr, ed., *The Kissinger Transcripts*, pp. 377-381.

[64] The fact of Kissinger's having informed Qiao is contained in "Normalization," an undated background paper prepared for Kissinger's October 1975 visit, p. 4, *National Archives*, box 373; the date of meeting is reflected in Burr, ed., *The Kissinger Transcripts,* p. 381.

CONSIDERING PARTIAL STEPS

Through the fall of 1975, in the run-up to Kissinger's next visit to China in October, during that visit, and even afterward, the U.S. side searched for a formula on the Taiwan issue that China might buy as representing "progress" even though it did not meet the terms necessary for full normalization. The Chinese were not interested.

When Kissinger advanced a proposal for "a partial step" during his October visit, characterizing it as "picking up the principle of the November 1973 Communiqué," Deng dismissed it as "a bit;"[65] Qiao Guanhua (by now Foreign Minister) called it "infinitesimal progress."[66] Though they continued to welcome the Ford visit without moving to normalization, the Chinese treated Kissinger brusquely, even rudely, and put forward hard-line rhetoric on Taiwan (and on other issues, as well) for use in a possible Ford communiqué.

One can only assume that the Chinese either missed the significance of Kissinger's proposal (which envisaged a direct American endorsement of the "one China principle") or felt that the gain wasn't worth the risk that the United States would rest at that point and not press ahead with normalization on the basis of the PRC's three conditions, which they stressed in their draft of the abortive communiqué. Or that political conditions in China were so unstable that they could not afford to move ahead on anything less than maximal terms. In any event, Beijing has not been offered a similar formal U.S. public affirmative statement on "one China" since, and given the political evolution in Taiwan in the meantime, they are unlikely to be presented with that opportunity unless and until cross-Strait agreement is reached on the nature of Taiwan's future association with the Mainland.

Ford's visit went well enough, including a lengthy meeting with Mao,[67] though little of substance was achieved and, in the end, no communiqué was issued. Deng made clear that the bilateral relationship would not be allowed to move forward until normalization had been completed, that is, until the Taiwan issues had been satisfactorily addressed. In response, Ford made a hedged commitment:

---

[65] Memorandum of Conversation, October 22, 1975 (3:40 pm-4:45 pm), p. 4, *NSA* 00373.

[66] General Brent Scowcroft, Memorandum for the President, "Secretary's Talks with Chinese Officials," October 23, 1975, p. 2, *NSA* 00374.

[67] Kissinger describes Ford as having been received with "impeccable courtesy" (*Years of Renewal*, p. 887).

...after the election [in 1976] we will be in a position to move much more specifically toward the normalization of relations, along the model perhaps of the Japan arrangement, but it will take some time, bearing in mind our domestic political situation.[68]

Deng rephrased that:

We have taken note of Mr. President's well-intentioned words, that is, that under suitable conditions you will be prepared to solve the Taiwan issue according to the Japanese formula [which Deng then specified as including the three principles on withdrawal of forces, abolishing the defense treaty and severing diplomatic relations with Taipei].[69]

When Deng argued that "other issues pertaining to Taiwan" would be resolved in accordance with the principle that it is the internal problem of China, Ford persisted:

It would have to be a peaceful solution, *which I understand is the understanding President Nixon made at that time.*[70]

Predictably, this set off Deng to repeat both the issue of principle (that it was an internal Chinese question) and, as Mao had repeated to Kissinger once again in October, that China did not believe in a peaceful transition. Each time this was repeated, of course, it deepened the record

---

[68] Memorandum of Conversation, December 4, 1975 (10:05 am-11:47 am), p. 4, *NSA* 00399. In his press conference that day, Kissinger pointed out that in the Shanghai Communiqué the United States committed to complete the process of normalization. He reported that President Ford had reaffirmed that commitment to the Chinese leader ("Excerpt from Secretary Kissinger's News Conference, Peking, December 4, 1975," in Department of State Office of Public Communications, *Selected Documents: U.S. Policy Toward China, July 15, 1971-January 15, 1979*, op. cit).

[69] Ibid. In recounting this conversation to Carter administration officials, Deng embellished it even further. He told Zbigniew Brzezinski in May 1978: "President Ford stated that if he was reelected he would move to full normalization according to the three conditions without any reservation"; see Memorandum of Conversation, May 21, 1978 (4:05 pm-6:30 pm), p. 6, Jimmy Carter Library.

[70] Ibid., p. 5. Emphasis added.

of Beijing's lack of commitment to peaceful resolution, complicating consideration of limiting arms sales to Taiwan.

THE END OF AN ERA

During 1976, as relations were stagnating, in important measure due to political developments in China,[71] hard-line PRC leaders took an increasingly outspoken stance on the low likelihood of peaceful "liberation" of Taiwan. In part, this was in response to the rising conservative voices in the United States opposed to normalizing with Beijing at Taiwan's expense. Symptomatic of this, the Republican Party platform, while endorsing improved ties with the PRC, also spoke of Taiwan policy in—to Beijing—provocative terms:

> Our friendly relations with one great power should not be construed as a challenge to any other nation, large or small. The United States government, while engaged in a normalization of relations with the People's Republic of China, will continue to support the freedom and independence of our friend and ally, the Republic of China, and its 16 million people. The United States will fulfill and keep its commitments, such as the mutual defense treaty, with the Republic of China.[72]

The Presidential debate in October did nothing to ease Beijing's concern. President Ford emphasized the U.S. "obligation" to the people in Taiwan and American insistence that cross-Strait issues be settled peacefully, "as was agreed" in the Shanghai Communiqué. Governor Jimmy Carter criticized Ford for "frittering away" the opportunity opened in 1972, but said: "I would never let that friendship with the People's Republic of China stand in the way of the preservation of the independence and freedom of the people on Taiwan."[73]

---

[71] Zhou Enlai's death in January 1976 and Mao's in September brought to a head the political tensions that had been brewing in Beijing for some time. In April, Deng Xiaoping was once again deposed, but by a month after Mao's death, the radical "Gang of Four" had been arrested and China resumed a more stable course with Deng once more "resurrected" in the months shortly thereafter.

[72] "Republican Party Platform of 1976," The American Presidency Project, University of California - Santa Barbara, online at http://www.presidency.ucsb. edu/site/docs/platforms.php.

[73] "Presidential Campaign Debate between Gerald R. Ford and Jimmy Carter,"

Shortly before the election, Kissinger met with his top China hands. Even though his aides predicted an improvement in U.S.-PRC relations in the wake of the recent shake-up in Beijing and the arrest of the radical Gang of Four, Kissinger indicated that even if Beijing had accepted the terms of normalization proposed in the past—including something on peaceful resolution—"it would be a fraud."

> Our saying we want a peaceful solution has no force. It is Chinese territory. What are we going to do about it?...For us to go to war with a recognized country where we have an ambassador over a part of what we would recognize as their country would be preposterous.[74]

Apparently reflecting his assessment of the political limitations on both sides, Kissinger said: "I never believed that normalization is possible." Despite all of his efforts, that view is understandable. As others have described the impossible situation, over all of those years both Nixon and Ford were

> ...trapped in a cross-strait conundrum. While it was clear that political reality was such that any further progress in the relationship with the PRC required that the status quo in relations with Taiwan be maintained, it was equally clear that a change in that status quo was the necessary prerequisite for Beijing's agreement to any further progress.[75]

After President Ford's defeat, PRC Liaison Office Chief Huang Zhen assured Kissinger that Mao's line on improving Sino-American relations remained intact, but, in what was likely intended as a warning to be passed on to the incoming Administration, he also cautioned that continuing improvement depended on strict observance of the Shanghai Communiqué by both sides. Any action counter to—or going back on—the principles of the communiqué would have "severe consequences."[76]

October 6, 1976, online at http://www.ford.utexas.edu/library/speeches/760854.htm

[74] Memorandum of Conversation, "Developments in China," October 29, 1976, in Burr, ed., *The Kissinger Transcripts*, p. 416.

[75] Steven M. Goldstein and Randall Schriver, "An Uncertain Relationship: The United States, Taiwan and the Taiwan Relations Act," *The China Quarterly*, no. 165 (March 2001), p. 170.

[76] Memorandum of Conversation, December 21, 1976 (4:35 pm-5:40 pm), p. 4,

Kissinger's last recorded comments on normalization as Secretary of State came in a luncheon he hosted in early January 1977 to introduce Huang Zhen to Carter's Secretary-designate, Cyrus R. Vance: "With respect to the Taiwan issue, we have confirmed our commitment to the principle of one China"[77]—a formulation that Vance echoed:

> As far as President Carter is concerned, let me assure you that he stands firmly behind the implementation of the Shanghai Communiqué as the guiding principle which should govern our bilateral relations...Let me say that I fully accept the principle of one China.[78]

Looking back over what was to be the last year of Mao's life and the last year of Ford's presidency, in light of the political circumstances in both countries, there was no possibility they could have bridged the gap in their approaches to Taiwan. Beijing had obviously dug in and rejected any terms that conflicted with the principle of "one China" as the PRC defined that. There would be no winks and nods on representation, no cutting corners on getting rid of the Mutual Defense Treaty, no commitments by Beijing to peaceful settlement, even though that was its preferred course.

And Ford, who had little flexibility to begin with, and who probably misunderstood the terms of the Shanghai Communiqué and thought there was agreement to peaceful resolution, lost whatever maneuvering room he had in the face of the conservative challenge. It seems pretty clear that Ford was prepared to move forward if he was re-elected, but on what terms will never be known.

Henry Kissinger, obviously very discouraged by the end about the prospects for normalization, nonetheless had laid an important foundation for later expansion of the relationship on a broad basis. If Watergate had not intervened, Nixon might well have created the political space to press ahead. But if so, it is not clear from what we have seen in the record how he would have dealt with the inherent contradiction between China's insistence that the United States had no role in determining the future of cross-Strait relations and the American

---

NSA 00438.

[77] Memorandum of Conversation, January 8, 1977 (1:15 pm-2:40 pm), p. 5, Carter Library.

[78] Ibid., p. 6. For his part, Huang voiced the same warnings he had given Kissinger in December.

insistence that, if the matter extended beyond politics to threatening peace and stability in the region, then it did.

As Kissinger carped when normalization finally occurred, he could have agreed to those terms years before.[79] But the fact is that under neither Nixon nor Ford was there an opportunity to move to totally (nominally) unofficial representation on Taiwan, nor is it clear that the Chinese were ready at that time to live with arms sales.

When Ford left office, the record pointed the way to what was necessary in terms of the principles and symbols of "one China" if normalization was going to take place. The issue was, in light of all of the new administration's other priorities, whether it would do the necessary.

---

[79] See his China-related remarks relayed in Lee Lescaze, "Kissinger Raps White House for Blaming Israel on Impasse," *Washington Post*, December 19, 1978, A18.

4

Normalization

"The United States of America recognizes the People's Republic of China as the sole legal government of China."

—Joint U.S.-PRC Communiqué, December 1978

Jimmy Carter came to the presidency determined to complete normalization of relations with the PRC,[1] even though his campaign rhetoric on preserving Taiwan's free and independent status may well have made Beijing nervous.

Once Carter was in office, in what was apparently his first briefing paper for the new President on China, National Security Adviser Zbigniew Brzezinski forwarded a memo from NSC Senior Staff Member Michel Oksenberg summarizing developments since 1969 and assessing their implications. Oksenberg assessed that, if parallel strategic interests vis-à-vis the USSR had been "the precipitant" of Sino-American détente, "the American accommodation vis-à-vis Taiwan was the enabling factor."[2]

In his first meeting with Carter, on February 8th, PRC Liaison Office Chief Huang Zhen went through the full litany of the "crucial" nature of the Taiwan question, the essentiality of fulfilling all three key conditions for normalization, and the requirement to observe the principles of the Shanghai Communiqué. In response, Carter set the tone that was to guide his administration's approach to normalization:

> We understand the Chinese position. This has been presented to us on many occasions. We believe the Taiwan question rests in the hands of the Peoples [sic] Republic of China and in the

---

[1] See Carter, *Keeping Faith,* op. cit., pp. 186-190.

[2] Michel Oksenberg, Memorandum for Zbigniew Brzezinski, "Sino-American Relations, 1969-1976, and Their Implications," February 4, 1977, p. 2, enclosed in Zbigniew Brzezinski, Memorandum for the President, "Meeting Next Week with the Representative of the PRC (Tuesday February 8)," February 4, 1977, Carter Library.

people of Taiwan. Nothing would please us more than to see a peaceful resolution of this question. We understand that this is an internal matter, but we have a long-standing hope and expectation that it can be settled in peaceful ways. I hope this can be resolved. I hope we can see strong movement toward normalization, and the principles of the Shanghai Communiqué are obviously the ones to which we are committed.[3]

CLOSING OUT OPTIONS: THE SECRETARY'S "RETREAT"

In late July, President Carter met with his senior national security team and discussed the strategic and domestic political implications of normalization at length. At the end of the meeting, the President decided he was prepared to move ahead in spite of the political risks.[4] In August, Secretary Vance went to Beijing carrying a message that "the time has come for both sides to take the necessary steps leading to the establishment of full diplomatic relations...to place our relationship on a new and more permanent basis."[5] However, in beginning his detailed discussion of normalization issues, Vance highlighted the two aspects that challenged the PRC concept of sovereignty and had plagued normalization efforts to that point—and that would continue to do so:

Provided that we can find a basis which will not lessen the prospects for a *peaceful settlement* of the Taiwan question by the Chinese themselves and which would enable *informal contacts with Taiwan* to continue, the President is prepared to normalize relations.

Under these circumstances, and in accordance with our undertaking in the Shanghai Communiqué, acknowledging the Chinese position that there is only one China and that Taiwan is a part of China, we are prepared to establish full diplomatic relations with the People's Republic of China, recognizing your Government as the sole legal government of China.[6]

---

[3] Memorandum of Conversation, February 8, 1977 (10:00 am), p. 4, Carter Library.

[4] Vance, *Hard Choices,* op. cit., p. 79.

[5] Memorandum of Conversation, August 22, 1977 (4:00 pm-6:40 pm), p. 2, Carter Library.

[6] Memorandum of Conversation with Huang Hua, August 23, 1977 (9:30 am-

Vance went on to say that, under these circumstances, the Mutual Defense Treaty would lapse and all U.S. military forces and installations would be withdrawn from Taiwan.

He amplified on the question of U.S. residual representation in ways that, while from an American perspective were different in some important respects from what had been proposed before, sounded very familiar to the Chinese:

> As you know, the nature and extent of our involvement in Taiwan is different from that of any other country. Taking into account our laws, administrative practices, and public and congressional views, we have concluded that *totally*, and I underscore *totally*, private arrangements are not practicable for us. We have concluded that, as a practical matter, i would be necessary for U.S. Government personnel to remain on Taiwan under an *informal* arrangements [sic].

> Whatever the name of such an office, it would be clear it would *not* be diplomatic in character and would *not* perform diplomatic functions or in any other way constitute recognition. No flags would be flown, no Government Seal would be on the door, and no names would appear in diplomatic lists.[7]

On the security issue, Vance, as had Kissinger before him, referred to the need to maintain both domestic political support for normalization and the credibility of American commitments abroad. He said that, while the United States had no desire "to make [itself] the arbiter of how the Chinese people resolved the relationship between Taiwan and the Mainland," it was necessary that "we not be placed in the position of appearing to jeopardize stability."[8] Thus, while he also noted that a statement by Beijing about peaceful resolution of the Taiwan question could be significant in selling normalization within the United States, in any event, the United States would reiterate its "concern and interest" in a peaceful settlement and express confidence that normalization would not lessen the prospects for such a settlement. Even if China reiterated

---

11:50 am), p. 19, Carter Library. Emphasis added.

[7] Ibid., pp. 21-22.

[8] Ibid., p. 22.

its position that this was an internal matter, it would be essential that it not contradict the U.S. statement or itself stress forceful liberation.[9]

The next morning, Foreign Minister Huang Hua embarked on the preliminary response to the Secretary's remarks. Citing American support for Chiang Kai-shek "in the slaughtering of Chinese people" during the civil war and its continuing support for Chiang after he moved to Taiwan, he said the United States owed two debts to China. "These are historical facts. They are not questions or matters for interpretation."[10]

Rebuffing Vance's statement regarding the need for efforts by both sides to bring about normalization, Huang asserted that, in light of the U.S. debt to China on Taiwan, "the question simply doesn't arise of the so-called reciprocal effort for the resolution of this issue." He charged Vance with paying mere lip-service to the three conditions China had laid down for normalization; he went on to assert that Vance had, in effect, "negated" the three conditions. In reality, the U.S. sought to maintain the right to interfere in China's internal affairs, he stormed. "How," he asked rhetorically, "can you reconcile your formula with the spirit and principles of the Shanghai Communiqué?" He went on: "You will continue to delay the normalization of relations between our two countries and, in doing so, you will continue to owe the debt to the Chinese people and the longer the delay the heavier the debt to the Chinese people."[11]

Deng rolled out the heavy guns that afternoon, scolding Vance for stating that the position the Secretary laid out was the "starting point." The starting point, Deng said, was the Shanghai Communiqué. Even President Ford had gone "a bit further on this issue." In Deng's opinion, what Vance proposed was "not a step forward from the original process of normalization. It is, on the contrary, a retreat from it." Reprising Huang's comment from the morning, Deng said:

> That prerequisite [for normalization] is that it is the United States which will have to make up its mind. It is not China that is called

---

[9] Ibid., pp. 23-24.

[10] Memorandum of Conversation, August 24, 1977 (9:30 am-12:20 pm), p. 8, Carter Library.

[11] Ibid., pp. 8-10.

upon to do that…[I]t is not China which owes a debt to the United States but the United States owes a debt to China.[12]

And on the question of a residual U.S. presence in Taiwan, Deng cited what the PRC characterized as President Ford's position, i.e., "to act along the Japanese arrangement" in normalizing.[13] Again—and again—Deng insisted that it was the United States that owed a debt to China and continued to seek to impose its will on China. As to the representation arrangement, he stated, "you want an Embassy that does not have a sign on its door."[14]

> The Secretary of State has just now said he hoped we would reconsider this proposal. Such a question does not arise…It is for the United States to make up its mind.

He added sardonically:

> As for the method by which we reunify Taiwan with the motherland, let us Chinese worry about that. We Chinese do have the ability to solve our own issues. There is no need whatever for American friends to worry themselves over such issues.[15]

Vance later said that, in a strategy agreed to by the President and the national security team, he presented the "maximum" position on representation to Beijing in the full expectation that the Chinese would reject it because he did not want to complicate processing of the Panama Canal Treaties, which were about to be signed and sent to the Senate.[16]

J. Stapleton Roy, later Ambassador to China was deeply involved in preparations for Vance's trip as Deputy Director of the Office of China

---

[12] Memorandum of Conversation, August 24, 1977 (3:00 pm-5:40 pm), p. 17, Carter Library.

[13] As seen above, President Ford's statement was not nearly as definitive as that, and Deng had rephrased it in repeating it back to Ford even at the time.

[14] Memorandum of Conversation, August 24, 1977 (3:00 pm-5:40 pm), p. 23.

[15] Ibid., p. 22.

[16] Vance, *Hard Choices*, p. 79. Brzezinski confirms that Vance carried with him a "somewhat ambivalent" position on normalization, and that Carter passed up an opportunity during Vance's time in Beijing to instruct the Secretary to take advantage of "any opportunity" to advance normalization (see Brzezinski, *Power and Principle,* op. cit., p. 201).

Mainland Affairs. He recalls that, because of the 1974 record, it was assumed that consulates were not obtainable. So, "basically" what Vance proposed "was an effort to trade embassies and liaison offices." This was justified on the basis that "a liaison office is not a diplomatic mission." Although it was recognized at the time that this, too, was unlikely to succeed, Roy noted, it was important to go through this step in order to move toward the ultimate position on "unofficial" representation.[17]

Another central participant, NSC Senior Staff Member Michel Oksenberg, judged that the lack of progress was due not only to the fact that the U.S. had pulled some of its punches on residual U.S. representation, but because, only a year after Mao's death, and with Deng yet to fully consolidate his power, China also was not politically prepared to make the difficult decisions that normalization would entail.[18]

ENGAGING IN EARNEST

Following Vance's departure and reconsideration in Washington of the U.S. position, U.S. Liaison Office (USLO) Chief Leonard Woodcock was instructed to indicate potential flexibility on the representation issue in a meeting with Foreign Minister Huang Hua:

> It would not be our intention to retain an 'Embassy without a flag' or a liaison office on Taiwan after normalization…We believe that we understand the nature of your concerns on the representation issue. Our position will take them into account.[19]

This new position was not only repeated twice during the meeting but was also the subject of a follow-up call from USLO to the Foreign Ministry.[20] Still, as Vance pointed out in his memoir, the United States essentially marked time over the next several months while it dealt with

---

[17] Interview by author.

[18] Michel Oksenberg, "Reconsiderations: A Decade of Sino-American Relations," *Foreign Affairs* 61, no. 1 (fall 1982), p. 182.

[19] State 259931, "Response to the Chinese on Normalization," October 31, 1977 and Peking 2654, "Meeting with Foreign Minister Huang Hua," November 14, 1977, both from Carter Library.

[20] Peking 2662, "Meeting with Foreign Minister Huang Hua," November 15, 1977, Carter Library.

other issues.[21] As Woodcock observed at the time, there was "very little more to talk about with the Chinese until we decide to establish diplomatic relations," and that would have to come by agreeing to the three PRC conditions, including with respect to a "non-official" presence on Taiwan.[22]

Woodcock also detected some flexibility in the Chinese position on the "Japanese formula" in the sense that normalization would be possible without, for example, agreeing on the issue of U.S. arms sales to Taiwan. The PRC would still oppose such sales, but he (correctly) foresaw that they could continue. However, his recommendation was that the U.S. should not try to discuss this issue with the Chinese, since they would be obliged to reject it.[23]

Although handling the political and security issues connected with a break with Taiwan was of central importance, throughout this period, no one was concentrating on the future of Taiwan; rather, the emphasis lay—strategically—on the future of U.S.-PRC relations.[24] Meanwhile, as the PRC indicated it would like to move ahead on normalization, it betrayed no special impatience, but rather adopted a strategy of outreach to congressional, business and cultural actors in the United States to help improve the atmosphere for the eventual steps that would need to be taken.[25] In a series of memos to Brzezinski, the NSC staff also recommended an American approach designed for the same purpose. Despite Woodcock's prediction, the one issue on which they seemed most unsure of Beijing's receptivity was continued U.S. arms sales to Taiwan.[26] Yet that was the "minimum demand," and the senior officials

---

[21] Vance, *Hard Choices,* p. 83.

[22] Peking 2662, "Meeting with Foreign Minister Huang Hua."

[23] Ibid.

[24] David Dean, interview by author.

[25] See, for example, Michel Oksenberg, Memorandum for Zbigniew Brzezinski, "Talking Points for Your Meeting with Ambassador Han Hsu on Monday, January 16, 1978," January 14, 1978, Carter Library. In his memo, Oksenberg details a number of the steps taken by Beijing in that direction (p. 2).

[26] See memoranda from Michael Armacost and Michel Oksenberg to Zbigniew Brzezinski: "Proposal for Adjustments in Asian Policy," March 13, 1978; "Strategy for Trying to Normalize Relations with the PRC in 1978," March 24, 1978; and "Recommendations for Your Monday Meeting on Asia Policy," April 7, 1978. See also Richard Holbrooke, Morton Abramowitz, Michael Armacost and Michel Oksenberg, Memorandum for Cyrus Vance, Harold Brown and

developing the plan noted that, "[I]f the PRC cannot agree to our minimum demands, normalization obviously cannot occur" since, while PRC sensitivities and legitimate security concerns needed to be taken into account, "[t]he ROC must continue to feel confident of its own future security."[27]

Brzezinski visited Beijing in late May 1978 to propose serious normalization talks starting in June. During that visit, the issue of Taiwan's security figured prominently. Deng predictably laid out for the National Security Adviser the three conditions for normalization, concluding with emphasis:

> And China cannot possibly give other concessions because this is a matter of sovereignty.[28]

Brzezinski responded that he was instructed "to confirm to you the U.S. acceptance of the three basic Chinese points."[29] He noted that the President was prepared to undertake "the political responsibility at home of resolving the outstanding issues between us" and continued: "In our relationships we will remain guided by the Shanghai Communiqué, by the principle that there is only one China and that the resolution of the issue of Taiwan is your problem."[30]

On peaceful resolution, Brzezinski raised the issue in familiar terms, describing the complex, difficult and very emotional issues involved in the historical legacy of U.S. relations with Taiwan.

Zbigniew Brzezinski, "Issues for Decision on Korea and China," April 4, 1978. All from the Carter Library.

[27] "Issues for Decision on Korea and China," pp. 9-11. At the same time, in a detailed paper on arms sales options for the April 11th meeting, it was noted that "as a practical matter Peking's attitude will make it harder to sell major systems after normalization" ("Arms Sales to the Republic of China," undated background paper prepared for the same meeting, Carter Library).

[28] Memorandum of Conversation, May 21, 1978 (4:05 pm-6:30 pm), op. cit., p. 3.

[29] Although President Carter's instruction had included the hope that there might be an opportunity to explore possible development of an "American model" (presumably less unofficial than a "Japanese model") for maintaining non-diplomatic relations with Taiwan, this does not appear to have been pursued. Nor could it have succeeded. As we shall see, within the month the U.S. was prepared to establish a totally private office in Taiwan.

[30] Memorandum of Conversation, May 21, 1978 (4:05 pm-6:30 pm), pp. 3-4.

That is why we will have to find some formula which allows us to express our hope and our expectation regarding the peaceful resolution of the Taiwan issue, *though we recognize that this is your own domestic affair* and that we do so in the spirit of the Shanghai Communiqué.[31]

Later he added in terms that were perhaps less familiar:

During that historically transitional period domestic difficulties in the U.S. would be far minimized if our hope and expectation that the internal and purely domestic resolution of Chinese problems would be such that it would be peaceful and that our own hopes in this respect would not be specifically contradicted.[32]

Carter's instructions to Brzezinski included the requirement that he make clear that "the United States will continue to provide Taiwan with access to military equipment for defensive purposes."[33] As a result, the National Security Adviser told Deng:

This consideration [expectation of peaceful resolution] must be borne in mind when resolving the issue of normalization and when defining the *full range of relations* during the historically transitional period of our relationship with the people on Taiwan.[34]

Later in this conversation and in other conversations, Brzezinski kept coming back to the phrase that was to stand as the codeword for arms sales. He said:

---

[31] Ibid., p. 4. Emphasis added.

[32] Ibid., p. 9.

[33] "President Carter's Instructions to Zbigniew Brzezinski for His Mission to China," May 17, 1978, p. 5, reproduced in Brzezinski, *Power and Principle*, Annex I. In *Power and Principle*, Brzezinski describes the goal as being to insist that the U.S. "would reserve for itself the right to provide arms to Taiwan, as it saw fit" (p. 208).

[34] Memorandum of Conversation, May 21, 1978 (4:05 pm–6:30 pm), p. 5. Emphasis added. As Patrick Tyler points out, even if Deng spoke English he could not have understood this sentence (*A Great Wall*, p. 255).

[D]uring the historically transitional period the maintenance of [the] *full range of commercial relations* with Taiwan would provide the necessary flexibility during the phase of accommodation to a new reality in the course of which eventually one China will become a reality."[35]

However elliptical the statements, the Chinese, in fact, seemed to grasp the U.S. intention to continue such sales. Linking this question to the repeated U.S. statements on peaceful settlement, CCP Chairman Hua Guofeng said to Brzezinski:

[T]he U.S. side invariably wants China to commit itself to solve the issue of Taiwan through peaceful means. At least the U.S. side thinks that it may issue a statement expressing its hope and expectation that China will solve this question by peaceful means and it would hope that China will not contradict it. Then it also means that the U.S. side is asking China to undertake a commitment not to use force to liberate Taiwan. If we undertake the commitment that China will not liberate Taiwan by arms, then on the other hand the U.S. side is helping and arming Taiwan with its military equipment. What will be the result of these actions? I think it is still the creation of one China, one Taiwan, or two Chinas. Taiwan is part of China's territory and the people in Taiwan are our compatriots. Does China insist on liberating Taiwan through arms? We think if Chiang Ching-kuo of Taiwan did not get U.S. equipment and weapons there might have been a quicker and better settlement of this.[36]

In reporting to the President, Brzezinski indicated that arms sales had not come up directly, but that the upshot of the indirect exchange, he judged, was that the Chinese offered a choice: continued arms sales to Taiwan after normalization without a Chinese statement regarding intent

---

[35] Ibid., p. 9; emphasis added. With Chairman Hua Guofeng, Brzezinski repeated a similar formulation: "There is going to be a period of historical transition during which presumably the United States will maintain *a full range of economic relations* with Taiwan and in the course of which many of the historical legacies of the past can then gradually be diluted, overcome or resolved." See Memorandum of Conversation, May 22, 1978 (5:25 pm-7:25 pm), p. 15, Carter Library. Emphasis added.

[36] Memorandum of Conversation, May 22, 1978 (5:25 pm-7:25 pm), p. 7, Carter Library.

to resolve the Taiwan issue peacefully, or a cessation of U.S. arms sales coupled with a Chinese statement of peaceful intent.[37]

On the representation issue, having taken on board the Chinese insistence that there could be no "official" office, the Administration fell back to creating a private corporation that would constitute a "fig leaf for certain relationships for which the U.S. Government—and the government in Taiwan—must ultimately be responsible."[38] Woodcock was to be instructed to tell the Chinese that there would be no official relations with Taiwan and no governmental representation after normalization—otherwise "the seriousness of our entire approach would be open to question."[39]

On arms sales, Vance argued in June that the Administration "must be in a position to state to the Congress that we will continue sales of defensive military equipment to Taiwan and that, although the PRC does not like that, it clearly understands our position and has proceeded with agreement on normalization anyway." In a statement that foreshadowed the diplomatic complexity of handling this issue, he said:

> In order to make that statement, the public and private record must sustain our characterization of Peking's position.[40]

Referring to Hua Guofeng's "delphic and ambiguous" statements to Brzezinski on arms sales in May, Vance judged that this was still the trickiest issue and a potential deal breaker. Nonetheless, with Hua

---

[37] Brzezinski, *Power and Principle,* p. 218. Deng Xiaoping appeared to give some further basis to the idea of a tradeoff—not between arms sales and a Chinese statement on peaceful resolution (he again rejected any such statement), but between arms sales and actual peaceful resolution—when he met with a Congressional Delegation led by Rep. Lester Wolff (D-NY) on July 9th. While praising an apparent U.S. decision to forego F-4 Phantom sales to Taiwan he said: "If such an action [i.e., the sale] is taken, it will obstruct reunification negotiations and settlement by peaceful means. If peaceful means are impossible, then armed force will have to be used" ("Transcript of CODEL Wolff Meeting with Teng Hsiao-p'ing," July 10, 1978, Carter Library). This was to become a familiar theme in the months ahead.

[38] Cyrus Vance, Memorandum for the President, "Next Moves on China: Woodcock's Approach," June 13, 1978, p. 3, Carter Library.

[39] Ibid., p. 4.

[40] Ibid., p. 5.

Guofeng having addressed it directly, the door was open to explore the limits of PRC tolerance.[41]

When Acting PRCLO Chief, Han Xu, called on Brzezinski on July 19th to warn against U.S. sale of F-4 fighter aircraft to Taiwan (as was still being reported in the press), Brzezinski withheld comment on the specifics and instead took the opportunity to refer once again to "a historically transitional phase" and certain "historical legacies." He took great care to place arms sales in a *commercial* context, thus taking them out of a category in which the United States Government would provide financial support as well as trying to put them under the rubric of "unofficial," "people-to-people" activities. In light of the fact that no one on the American side was considering moving ahead with normalization without continuing arms sales to Taiwan, it was crucial to find a way to make those sales at least minimally acceptable to China. As Brzezinski put it:

> [O]ur acceptance of the principle of one China and our willingness to move forward on normalization within the context of your three points do not preclude the maintenance of full economic relations with the people on Taiwan.[42]

NEGOTIATING NORMALIZATION

Meanwhile, Leonard Woodcock in Beijing began on July 5th to discuss normalization issues in earnest with Foreign Minister Huang Hua. In his conversations through early August, he laid out the U.S. position on a number of fronts. The U.S. would:

- terminate the Mutual Defense Treaty, end diplomatic/official relations, withdraw all U.S. forces and installations from Taiwan, all in accordance with the so-called "three principles";

- recognize the PRC as the sole legal government of China;

- acknowledge the Chinese position on "one China" and Taiwan's role in it, (and not seek to create any variant of "two Chinas" or "one China, one China");

---

[41] Ibid., p. 6.

[42] Memorandum of Conversation, June 19, 1978 (11:30 am-12:00 noon), p. 2, Carter Library.

- radically alter post-normalization U.S. representation in Taiwan (i.e., it would be private, though it would have government funding and, in order to maintain certain unofficial relations with Taiwan, legislative authorization); and

- at the time of normalization, in addition to the joint communiqué, seek parallel public statements to be issued by the U.S. and PRC governments, incorporating familiar formulations on both sides regarding peaceful resolution, but ensuring that neither side directly contradicted the other.[43]

Woodcock had also proposed to discuss U.S. trade with Taiwan after normalization, which, as noted, was the rubric under which arms sales would continue. As we have seen, Chinese protests confirmed that, at least in the early stages of the talks, the Chinese understood the intention to continue arms sales (though whether they understood Brzezinski's codeword phrase—"full range of commercial relations"—is not known). As time went on, however, concern grew in Washington that Beijing might have thought it had successfully rebutted this plan. Thus, before Woodcock got to discuss this issue in any detail, it was decided that Assistant Secretary of State for East Asian and Pacific Affairs, Richard Holbrooke, should "set the stage" for that conversation by being direct with PRCLO Deputy Chief Han Xu about the subject.[44]

When Han called at the State Department on September 7th, Holbrooke argued to him that the U.S. had been consistent in stating it would exercise "great restraint and discretion" in arms sales to Taiwan, that such sales would be "defensive" in nature, and that all U.S. actions in this regard had been and would continue to be in conformity with the principles of the Shanghai Communiqué. He went on to clarify that arms sales would indeed continue after normalization, employing both euphemisms and plain phrases:

---

[43] This discussion is drawn from a number of documents from the period, including Woodcock's cables of instruction and reporting cables, all at the Carter Library. For a good summary of the conversations up to that point, see Richard Holbrooke, Leonard Woodcock and Michel Oksenberg, Memorandum for the Secretary, "Your Meeting with Huang Hua," October 2, 1978, Carter Library.

[44] As already noted, Brzezinski had repeated his allusion to "full economic relations" when Han presented a démarche on military sales to Taiwan in June, and Han had made a démarche to Holbrooke in response on August 21st.

When we enter this period of historical transition *following normalization*, it will be of critical importance for the United States to maintain a *full range of commercial relations* with Taiwan that will be conducted without official government representation on Taiwan and without formal governmental relations. *Sale of defensive military equipment would continue* only in this context.[45]

Apparently primed for Holbrooke's presentation, Han responded from prepared notes that U.S. arms sales to Taiwan were not in conformity with the spirit of the Shanghai Communiqué, that the U.S. intention to continue sales was contrary to Brzezinski's pledges on the President's behalf that the U.S. wanted to move ahead to normalize on the basis of "one China" and accepting China's three principles, and that if one wanted to speak of historical legacies, one needed to keep in mind American support for Chiang Kai-shek in "slaughtering Chinese people." He warned that the U.S. position would "not help push forward normalization of relations between our two countries."[46]

Han returned to Holbrooke's office five days later to repeat PRC objections. He called the U.S. position "untenable" and an "obstacle" to normalization. Asserting that the United States "recognizes" that there is but one China and Taiwan is part of China, Han claimed that U.S. insistence on supplying military equipment to Taiwan after normalization was simply an attempt to continue to interfere in China's internal affairs. In this circumstance, the U.S. acceptance of China's three conditions for normalization was "mere lip service."[47]

On September 19th, President Carter met with the recently arrived PRCLO Chief, Chai Zemin, in the President's first substantive meeting with a Chinese official since he had met with Chai's predecessor, Huang Zhen, in February 1977, some nineteen months earlier. Brzezinski's briefing memorandum to Carter underscored the importance of the meeting at that point in normalization negotiations:

The session takes place at a critical juncture in our relations with Peking. After cultivating a positive atmosphere, you are now

---

[45] Memorandum of Conversation, September 7, 1978 (4 pm), p. 2, Carter Library. Emphasis added.

[46] Ibid., pp. 3-5.

[47] Memorandum of Conversation, September 12, 1978 (4:30 pm), Carter Library.

bluntly telling them if they want normalization within the framework of their three points, they must be prepared to tolerate continued U.S. arms sales to Taiwan and must not contradict our statement that we are confident the Taiwan issue would be settled peacefully by the Chinese themselves. Never before has our bottom line been as clearly spelled out, and the session with you will be important to place Leonard [Woodcock]'s talks in the appropriate overall context.[48]

Carter reviewed for Chai the state of play in the negotiations and noted that he personally approved Woodcock's instructions; the USLO Chief spoke for him. In reprising the U.S. position, the President observed that the United States would continue to trade with Taiwan, "including the restrained sale of some very carefully selected defensive arms." In so doing, he raised the specter of Taiwan otherwise turning to other arms suppliers or acquiring "dangerous weapons" that could be threatening to the PRC, including nuclear weapons.[49]

Although Chai responded only briefly—citing discussions of this issue in Beijing as well as Han Xu's talks with Holbrooke—a more authoritative response came in Vance's meeting with Foreign Minister Huang Hua at the UN two weeks later. Huang accused the United States of seeking to "reproduce in a new form" the positions already rejected by China. Insistence on arms sales after normalization contravened the spirit of the Shanghai Communiqué, Huang charged, constituted interference in China's internal affairs, and showed that the U.S. had not yet made up its mind to normalize relations.

The U.S. should clearly understand that this is a question concerning China's sovereignty and territorial integrity and that it is an important matter of principle. The Chinese side has always been firm and unshakeable on matters of principle...It is our hope that the U.S. side will no longer indulge in unrealistic thinking.[50]

---

[48] Zbigniew Brzezinski, Memorandum for the President, "Talking Points for Your September 19, 11:30 a.m. Meeting with Ambassador Ch'ai Tse-min," September 19, 1978, p. 1, Carter Library.

[49] Memorandum of Conversation, September 19, 1978 (11:35 am-12:12 pm), p. 3, Carter Library.

[50] Memorandum of Conversation, October 3, 1978 (6:55 pm-11:55 pm), pp. 18-19, Carter Library.

Woodcock, who attended the October 3rd Vance-Huang meeting, did not mention arms sales specifically when recapping the U.S. position with Huang in Beijing on November 2nd as he handed Huang a draft normalization communiqué,[51] but he did so when he met with Acting Foreign Minister Han Nianlong on December 4th.

At the December meeting, Han handed over, in both English and Chinese versions, a PRC redraft of the communiqué Woodcock had given to Huang Hua on November 2[d]. The PRC redraft included a statement that the United States "recognizes that the Government of the People's Republic of China is the sole legal government of China and that Taiwan is a province of China," that the United States was breaking relations with the "Jiang Jingguo [i.e., Chiang Ching-kuo] regime in Taiwan," that it was "abrogating" the U.S. Mutual Defense Treaty, and that it declared "null and void" all other treaties and official agreements with Taiwan,[52] "which," Han expanded orally, "are illegal in the first place."[53]

In what Woodcock described as a "relaxed and friendly" meeting,[54] Han also read a prepared statement that expanded on the two key security issues: arms sales and peaceful settlement. On arms sales:

We have clearly stated our emphatic objection to the U.S. expressed intention of continuing its arms sales to Taiwan after normalization. Such sales would only convince the Chinese people that the U.S. government is still using armed force to support the Chiang clique's actions against them and is still interfering in China's internal affairs. Since the U.S. side is going to establish diplomatic relations with China and change its former China policy, why must it continue to arm the Chiang clique which has long been spurned by the 800 million Chinese people? As regards the U.S. assertion that such a move is meant to prevent the Chiang clique from obtaining atomic weapons, we

---

[51] For Woodcock's instructions from Washington, see WH 81342, "Instructions for Woodcock's Fifth Round," October 19, 1978, Carter Library.

[52] Peking 215, "Normalization Communiqué: Chinese Draft," December 4, 1978, Carter Library.

[53] Peking 216, "Sixth Session: December 4 Meeting with Han Nien-lung," December 4, 1978, p. 4, Carter Library.

[54] Peking 217, "December 4 Meeting with Han Nien-lung: Atmospherics," December 4, 1978, Carter Library.

must point out first that the U.S. side should stand by its own promise and refrain from letting the Chiang clique make or acquire such weapons. Second, if the Chiang clique should possess such weapons, it is not something for the U.S. to worry about. We know how to deal with it.

And on peaceful settlement:

The U.S. side has always sought to make us somehow commit ourselves to the peaceful liberation of Taiwan. I would like to make it clear to the U.S. side once again that this cannot be done because it amounts to asking the Chinese side to forego its sovereignty. Furthermore, in terms of the consequences, if China should really make such a commitment, it would only feed the arrogance of the Chiang clique…thus destroying any possibility of restoring Taiwan to the motherland by peaceful means…We are willing to understand your need to say something to the people of the United States. We can refrain from raising objections to statements by U.S. government leaders expressing their hope to see a peaceful solution of the Taiwan issue. But in that event the Chinese side will issue a statement declaring that the way of bringing Taiwan back to the embrace of the motherland and reunifying the country is wholly a Chinese internal affair.[55]

So here we have a situation where, as the PRC saw it, the U.S. had accepted to the letter the "three conditions" Beijing had laid down, but where the U.S. intention to continue providing arms to Taiwan cut across the very essence of the Beijing's conception of the sovereign principle of "one China" by providing Taipei the means to continue to resist coming to the table, vitiating the U.S. "acceptance" of the PRC conditions. From an American perspective, on the other hand, even setting aside the usual domestic and international factors at play, it was unpersuasive to argue that the United States should stop providing the means for seventeen million people, living peacefully in a friendly society with a burgeoning economy, to maintain their security, instead allowing them to be coerced by a Communist regime, especially one that regularly engaged in political suppression and human rights violations. Moreover, their sense of security could eventually facilitate cross-Strait political dialogue.

---

[55] Peking 216, "Sixth Session: December 4 Meeting with Han Nien-lung," pp. 4-5.

In any case, for the first time in the negotiation, Han told Woodcock that China "welcome[d]" the U.S. approach to normalization on the basis of "one China" and the three Chinese conditions. In so doing, he claimed that the U.S. had "reaffirmed" that there is only one China and that Taiwan is "a province of the People's Republic of China." (As we shall see, PRC efforts to redefine the U.S. position did not end there.) Finally, Han indicated that Deng Xiaoping wanted to meet with Woodcock, a clear signal to the Americans that they were in the final stages of the negotiation.

In his marginal comment on Woodcock's reporting cable, Carter noted that, with respect to "one China" and Taiwan's place in it, the U.S. should stick with the Shanghai Communiqué language.[56] Woodcock was instructed: "Under no circumstances are you to say that Taiwan is 'a province of China'" [or, by extension, of the PRC].[57]

In the wake of the Woodcock-Han meeting, Brzezinski tended to believe that the Chinese understood and agreed to the arms sales kabuki, recognizing that such sales would go forward even as they expressed outrage and total disapproval at the very thought. He told the President that they would find a way for Woodcock to test the accuracy of this reading.[58] As has been described in detail elsewhere, intense discussions over the next ten days revolved around this issue right up until the very eve of the normalization announcement.[59]

The upshot was that Deng may have genuinely thought the arms sales had been turned off, and that he only realized at the last minute this was not the case. Both Leonard Woodcock and his deputy, J. Stapleton Roy reported to Washington that they had "no doubt...that we have clearly put on the record our position with respect to arms sales."[60] Nonetheless, after being instructed to go back in to see Deng one more time to make absolutely sure there were no missed signals, Roy emerged

---

[56] Peking 215, "Normalization Communiqué: Chinese Draft."

[57] WH 81595, "Instructions for Woodcock's Meeting with Teng Hsiao-p'ing," December 12, 1978, p. 2, Carter Library.

[58] Zbigniew Brzezinski, Memorandum for the President, "Leonard's December 4th Meeting," December 5, 1978, p. 1, Carter Library.

[59] See Tyler, *A Great Wall,* pp. 261-271; Carter, *Keeping Faith*, pp. 197-200; Brzezinski, *Power and Principle*, pp. 230-233; and Vance, *Hard Choices*, pp. 118-119.

[60] Peking 229, "December 14, 1978, para. 10, Carter Library.

from the conversation with an enraged Deng convinced that his own original judgment had been in error, and that Deng in fact had not grasped the U.S. intention to resume sales in 1980 after a one-year hiatus while the Mutual Defense Treaty termination clock was ticking.[61]

There is also a possibility that Beijing was handling the issue in much the same way Washington had at first. That is, it put its position on the record and, if it received no definitive rebuff, it assumed it had laid a sufficient foundation to conclude—and, if need be, to later insist— that its position had been understood and accepted by the other side. When Woodcock went back to clarify the record, Deng may have had no choice but to express what was no doubt genuine anger, but perhaps tinged by a greater sense of surprise than the Chinese leader actually felt.

In any event, Deng agreed to proceed to establish diplomatic relations—presumably because of the central importance normalization played in his plans to promote a major economic reform program, as well as, to a lesser degree, because China had determined on a course of military "punishment" of Soviet-backed Vietnam and wanted to bolster its own strategic situation. But Deng made clear that China considered U.S. arms sales to Taiwan a violation of the most basic principles of normalization to which the United States had agreed, and that China would raise the arms sales issue again.

In light of subsequent developments, it is noteworthy that in this conversation, as he had during the earlier phase of the negotiation, Deng underscored two circumstances in which the Mainland would resort to force against Taiwan. One was if the Soviet Union should seek to control Taiwan. The other was if Chiang Ching-kuo

> ...should lean on certain powerful support, say the provision of arms, and refuses to talk to us about the problem of reunification of the country.[62]

The communiqué announcing establishment of relations was issued on December 15, 1978.[63] In the background briefing given by Brzezinski

---

[61] Interview by author.

[62] Peking 237, "Full Transcript of December 15 Meeting with Teng," December 15, 1978, para. 32, Carter Library. Those who follow the issue closely will detect the forerunner of the "third 'if'" of the February 2000 Taiwan White Paper, discussed later.

[63] "Joint Communiqué on the Establishment of Diplomatic Relations Between the United States of America and the People's Republic of China, January 1,

on the night of the announcement, he was asked about arms sales. He responded:

> I think it is quite clear from the statement that is being made that the United States will continue the full range of commercial relations with Taiwan. As the treaty is being abrogated,[64] we will continue to deliver to Taiwan all the items that have been committed or have been contracted for. And beyond 1979, we will, of course, make our judgments in the light of the prevailing situation, which we hope will be peaceful. But we will, as I said earlier, retain the full range of commercial relations with Taiwan...[w]hich includes, if necessary and the situation warrants, selected defensive weaponry. [65]

Perhaps feeling he had been overly euphemistic in deference to Chinese sensitivities and too elliptical for his U.S. and Taiwan audiences, Brzezinski returned to the subject:

> Let me answer it again so that there is no doubt [about reserving the right to supply military equipment to Taiwan]...After the treaty is terminated at the end of 1979, the United States will give Taiwan access to arms of a defensive character and do so on a restrained basis so as to promote peace and not interfere with peace in that area.[66]

PRC Chairman Hua Guofeng laid out the Chinese view in a December 16th press conference:

> During the negotiations the U.S. side mentioned that after normalization it would continue to sell limited amount of arms to Taiwan for defensive purposes. We made it clear that we absolutely would not agree to this. In all discussions the Chinese side repeatedly made clear its position on this question. We held that after the normalization continued sales of arms to Taiwan by the United States would not conform to the principles of the

---

1979," the text of which appears in the appendix.

[64] Later in the briefing it was clarified that the treaty was being "terminated" in accordance with its own provisions, not abrogated.

[65] "Background Briefing at the White House at 9:20 pm EST," December 15, 1978, pp. 6-7, Carter Library.

[66] Ibid., p. 7.

normalization, would be detrimental to the peaceful liberation of Taiwan and would exercise an unfavourable influence on the peace and stability of the Asia-Pacific region. So our two sides had differences on this point. Nevertheless, we reached an agreement on the joint communiqué.[67]

The two governments issued individual statements, the U.S. reiterating American "interest" in—and "expectation" of—peaceful resolution of the Taiwan issue by the Chinese themselves, the PRC underscoring that the way of unifying with Taiwan was "entirely China's internal affair."[68]

TWO KEY ISSUES: UNDERSCORING THE U.S. POSITIONS

In addition to arms sales, two other issues merit further comment: peaceful settlement of the Taiwan question and the U.S. position on "one China."

Peaceful Resolution

Despite the PRC position that it could not commit to not use force, and despite its argument that U.S. arms sales would make peaceful resolution far less likely or even impossible, at the Third Plenum of the 11th Central Committee in the days immediately following the normalization announcement, Beijing formulated its position on "peaceful reunification"[69] and on New Year's Day it issued a message extending an olive branch to Taiwan.[70]

The message gave no ground on the assertion that "Taiwan has been an inalienable part of China since ancient times" and held little appeal to people on the island in its claim that early reunification was the common

---

[67] *Peking Review* 21, no. 51 (December 22, 1978), cited in Hungdah Chiu, ed., *China and the Taiwan Issue* (New York: Praeger, 1979), p. 259.

[68] Texts in Hsiao and Witunski, *Sino-American Normalization,* op. cit., Appendix B.

[69] As related by Deng to Seton Hall Professor L. Y. (Winston) Yang on June 26, 1983; see "Deng Xiaoping on China's Reunification," *Xinhua,* July 29, 1983, carried by FBIS (OW291552) on August 1, 1983, in its report on China, PRC Media on Taiwan Affairs, p. U1. It was at the Third Plenum that ascendancy of Deng and his reform program was consolidated.

[70] "NPC Standing Committee Message to Compatriots in Taiwan," January 1, 1979, online at http://www.fmprc.gov.cn/eng/5044.html.

desire of all the people of China, "including all compatriots in Taiwan." But while it sought to create pressure on the island by noting—in the immediate wake of U.S.-PRC normalization as well as of the Sino-Japanese Treaty of Peace and Friendship—that the "world in general" recognized only one China with the PRC government as the sole legal government, it also offered carrots. Those included PRC leaders' pledges to

> ...take present realities into account in accomplishing the great cause of reunifying the motherland and respect the status quo on Taiwan and the opinions of people in all walks of life there and adopt reasonable policies and measures in settling the question of reunification so as not to cause the people of Taiwan any losses.

The statement expressed great hope in the people of Taiwan "and also the Taiwan authorities," noting that the latter had always supported "one China" and opposed an independent Taiwan.

After announcing the cessation of bombardment of Jinmen (Quemoy) and the other offshore islands,[71] the statement called for discussion between the PRC government and the authorities in Taiwan "to create the necessary prerequisites and a secure environment" for contacts and exchanges in different areas. It was in this statement that the first call was made for the "three links" across the Strait in trade, transportation and postal exchanges, as well as visits and exchanges in academic and cultural areas, and sports and technological interchange.

In this same time frame, Deng met with a visiting U.S. congressional delegation. He reiterated the New Year's Day message themes of conciliation, but he also took the occasion to repeat something less conciliatory that he had said to Woodcock. China could not, he argued, foreswear the use of force—even unilaterally, not just as a commitment to someone else—because Taiwan would then refuse to talk. But Deng then added a new consideration: a deadline. While it would be all right for Taiwan to refuse talks for one or two years, if the refusal persisted a long time, for example ten years, then it would necessarily lead to settlement by use of force.[72]

---

[71] Shelling of the offshore islands had been going on in symbolic manner on alternate days since 1958.

[72] Peking 162, "Codel Nunn Meeting with Deng Xiaoping," January 11, 1979, Carter Library.

Deng repeated this position to President Carter during his visit to the United States in early 1979. As he put it to Carter:

> I said previously that there are two conditions under which we will be forced not to use peaceful means. One situation is when the Taiwan authorities just absolutely refuse to talk with us… over a long period of time…With regard to Taiwan, I will reiterate that we will adopt a fair and reasonable policy and will try our very best to use peaceful means to solve the Taiwan question. And on this question we have patience, but this patience cannot be unlimited. [73]

What we see here is that, by "resolving" the Taiwan issue with the United States,[74] normalization allowed Beijing to frame its cross-Strait policy in a more "generous" way as an "internal" matter no longer burdened by foreign challenges to its claims to sovereignty. This approach, in what later became the "one country, two systems" proposal, was not only transmitted to Taiwan audiences through the New Year's Day message, but also to American audiences in a Deng Xiaoping cover story interview with *Time* magazine that appeared while he was in the United States.[75]

Deng repeated to *Time* what he had said to the Nunn delegation: that ten years was too long to wait for reunification. Although his remarks were tinged with concern about U.S. arms sales, a concern also reflected in his comments to President Carter, Deng sought overall to project an image of self-confidence based on the new U.S.-China relationship created by normalization. While he noted that this had great significance from the perspective of "global strategy," it was clear that he also thought it would promote reunification.

---

[73] Memorandum of Conversation, January 30, 1979 (9:40 am), p. 10-11, Carter Library.

[74] The PRC Government statement that accompanied the normalization communiqué stated: "The question of Taiwan was the crucial issue obstructing the normalization of relations between China and the United States. It has now been resolved…" ("Statement of the Government of the People's Republic of China in Connection with the Establishment of China-U.S. Diplomatic Relations," reproduced in Harding, *A Fragile Relationship*, op. cit., p. 381).

[75] "An Interview with Teng Hsiao-p'ing," *Time,* February 5, 1979, pp. 32-35.

Word Games

The other issue that has generated much comment over the years was the adoption in the Chinese-language version of the normalization communiqué of new wording to express the U.S. position on "one China." In the Shanghai Communiqué, the United States had "acknowledged" the Chinese position on "one China" and on Taiwan being a part of China. The Chinese term used to translate "acknowledge" in 1972 was *renshidao,* accepted by all concerned as an appropriate translation. Indeed, although Henry Kissinger had argued that one advantage of having negotiated the communiqué in English was that the English version was then binding in case of dispute, in his memoirs Kissinger cited a note from NSC staff member Richard Solomon that indicated the Chinese had bent over backward to capture the flavor of the U.S. intent. According to Solomon:

> Regarding the future of Taiwan, the Chinese version conveys even less of a sense of U.S. acceptance of the PRC [Peking] view that the island is Chinese territory than does the English. It more strongly conveys the idea that we do not wish to get involved in a debate regarding the Chinese position on Taiwan, and strengthens the sense of our concern that there be a peaceful resolution of the Taiwan question. [76]

The same could not be said in 1978. As noted earlier, Acting Foreign Minister Han Nianlong had on December 4[h] handed Woodcock both an English- and a Chinese-language version of a draft communiqué. In that draft, it said, in a single thought, that the United States "recognized" the government of the PRC as the sole legal government of China *and that Taiwan was a province of the PRC.*[77] A copy of that draft in Chinese is not available, but it is a fair presumption that it used one verb to cover the entire thought, and that the verb used was *chengren,* which commonly is translated as "recognize."

However, when the final text emerged, the above thought had been divided into two pieces. One was the concept of "recognizing" the government of the PRC as the sole legal government of China. The other was the U.S. "acknowledgement" of the Chinese position on "one China" and on Taiwan being a part of China, essentially reiterating the Shanghai

---

[76] Cited in Kissinger, *White House Years,* p. 1085.

[77] See the earlier discussion of the communiqué starting on p. 91.

Communiqué position. That negotiation took place in English, without further reference to Chinese texts. J. Stapleton Roy, who was dealing with the fine points of the texts, recalls that in reconciling the English and Chinese texts after the negotiation had been completed in English, he insisted on utilizing the same Chinese phrase—*renshidao*—as in the Shanghai Communiqué to express the term "acknowledge." The Chinese side, however, argued to him that *chengren* was a more accurate way of expressing "acknowledge." An argument ensued and dictionaries were consulted. Roy was finally persuaded that his counterparts' point was valid when a dictionary entry was found as substantiation.[78]

When the Chinese-language version reached Washington, however, and the change was noted, there was consternation. Roy in later years said he regretted allowing the change if only because of this reaction, but he said it was inconceivable that Chinese agreement to normalization hinged on this issue. The Chinese were very clear at the time not only that was there no change in the U.S. position, but that the English-language version, as in 1972, was binding since that was the language in which the communiqué was negotiated and, in this case, since the term under discussion was an expression of the U.S. position.

Even so, over the intervening years, this evolution in the Chinese-language version has been the focus of some commentary. Richard H. Solomon, who observed in 1972 how meticulous the Chinese had been about translating the Shanghai Communiqué, noted that in the case of the normalization communiqué, they essentially engaged in word games.[79] China scholar Andrew J. Nathan wrote that:

> The difference between the two versions is conspicuous. The English version leaves room for the idea that the United States has only noted, not adopted, the Chinese position. The Chinese text does not.[80]

Nathan goes on to say that the U.S. claim that the English text is binding "left holes through which it would be possible to draw gossamer threads

---

[78] Interview by author.

[79] Richard H. Solomon, *China's Political Negotiating Behavior, 1967-1984* (Santa Monica: RAND, 1995) pp. 126-129.

[80] Andrew J. Nathan, "What's Wrong with American Taiwan Policy," *The Washington Quarterly* (spring 2000), p. 105, note 1.

of argument that the United States had never really changed its position on the status of Taiwan."[81]

Chas. W. Freeman, Jr., was sitting in Washington at the time and caught the change, later drafting press points explaining that there was "no change" in meaning. Nonetheless, he has since argued that the change in language was, in fact, meaningful. Whatever the American position is about there having been no change from the Shanghai Communiqué, Freeman says, what the U.S. did in the normalization communiqué clearly led the Chinese to believe that the Washington had in fact changed its position. The point, he says, is that, not only did the U.S. meet the three Chinese conditions, but it did so "in the context of resolving the ambiguity of Taiwan's relationship to the Mainland."[82]

One major problem created by the discrepancy in language between the two communiqués is that a generation of scholars and officials in China has grown up reading the normalization communiqué in Chinese. While those who have used the English-language text will have insight into this question, those who only read the Chinese version could well mistakenly believe the United States went further than it really did in accepting the PRC's "one China principle"—and, by extension, the PRC's position on sovereignty over Taiwan.

---

[81] Ibid.

[82] Interview by author. Freeman also argues that, whatever the U.S. Government's position on the "authoritativeness" of the English text, as a matter of international law, the two versions have equal validity.

IMPLEMENTING NORMALIZATION

"We hope that the American side will strictly implement all the principles in the Sino-American agreement on the establishment of diplomatic relations, remove certain obstacles that hamper the process of developing our normal relations and refrain from any action harmful to the return of China's territory Taiwan to the motherland, so that Sino-American relations will continuously progress in a direction that conforms to the wishes of the people of both countries."

—Chairman Hua Guofeng
Report to the Fifth National People's Congress, June 1979

5

One China, Respective Interpretations

"The question of Taiwan was the crucial issue obstructing the normalization of relations between China and the United States. It has now been resolved between the two countries in the spirit of the Shanghai Communiqué."

—PRC statement in connection with normalization, December 1978

At this point our focus shifts from the achievement of normalization, and what it took to get there, to implementation of the understandings and commitments that made it possible. But in assessing this period, a basic truth must be understood. Normalization did not resolve the underlying Taiwan-related issues. Instead, it was based on an approach sufficiently ambiguous so that each side could justifiably argue that its own requirements had been met.

The United States broke diplomatic and other official ties with Taiwan, committed to removing the remaining forces on the island, and gave one year's notice to terminate the Mutual Defense Treaty on its own terms. But Washington did not accept the Chinese claim to "one China" of which Taiwan was a part—and of which the PRC was the sole legal government. Rather it recognized the government of the PRC as the sole legal government of China, but it did not go beyond *acknowledging* Beijing's claim to sovereignty over Taiwan and certainly did not buy into the proposition that the PRC government spoke for the people in Taiwan. Moreover, the U.S. had reserved the right to supply arms to Taiwan to help maintain the military balance, and, while not touting it, had not given up the right to come to Taiwan's aid in case of a military contingency, thus providing a level of deterrence that it hoped would ensure that there would be no use of force in an attempt to resolve cross-Strait issues.

The PRC, on the other hand, felt that it had obtained, through American actions and words, solemn American commitments to Beijing's status as the sole legal government of China, and by extension, through the American acknowledgment of the "Chinese position" that there is only "one China" of which Taiwan is a part, that the U.S. accepted that the writ of that government to represent China in the international community extended to Taiwan as well. At a minimum, the U.S. would no longer support Taipei's claim to participate as a state in the international community, and it would not provide a security guarantee. While this last point was somewhat vitiated by the U.S. plan to continue selling limited quantities of carefully selected defensive weapons, without the backing of a U.S. security commitment Taiwan could not match the growing Mainland capabilities. Taipei would eventually have to come to the negotiating table.

Given these very different perspectives, for normalization to work, the arrangement would require—and continues to require—not just finesse and sensitivity, but a clear understanding about the nature of the ambiguity, the issues it left unresolved, the commitments that permit it to function, and the redlines that could cause it to collapse. Over the two decades since normalization, whenever such understanding has been lacking, or when the terms of the deal have been ignored, fundamental issues of trust and sincerity have come under challenge, threatening the durability of the overall arrangement. That is, when either side has seemed to disregard or reject the other side's basic premises of normalization, trouble has ensued.

For China, that has meant that threatening Taiwan has set off a chain of consequences with very broad ramifications in terms of U.S. policy. For the United States, taking steps that frontally challenged China's position on sovereignty and "one China" has set off a similar set of reactions on the other side. In the course of normalization, neither side endorsed the legitimacy of the other side's claim, though each at least tacitly agreed to respect it.

LAYING DOWN THE LAW: THE TAIWAN RELATIONS ACT

This is not a study of the Taiwan Relations Act (more popularly known by its initials: the TRA); many in-depth studies already exist.[1] But we recount here some of the history of the U.S.-PRC exchanges on this matter precisely because they laid a predicate for the continuing

---

[1] For but two examples, see: Lester L. Wolff and David L. Simon, eds., *Legislative History of the Taiwan Relations Act* (Baltimore: OPRSCAS, 1982) and Goldstein and Schriver, "An Uncertain Relationship: The United States, Taiwan and the Taiwan Relations Act," op. cit. The text of the relevant portions of the TRA is included in the appendix to this study.

controversy over the very principles of normalization that has continued to plague U.S.-PRC relations over the past twenty-five years.

As is well known, the dry, technical bill introduced on behalf of the Carter Administration in late January 1979 "to promote the foreign policy of the United States through the maintenance of commercial, cultural and other relations with the people on Taiwan on an unofficial basis, and for other purposes"[2] was, by the time of the bill's enactment in April, transformed by Congress into a quasi-guarantee of Taiwan's security.

The basic driving force behind that transformation was congressional anger at the way Members perceived Taiwan to have been treated and, perhaps even more significant, the way they felt that Congress itself had been treated. Especially important for a number of Members was the lack of formal consultation on the Hill before the President announced termination of the U.S.-ROC Mutual Defense Treaty.[3]

Throughout the legislative process, as the shape of the bill became increasingly clear, China made a series of démarches in both Washington and Beijing. It protested language added by Congress that seemed to effectively reconstitute the U.S.-Taiwan Mutual Defense Treaty. And instead of allowing discreet handling of the arms sales issue, the importance of which Deng had impressed upon Woodcock in their final conversation in December, the TRA highlighted the U.S. intention to continue providing whatever arms Taiwan needed.

In protesting the TRA's statement of "policy"—especially the provision that the decision to establish diplomatic relations with the PRC "rests upon the expectation that the future of Taiwan will be determined by peaceful means" and the enumeration of possible responses to the "grave concern" that would be created if the PRC resorted to "non-peaceful" means to determine Taiwan's future—Beijing complained that these provisions "clearly contravene[d]" the normalization agreement

---

[2] S. 245, 96th Cong., 1st sess., introduced January 29, 1979.

[3] The constitutionality of the President's action was later upheld by the courts, with the Supreme Court declining to overrule a lower court decision. Still, as Cyrus Vance recounted, there was a debate within the Administration about consulting with Congress toward the end of the process, and he regretted afterward that that had not been done (*Hard Choices*, p. 118.) As his then-Deputy, Warren Christopher, put it: "This illustrated again the axiom that if you succeed in circumventing the Congress on a foreign policy issue, Congress will neither forgive nor forget your success" (*Chances of a Lifetime*, p. 91).

and stood in violation of the principle of non-interference in other countries' internal affairs. In so doing, Beijing drew on the negotiating record of private statements that had gone beyond U.S. public statements.

Foreign Minister Huang Hua called in Ambassador Woodcock in mid-March, for example, to issue a formal protest:

> At the time of the establishment of diplomatic relations between China and the U.S., the U.S. side explic itly undertook to recognize the government of the People's Republic of China as the sole legal government of China *and acknowledged that Taiwan is part of China* and only unofficial relations would be maintained with the people of Taiwan.

> At the same time, *the U.S. side further acknowledged that the return of Taiwan to the motherland was a matter within the scope of China's sovereignty*.[4]

In fact, though Huang took them out of context, both of these things had been addressed in one way or another privately during the normalization negotiations. Brzezinski had said that peaceful settlement of the Taiwan issue was China's "domestic affair" in May 1978 when trying to create an acceptable context for the PRC to make a unilateral statement on peaceful resolution.[5] And Woodcock had spoken of how the President would tell the American people that "there is one China and that Taiwan is part of that one China" when seeking to persuade Deng Xiaoping at the last moment that arms sales would not obstruct progress but would, rather, lead to a change in American attitudes that would redound to the benefit of eventual reunification.[6] At the same time, not only were the public commitments in the normalization communiqué—as in the Shanghai Communiqué—far more rounded, but it was always clear that, in American minds, the repeated expression of U.S. "abiding interest" in peaceful resolution opened the door to intervention if necessary. So while the congressional language was provocative to China, and in that sense diplomatically unhelpful, it did not, in fact, change long-standing U.S. policy.

---

[4] Beijing 1469, "PRC Reaction to Taiwan Legislation," March 16, 1979, paras. 4-5, Carter Library. Emphasis added.

[5] See excerpt on p. 85.

[6] Peking 237, "Full Transcript of December 15 Meeting with Teng," op. cit.

In another conversation, having repeated the Foreign Minister's claim that the U.S. had "acknowledged there is but one China and that Taiwan is a part of China," then-Director of the Foreign Ministry's Bureau of American and Oceanian Affairs Han Xu asked rhetorically:

> What right does the U.S. have to meddle in this affair, much less to contemplate taking action?[7]

The response that Deputy Chief of Mission (DCM) J. Stapleton Roy gave Han is relevant to understanding later internal American debates about what has been called "strategic ambiguity." Roy noted that in the normalization agreement itself, the United States had expressed its continuing interest in peaceful resolution of the Taiwan question.[8] He went on:

> While the Congress added some language on this question, in essence it amounted to an expression of this interest *but without committing the U.S. to any particular action*. As a result, it was not inconsistent with the normalization agreement.[9]

In other words, if the United States took a formal, concrete stance that "we will do thus and so," then there might be a case to be made that the U.S. was not respecting—indeed was contradicting—the Chinese claim to sovereignty. But as long as the United States confined its statements to the level of principle, while the potential for intervention existed—and, indeed, it was hoped that China would take that potential very seriously—it did not breach the normalization agreement.

Also of relevance to later debates—and recent actions—was a written response given to Ambassador Chai Zemin by Deputy Secretary of State Warren Christopher regarding various PRC complaints about the TRA. In rebutting the Chinese charge that the Act gave "official status" to future U.S.-Taiwan relations, Christopher said: "The American Institute in Taiwan will not have any US Government employees, nor

---

[7] Beijing 1779, "PRC Reaction to Taiwan Legislation," March 31, 1979, para. 4, Carter Library.

[8] In fact, this point was not in the normalization communiqué, but it was obviously central to the normalization negotiations and was a key element of both President Carter's statement on December 15th announcing normalization and the formal U.S. Government statement that accompanied the announcement.

[9] Beijing 1779, "PRC Reaction to Taiwan Legislation," para. 5. Emphasis added.

will it perform official acts."[10] As we shall see, while the latter claim is still part of the U.S. position, the situation regarding staffing has now changed.

While the Taiwan issue did not disappear, over the year following passage of the TRA, bilateral discussions generally shifted away from that question, focusing even more than before on international strategic issues such as Korea and on areas such as trade and nonproliferation where bilateral cooperation was sought. But Taiwan remained on the agenda and proved to be, whenever it arose, a subject of more formal and testy exchanges. When Vice Foreign Minister Zhang Wenjin visited the United States in March 1980, for example, the State Department noted that "the only time in four days of talks in Washington that the Chinese adopted a stiff, formal tone" was when the conversation turned to a new U.S.-Taiwan maritime agreement. Zhang related it to the TRA. As he explained, China had all along expressed opposition to the TRA:

> And what is more and what is very important is our reason for our position. One of our points of opposition to that Taiwan Relations Act was the fact that that act declared the various agreements and treaties, with the exception of the defense treaty, which the U.S. had with the so-called Republic of China, will continue to be effective. That is one of our main objections to that Act.[11]

Throughout this period, Beijing continued to raise the issue of arms sales to Taiwan, calling them "unwise" and "not conducive to peaceful reunification or to regional stability."[12] But there was no serious clash of interests. The real trouble was brewing in another quarter: the presidential campaign of Ronald Reagan.

---

[10] "PRC Concerns," p. 2, handed to Chai by Christopher on March 27, 1979; see State 077424, "PRC Reaction to the Taiwan Legislation," March 28, 1979, Carter Library.

[11] State 077998, "PRC Vice Foreign Minister Zhang Wenjin's Visit—Taiwan," March 25, 1980, Carter Library.

[12] See, for example, Beijing 6156, "Chinese Comments on Taiwan Arms Sales, Related Issues," July 5, 1980, released to author by the Department of State pursuant to a Freedom of Information Act request (all such documents hereafter *FOIA*).

"Officiality" and the 1980 Presidential Campaign

In December 1978, in the immediate aftermath of the normalization announcement, Ronald Reagan denounced the agreement in a radio commentary. Arguing that the U.S. had gained "virtually nothing we didn't already have" he said:

> The 'breakthrough' the Pres[ident] announced on Dec[ember] 15th was…not a breakthrough at all. We simply gave in to Peking's demands.[13]

At that time, Reagan called for maintaining diplomatic relations with Taiwan even while proceeding to normalize relations with Beijing. Although he eventually backed away from that stance, still, in mid-May 1980, when he had virtually sewn up the Republican nomination, he called for restoration of "official" relations with Taiwan.[14] He told reporters in Cleveland:

> I see no reason why, with an embassy in Peking instead of Taiwan, we could not now have an official liaison office in Taiwan, the same as we had in Peking before the change occurred.

Others in the Party, as well as in Reagan's own camp, sought to contain the potential damage from the controversy Reagan's statements were stirring up with China, and the Republican Party platform tried to stick closely to positions blessed in the TRA.[15] Nonetheless, the issue

---

[13] "Taiwan II, January 1979," in Ronald Reagan, *Reagan In His Own Hand* (New York: The Free Press, 2001), p. 45.

[14] Donald M. Rothberg, "Reagan Courts Ethnic Vote in Detroit," *Associated Press,* May 18, 1980.

[15] See "Republican Party Platform of 1980," The American Presidency Project, online at http://www.presidency.ucsb.edu/site/docs/doc_platforms.php?platindex=R1980. The platform plank on Taiwan read: "…we deplore the Carter Administration's treatment of Taiwan, our long-time ally and friend. We pledge that our concern for the safety and security of the 17 million people of Taiwan will be constant. We would regard any attempt to alter Taiwan's status by force as a threat to peace in the region. We declare that the Republican Administration, in strengthening relations with Taiwan, will create conditions leading to the expansion of trade, and will give priority consideration to Taiwan's defense requirements." The *Washington Post* reported that the plank had been so worded at the direction of the Reagan camp (Don Oberdorfer, "Advisers Failed to Soften Reagan Taiwan Stand," August 20, 1980, A-3).

festered, and, at the urging of Reagan's foreign policy adviser, Richard V. Allen, vice presidential candidate George H.W. Bush—former ambassador to the United Nations, where he had dealt with the PRC quite frequently, and former head of the U.S. Liaison Office in China— was called upon to go to Beijing with Allen and others to reassure the Chinese about Reagan's position and heal the wounds that had been created.[16]

But on August 16, 1980, on the very eve of Bush's departure for China, Reagan reopened the issue—and the sore. At a joint press conference with Bush, Reagan said that he had been misinterpreted as proposing "diplomatic relations" with Taipei; echoing his mid-May remarks, he said that "all" he was proposing, as one report paraphrased it, was "the same level of government liaison that existed with the People's Republic of China before the United States officially recognized China and opened an embassy in Peking."[17] "Clarifying" his position, Reagan explained:

> What I said was, under the Taiwan Relations Act there are provisions for governmental relations. They just haven't been implemented. But, at all times, I stressed that we also intended to continue working toward increasing our relationship with the People's Republic of China.[18]

While Reagan had almost certainly not seen the record of negotiations, he was a person who paid close attention to this issue and he could not have been unaware of Chinese insistence on eliminating all vestiges of officiality in U.S.-Taiwan relations before agreeing to normalize. He just did not agree with it. Further, while he characterized his positions as being within the spirit of the TRA, in fact what he called for contradicted the wording of that Act, which authorized unofficial relations with the people in Taiwan.

BUSH IN BEIJING

George Bush, no doubt, was uncomfortable with this stance, but the best he could do, given Reagan's approach, was to try to square the circle by playing down, for the Chinese, Reagan's call for officiality and to

---

[16] Richard Allen, correspondence with author.

[17] Doug Willis, (untitled), *Associated Press*, August 16, 1980.

[18] Ibid.

argue that "the plan for Taiwan is to improve relations with Taiwan and to improve relations with China. There is nothing inconsistent with that."[19]   Bush predicted that Beijing would be satisfied with the explanation that calling for official ties with Taiwan did not mean closing the Embassy in Beijing.[20]   Bush also said—perhaps wishfully— that the subject was not on the agenda for his visit.

People's Daily, the authoritative Chinese Communist Party newspaper, lost little time in responding.   It termed Reagan's plan to restore "official" relations with Taiwan while maintaining diplomatic relations with the PRC "sheer deception" and said any such move would destroy the basic principle of normalization, thereby "surely affect[ing]" U.S.-PRC relations.   As to Bush's statement that this issue would not be discussed during his visit, *People's Daily* asked sarcastically how Reagan's running mate "could...possibly evade the issue."[21]

As the then-DCM in Beijing, J. Stapleton Roy, recalls it, when they arrived in China, it was clear the Bush party had not been briefed by the Carter Administration and it even seemed that they had not read the normalization communiqué; they certainly had not brought a copy along. Woodcock, still Carter's envoy in China, perceived the Reagan team as seeking to undo normalization in which he had played such a central role.   While the ambassador made himself available to answer any questions, he volunteered no information to Bush.[22]

Bush reportedly informed Foreign Minister Huang Hua on the 21st that Reagan had been "misinterpreted" and that, if elected, the Californian had no intention of upgrading the unofficial status of U.S. relations with Taiwan.[23]   However, during his meeting with Deng Xiaoping the next day, one of Deng's aides came running in with the report of an inflammatory statement by Ray Cline, a person close to Taiwan and identified as Reagan foreign policy adviser.   Cline's statement promoting "officiality" of relations with Taiwan prompted an

---

[19] Ibid.

[20] Howell Raines, "Reagan Denies Plan to Answer Carter," *New York Times,* August 17, 1980, sec. 1, p. 1.

[21] "People's Daily Warns Ronald Reagan Not to Miscalculate," *Xinhua,* August 19, 1980, reporting a "commentary" of that date.

[22] Roy, Interview by author.

[23] James P. Sterba, "Bush Reception in China Warms Up After Cool Start," *New York Times,* August 22, 1980, B-8.

outburst by Deng.[24] Moreover, at about the same time, just as Bush was trying to reassure his Chinese hosts that Reagan did not favor a "two Chinas" policy and that a Republican administration would have "no government relations in the diplomatic sense" or even "official" relations with Taiwan—"if by official you mean governmental"[25]—Reagan was telling an evangelical gathering in Dallas that he stood by his press conference statement of the 16th, even though he, too, denied this represented a "two Chinas" stance.[26]

The net effect of all of this was that, after Bush's meeting with Deng, the official Chinese news agency, *Xinhua*, blasted Reagan and raised the specter of a reversal of Sino-American relations.[27]

And, in fact, in a detailed report to Woodcock on their conversations, the Chinese reported that they had told Bush not only that the Republican Party platform represented a step backward in its advocacy of strengthening Taiwan's armed forces, but also that Reagan's campaign statements would, if they became policy, lead to a retrogression in bilateral relations. They said:

> [I]f the United States should reestablish any official relations with Taiwan, if the United States should establish a liaison office in Taiwan or a disguised official liaison office under any other name...it would not...be possible to maintain [U.S.-PRC] relations at their present state.[28]

As the press widely reported, Bush also conveyed to the Chinese the argument that, because of U.S-PRC common interests vis-à-vis the

---

[24] James R. Lilley, interview by author.

[25] Quoted in Victoria Graham, "Rules Out Diplomatic Relations with Taiwan," *Associated Press*, August 22, 1980.

[26] Kathy Sawyer, "Reagan Sticks to Stand on Taiwan Ties," *Washington Post*, August 22, 1980, A-1.

[27] "Commentary by Xinhua Correspondent: No Compromise on Matters of Principle—On Reagan's Remarks Concerning Sino-American Relations," *Xinhua*, August 22, 1980. See Tyler, *A Great Wall*, pp. 289-296 for an insightful account of how these conversations and the Bush mission related to the campaign and Republican party politics, while China's reaction was conditioned by the difficult end-game conversations over normalization—and especially Taiwan arms sales—only twenty months earlier.

[28] Beijing 8226, "Briefing by Vice Foreign Minister Zhang Wenjin on the Bush Visit to China," August 27, 1980, para. 7-10, Carter Library.

Soviet Union, the PRC should be more flexible with regard to Taiwan.[29] Given what we know about PRC attitudes toward the normalization understandings, it is not surprising that Beijing rejected this argument, characterizing as "sheer daydreaming" the thought that China had to beg for help from the United States out of fear of the USSR and that therefore "China would have no other alternative but to swallow it" if the platform and Reagan's remarks regarding Taiwan became policy. If they did become policy, they retorted, "the Chinese Government would certainly make a firm and strong response." And if that response disrupted the global strategic situation, so be it. "[W]e Chinese would not be afraid, no matter what the consequences might be."[30]

The net result was that, in the blunt words of an official *Xinhua* commentary, Bush "failed to reassure China" about Reagan's Taiwan policy, his effort to do so having been "cancelled out" by Reagan's renewed call for official governmental relations with the island.[31]

On Bush's return, an effort was immediately made in yet another joint press conference with Reagan to put this issue to rest. Although in that session Reagan denied any intention to establish a liaison office or other representative establishment labeled "official," it was, at best, a mixed performance from the PRC perspective. After criticizing Jimmy Carter for normalizing relations without obtaining agreement to retain a liaison office on Taiwan "of equivalent status to the one which we had earlier established in Peking," Reagan tried to move on: "But that is behind us now." He pledged fidelity to the TRA. Noting that that law provided for administering U.S. relations through the American Institute in Taiwan (AIT), he sought to infuse the establishment and operation of AIT with as much officiality as he could:

- The TRA "provides the *official* basis for our relations with our longtime friend and ally."

---

[29] Reagan reiterated this point on August 21st in Los Angeles, which was reported in time to be relayed to Deng Xiaoping before his meeting with Bush; see Sterba, "Bush Reception in China Warms Up After Cool Start."

[30] Beijing 8226, "Briefing by Vice Foreign Minister Zhang Wenjin on the Bush Visit to China," para. 11-12.

[31] Zhou Lifang and Zhou Cipu, "George Bush's Difficult Mission," *Xinhua*, August 23, 1980; see John Roderick, "Reagan China Policy Angers Peking," *Associated Press*, August 24, 1980.

- "It declares our *official* policy to be one of maintaining peace and promoting extensive close and friendly relations" with the people on Taiwan and on the mainland.

- "It specifies that our *official* policy considers any effort to determine the future of Taiwan by other than peaceful means a threat to peace and of grave concern to the United States" and, "most important," spells out the weapons sales policy and mandates that the U.S. maintain the means to resist any use of force or other coercive measures.

- It spells out how the President of the United States, "our highest elected *official*" shall conduct relations with Taiwan, leaving him great discretion.

- It details how "our *official* personnel, including *diplomats*" are to administer relations with Taiwan through AIT.

- It makes "crystal clear" the intent of Congress: "Our *official relations with Taiwan* will be *funded by Congress with public monies*" *audited by the Comptroller and monitored by congressional committees.*

Capping this recitation in officiality, and saying he would end such "petty…inappropriate and demeaning" practices of the Carter Administration as not seeing Taiwan officials in U.S. or Taiwan government offices, Reagan addressed the question of what he would do differently:

> I would not pretend, as Carter does, that the relationship we now have with Taiwan, enacted by our Congress, is not official. I am satisfied that this act [the TRA] provides an official and adequate basis for safeguarding our relationship with Taiwan. And I pledge to enforce it.[32]

Richard Allen sought to put the campaign controversy over Reagan's Taiwan statements to bed, labeling the candidate's August 25th statement "official and a definitive statement of the Reagan-Bush policy."[33] He

---

[32] Above all taken from "Excerpts from Reagan's Statement on Ties to China and Taiwan," *New York Times*, August 26, 1980, B-7. Emphasis added throughout.

[33] Howell Raines, "Reagan, Conceding Misstatement, Abandons Plan on Taiwan

succeeded as far as the campaign was concerned.[34] But for Beijing, having this stand as the last word was not positive news.

Leonard Woodcock was so appalled by the implications of all of this for U.S.-PRC relations that, at his own initiative and not on instruction from Washington, he called a press conference. He declared that Reagan's statements on Taiwan endangered the carefully crafted Sino-American relationship and ran the risk of "gravely weakening" the U.S. international position at a "dangerous time."[35]

Office," *New York Times,* August 16, 1980, A-1.

[34] Richard Allen, correspondence with author.

[35] James P. Sterba, "Woodcock Says Reagan Assertions on Taiwan Endanger China Links," *New York Times,* August 27, 1980, A-1. Stapleton Roy recalls that, as a result, when Reagan won, although Woodcock initially received a standard cable asking him to stay in place until a replacement was chosen, the next day he received one telling him to leave right away (interview with author).

6

Arming Taiwan

"The United States will make available to Taiwan such defense articles and defense services in such quantity as may be necessary to enable Taiwan to maintain a sufficient self-defense capability."

—Taiwan Relations Act

The events surrounding the 1980 campaign laid the foundation for the crisis in U.S.-PRC relations that erupted only a few months into the Reagan Administration, in early fall of 1981, and was to last for almost a full year until "resolved" by the joint communiqué of August 17, 1982. It was a crisis that reflected the clash between Ronald Reagan's ideological disdain for the PRC, his underlying sense that Taiwan had been badly treated—as well as his concern over its future security, and, on the other side, Beijing's determination not to accept any meaningful compromise on the hard-won principles of normalization. Moreover, Beijing harbored both anger and suspicion over U.S. intentions toward continuing arms sales to Taiwan. These sharply divergent perspectives and interests became fused in a dispute over the possible sale to Taiwan of a "follow-on aircraft" for Taiwan's deteriorating fighter aircraft fleet.

The story, of course, has been told in various places in great detail.[1] What is worth examining in the context of this study is what led to the crisis. Was it the product of misunderstandings and miscommunication, differing interpretations of what had already been agreed, or simply a determination to bypass or "reinterpret" previous commitments?

ADVANCED FIGHTER AIRCRAFT (I): THE FX

Noting the central role that arms sales played in normalization and their persistently contentious nature ever since, AIT's first Director in

---

[1] See, for example, Tyler, *A Great Wall*, pp. 298-327; Mann, *About Face*, pp. 118-133; Holdridge, *Crossing the Divide*, pp. 199-241; Haig, *Caveat*, pp. 204-215; Shultz, *Turmoil and Triumph*, pp. 383-385; and Harding, *A Fragile Relationship*, pp. 108-118.

Taipei, Charles Cross, summed up their symbolic importance to all three concerned parties:

> For the Chinese in Beijing, arms sales have been a recurring symbolic reminder that the United States stands against their ruling Taiwan. For the Chinese in Taipei, the arms have been symbols of moral support…To the United States, providing arms to Taiwan has been symbolic of our fiat that the Chinese must settle Taiwan's status peacefully.[2]

Given Reagan's strong history of advocating arms sales to Taiwan, his election gave hope to Taipei that the new American president would provide advanced fighter aircraft to replace the aging, short-range F-5Es on which it primarily depended. Although the need for a "follow-on" aircraft was unclear in the minds of many U.S. experts, Taiwan was encouraged by various "friendly" voices in Washington to think that it would at least get a newly designed export fighter known generically as the FX or possibly even the front-line F-16.[3]

In later years, Cross recalled that he had been concerned by comments from some figures close to Reagan spinning out extravagant arms sales scenarios that, if implemented, would have created unnecessary problems for Washington's China policy. He suggested early on to the new administration that Taipei be allowed, sooner or later, to purchase the FX in order to avoid a Taiwan public relations campaign that would risk turning aircraft sales into a lightning rod for PRC complaints.[4]

---

[2] Charles T. Cross, *Born a Foreigner: A Memoir of the American Presence in Asia* (Boulder: Rowman & Littlefield, 1999), p. 263.

[3] President Carter had encouraged airplane companies to compete in developing an export fighter plane—which came to be called the "FX"—with lower capabilities than the front-line F-16, but, according to some accounts, in the end he declined to choose between California- and Texas-based manufacturers during the 1980 presidential campaign and never decided on any such s ales. The whole question of export aircraft was thus in limbo when Reagan assumed office. But Richard Allen observes that Taiwan bears some responsibility for the lack of a sale under Carter. He notes that Taiwan held off making a decision between the different versions of the FX in the hope that Reagan would be elected and would offer Taipei a better aircraft. If that did not pan out, they figured, they would still have the two FX versions to choose from. It did not turn out that way (correspondence with author).

[4] Cross, *Born a Foreigner*, pp. 264-266.

But nothing happened as Washington debated these matters, and within a few months after Reagan took office, reports began to come out of Taiwan that the island's "great expectations" were "wearing thin" and that it feared Reagan's campaign rhetoric on arms sales would prove to be just that—campaign rhetoric.[5]

As this issue was being considered on one track, Secretary of State Alexander M. Haig had been pressing on a parallel track for a broader military-to-military relationship with the PRC, including provision of dual civilian/military use technology and even arms. A leak to the press in early June reported that the NSC had decided to proceed with a plan approved under Carter, but never implemented, to place China in a more lenient export control category than that governing sales to the Soviet Union and its allies.[6] Accompanying that report, there was more than a whiff of a suggestion that the administration planned to play these two tracks off against one another, hoping that engaging Beijing in a new security relationship would reduce PRC opposition to provision of new arms to Taiwan.

It was against this backdrop that Secretary Haig went to Beijing in mid-1981. In advance of his June 14th arrival, however, Beijing launched a media blitz carried on the front page of every major Chinese newspaper casting doubt on American motives. The articles quoted a Foreign Ministry spokesman:

> We have time and again made it clear that we would rather receive no U.S. arms than accepting continued U.S. interference in our internal affairs by selling arms to Taiwan, to which we can never agree.[7]

Although the article expressed China's appreciation for statements by senior American officials in support of strengthened U.S.-PRC strategic relations, it also commented:

---

[5] Henry Kamm, "Taiwan Disappointed in Reagan Policy," *New York Times,* June 4, 1981, A-3.

[6] Bernard Gwertzman, "Reagan Decides to Relax Curbs on China Trade," *New York Times,* June 6, 1981, sec. 1, p. 1. See Tyler, *A Great Wall,* pp. 304-311, for a rendering of this entire issue from various insider accounts.

[7] Quoted in "Propaganda Blitz Scores Taiwan Arms Sales," *Associated Press,* June 11, 1981.

The crux to further strategic relations between the two countries remains that the United States stop developing all contacts with Taiwan that go beyond nongovernmental relations in keeping with the principles laid down in the China-U.S. joint communiqué on the establishment of diplomatic relations. For the moment, the outstanding issue is about the U.S. arms sales to Taiwan.[8]

According to Western diplomats, this line represented a hardening of Beijing's position, which, only a few weeks earlier had appeared open to the "quiet replenishment" of Taiwan's military stocks *if* the U.S. would forego selling the FX to Taiwan.[9] Whether this apparent toughening was due to anticipated PRC leadership changes[10] or because there were insistent signals about an impending FX sale was unclear. The Chinese message, however, was unambiguous.

In his meeting with Foreign Minister Huang Hua on June 15th, Haig informed the Chinese side of the Administration's intention to ease export controls on China. At the same time, he also made clear to Huang that, "for the foreseeable future," the United States would proceed with the sale of certain "modest defensive weaponry" to Taiwan. Haig reported that no decision on the type of fighter aircraft to be provided Taiwan would be taken before the end of the year, though he indicated that some new planes would be required in 1982 to replace Taipei's deteriorating fleet.

The Secretary was quick to dismiss any suggestion of linkage between Taiwan sales and sales to the PRC, telling Huang that press reporting on the subject was "speculation." He called for "tolerance" and "understanding" from Beijing about U.S. interactions with Taiwan. Moreover, he reassured Huang that "there [could] be no question" but that the President and his entire Administration were committed to the framework of relations laid out in the normalization communiqué and that Washington's dealings with Taiwan would "remain unofficial— people-to-people, as established in that communiqué."[11]

---

[8] Quoted in James P. Sterba, "China Cautions U.S. on Arms for Taiwan," *New York Times,* June 14, 1981, sec. 1, p. 17.

[9] Ibid.

[10] Bernard Gwertzman, "Haig Flies to China; Sees a Mutual Goal to Resist Russians," *New York Times,* June 14, 1981, sec. 1, p. 1.

[11] Super Sensitive 8118399, June 17, 1981, *NSA* 00592. (Not otherwise

Haig reported to Washington that his conversation with Deng Xiaoping "strongly confirmed" the upbeat attitude of his earlier session with the Foreign Minister and "underscored the overriding value to China of continued U.S.-Chinese accord on strategic issues."[12] However, William F. Rope, then Director of the Office of Chinese Affairs at the State Department, who accompanied Haig, recalls a substantially different tenor when the discussions turned to Taiwan arms sales. Huang Hua railed against such sales—"One billion Chinese people will never be bought off!"—and Deng was adamantly opposed to sale of the FX. Intriguingly, however, Deng's presentation seemed to convey an implicit message that, even though every U.S. arms sale to Taiwan was unacceptable "in principle," provision of less advanced weapons would not create a crisis in U.S.-PRC relations.[13]

Here again was an example of Deng's ability to balance strict adherence to the principle of "one China," as the basis of normalization, with pragmatic flexibility in day-to-day implementation.

Before departing for Washington, Haig held a press conference in Beijing on June 16th and announced that the U.S. had decided "in principle" to sell arms to the PRC. He reported that PLA Deputy Chief of Staff Liu Huaqing would visit the United States in August to explore specific items.[14] Although not presented to the press or the PRC as a decision linked in any way to Taiwan arms sales, the suggestion of a

---

identified, this appears to be the draft of a cable transmitting the memorandum of conversation on Taiwan and bilateral issues in Haig's June 15th meeting with Huang Hua. The control number was assigned by the State Department Executive Secretariat.)

[12] SECTO 04078, "Meeting with Deng Xiaoping," June 16, 1981, *NSA* 00587.

[13] Rope interview with author.

[14] Bernard Gwertzman, "U.S. Decides to Sell Weapons to China in Policy Reversal," *New York Times,* June 17, 1981, A-1. Although Haig's announcement went beyond what the NSC had agreed should be disclosed before adequate consultations with Congress (and, presumably, Taiwan), Reagan at a press conference on the 16th backed up Haig's statement, noting that selling Beijing "certain technology and defensive weapons" was a "normal part of the process of improving our relations" with China. At the same time, he was careful to deny any connection to Taiwan policy and reaffirmed his commitment to arms sales under the TRA ("Transcript of the President's News Conference on Foreign and Domestic Affairs," *New York Times,* June 17, 1981, A-26). The Taiwan-related portions of this presidential statement, according to Rope, led to a last-minute airport protest by Zhang Wenjin (interview by author).

trade-off pervaded press accounts of the announcement and, over the next four months, such linkage deepened in the thinking of both sides.

In Taiwan, meanwhile, although welcoming Reagan's "show of friendship toward the Republic of China" and the reiteration of his commitment to arms sales under the TRA, the government struck a rhetorical pose on the U.S. decision to sell weapons to Beijing, lamenting that "[a]ny means that will prolong the Chinese Communist regime can only bring the Chinese people more suffering."[15]

During the course of the summer, an intense debate raged in Washington over what weapons systems could be sold to Beijing and whether the FX should be sold to Taiwan.[16] As Rope recalls, Beijing's queries about both the menu of arms to be offered Liu and the fate of the FX decision became more insistent and more focused as the weeks passed. But, reflecting the roiled internal state of play in Washington, American interlocutors parried these inquiries. American officials responded with vague statements that Liu would be "well taken care of" while providing no answer at all on the FX.[17] Liu's visit was then delayed pending receipt of satisfactory answers, and, when none were forthcoming by September, China called it off.

How Beijing actually viewed the pairing of arms sales to the PRC and to Taiwan is a matter for speculation. While it was clear that U.S.-PRC strategic cooperation was growing[18]—and Haig's visit sought to foster further developments in that direction—Rope remains convinced that the FX represented an absolute "redline" item for China that could not be swallowed.[19] He recalled that the Chinese had downgraded relations with the Netherlands the previous December over Dutch submarine sales to Taiwan. On the other hand, Rope acknowledges that

---

[15] Foreign Ministry spokesman, cited in "Taiwan Assails U.S. Arms Policy," *New York Times*, June 18, 1981, A-14.

[16] Patrick Tyler describes these developments, linking the efforts to persist with an FX sale to both political and financial considerations (*A Great Wall,* p. 308).

[17] Interviews by author.

[18] For example, just after Haig left Beijing, the *New York Times* reported that the U.S. and China had been jointly operating an electronic intelligence-gathering station in western China near the Soviet border since 1980 (Philip Taubman, "U.S. and Peking Join in Tracking Missiles in Soviet," June 18, 1981, A-1).

[19] Chas Freeman later confirmed in conversations with Chinese officials that Beijing had been fully prepared to downgrade relations if the FX were sold to Taiwan (interview by author).

by linking these two issues in their inquiries, the Chinese left the impression in the minds of some U.S. officials that Beijing was amenable to a trade-off, and that impression probably contributed to the persistent pursuit of such a course in Washington over the next few months.[20]

Tensions with Beijing over the possibility of FX sales continued to rise, culminating in a crescendo of escalating demands that the United States commit not to provide any advanced fighters to the island and eventually, in October 1981, the demand that the United States end *all* arms sales to Taiwan.

Arising so close on the heels of normalization in which Taiwan arms sales were such a critical—and unresolved—factor, the dispute over follow-on aircraft for Taiwan acquired special importance for Beijing because of the political context in which it arose. The issue was not "merely" arms sales, where the U.S. commitment to show "restraint" and to provide only "carefully selected defensive equipment" seemed to have gone out the window. Because of Reagan's campaign rhetoric on upgrading the level of officiality of American ties to the island, in Beijing's mind it engaged the issue of sovereignty, and hence the entire premise of normalization. It was against this background that China apparently determined the time had come to resolve this unsettled remnant of the normalization negotiation once and for all.

INDUCEMENTS AND THREATS: MOVING TOWARD AUGUST 17

A critical new factor affected not only Beijing's subsequent approach to forestalling an FX sale, but the resolution of the entire arms sales issue. That was the "nine-point proposal" made by National People's Congress (NPC) Standing Committee Chairman Ye Jianying in an interview with *Xinhua* on September 30, 1981.[21]

In it, the NPC Chairman laid out what *People's Daily* editorially called "our steadfast policy...not an expedient measure," that "takes into consideration both basic national interests and the present situation in Taiwan."[22] Echoing much of the general rhetoric of the 1979 New

---

[20] Interview by author. Rope confirmed that, though he was convinced by Deng's remarks that Beijing would have no choice but to downgrade relations in the event of an FX sale, Haig continued to pursue a trade-off strategy for four more months.

[21] Full text available at http://un.fmprc.gov.cn/eng/4293.html.

[22] "Struggle Jointly for Taiwan's Return to the Motherland and the Realization of the Great Cause of Reunification," *BBC Summary of World Broadcasts*,

Year's Day "Message to Compatriots,"[23] Ye reiterated the proposal for the three links, called for party-to-party (Communist-to-Nationalist) talks "on a reciprocal basis," promised a high degree of autonomy to Taiwan after reunification including retention of Taiwan's armed forces, and pledged non-interference by Beijing in Taiwan's social, economic, legal or other local affairs. Ye's appeal for cooperation in this endeavor was addressed both to "people in authority" as well as to private citizens in various circles within Taiwan.

When Vice Foreign Minister Zhang Wenjin called on National Security Adviser William Clark at the White House four days later, he based his argument against the FX in part on Ye's proposal, calling this newly refined approach to peaceful reunification a "fundamental policy that would not change."[24]

This did not lead to a new U.S. position, however, and a pair of testy exchanges followed between Haig and Foreign Minister and Vice Premier Huang Hua—first in Cancun, Mexico on October 23rd and then about a week later when Huang traveled to Washington. Huang demanded that the United States establish a firm schedule to end all Taiwan arms sales and, pending agreement on such a schedule, that Washington suspend any new sales. He threatened serious consequences if the U.S. did not comply. While the United States did not accept these conditions, arms sales were, in fact, suspended and the two sides convened discussions in Beijing that eventually produced the August 17, 1982 Communiqué.

It was in the Haig-Huang conversation in Washington that the Secretary, in a formula that would eventually end up in the August 17 Communiqué, first agreed to limit the quality and quantity of arms sales to Taiwan to levels that had prevailed in the years since normalization.

October 3, 1981, reporting the full text of the *People's Daily* editorial which appeared on October 2, 1981.

[23] See p. 96.

[24] Rope, interview by author. This point is substantiated in L. Paul Bremer, Memorandum for Ms. Nancy Bearg-Dyke, The White House, "Key Statements on Taiwan Arms Sales," July 15, 1982, *FOIA*. An attachment, entitled "Taiwan Arms Sales: Communiqué Language," laid out the then-current state of the second draft of the communiqué as presented to the Chinese in February. Without providing a specific source for the statement, it read in part: "The next three paragraphs restate China's 'fundamental policy of striving for peaceful reunification' which is termed 'a national policy that will not change.'"

On the one hand, this "limitation" was acceptable to the U.S. because the quantity of arms sold to Taiwan since 1979 had in fact been very high, and hence the pledge was not seen to sacrifice anything. On the other hand, it also reflected the realization, after Cancún, that the FX deal was dead.[25]

The formal decision to kill the FX did not come for several more weeks, though, and was only forced through after Richard Allen, a staunch FX proponent, left the White House at the end of 1981. The State Department had been frustrated by what it perceived to be an overly ideological fixation in the NSC on bolstering Taiwan's arsenal against the Mainland, unbalanced by broader strategic considerations.[26] Seizing on what he saw as a window of opportunity, Rope pushed forward a decision memorandum under Haig's signature, which Reagan approved in early January.[27] As it was explained by Deputy Secretary of State-designate Walter Stoessel to friendly ambassadors in Washington:

> The President has accepted the recommendation [of State, Defense and other national security agencies] that no advanced aircraft sale is required for Taiwan because no military need for such aircraft exits.
>
> The military and intelligence communities agree that for the foreseeable future Taiwan's legitimate defense needs can be fully met, by continuing the F-5E co-production line on Taiwan with the possibility in addition of replacing older worn out aircraft with used aircraft of a comparable type.[28]

However, Stoessel told the Senate Foreign Relations Committee in late January 1982 that the FX sale was called off because of a "real danger of rupture" in Sino-American relations. He noted that the Administration had been planning a military spare parts sale to Taiwan later in 1982, but that (unspecified) developments forced the acceleration

---

[25] Interview with William Rope.

[26] Scott Hallford, interview by author. At the time, Hallford was the Deputy Director of the State Department's Office of China Affairs.

[27] Mark Mohr, interview by author. Mohr was on the Taiwan desk at the time.

[28] State 007065, "Taiwan Arms Sales: Deputy Secretary-Designate's Talking Points and Press Guidance," January 11, 1982, *FOIA*. In fact, according to Rope and Lilley, the intelligence community had concluded some weeks before that the FX was not militarily required (interviews by author).

of that calendar to December, which then led to a sharp reaction from Beijing and a demand that the U.S. halt all Taiwan arms sales.[29] Stoessel also cited "strategic implications" of a U.S.-PRC split, a reference to the tensions over the imposition of martial law in Poland.[30]

When Assistant Secretary of State for East Asia John Holdridge went to Beijing in January to explain the airplane decision, the Chinese inclination at first was to criticize the extension of F-5E co-production rather than to embrace the decision to shelve the FX. An authoritative, if pseudonymous, *Xinhua* commentary by "Mei Ping" attacked the "unilateral" U.S. decision as "an encroachment on China's sovereignty and interference in her internal affairs." Mei decried as "untenable" the effort "to create a false impression" that the decision to proceed with F-5Es rather than F-16s or FXs was a "concession." The article concluded that whether there was to be retrogression in relations depended on whether Washington decision makers made the "wise choice" of showing respect for China's sovereignty.[31]

---

[29] John H. Holdridge reports the PRC's December protest in *Crossing the Divide,* p. 221.

[30] State 023622, "January 28 EA Press Summary," January 28, 1982, *FOIA,* citing various stories. About ten days earlier, former *New York Times* correspondent Tad Szulc had reviewed this question in some detail and had come up with a decidedly *realpolitik* assessment of what had happened. Szulc cited a forceful memorandum Haig had sent to the President at the end of November 1981, reviewing the deteriorating state of U.S.-PRC relations, particularly as a result of the FX issue. Haig had written that, against the background of the campaign rhetoric as well as subsequent actions with Taiwan and the PRC, the President had created the impression that the U.S. was reverting to a "two Chinas" policy. That, the Secretary argued, had "transformed the aircraft replacement question, which might otherwise have been manageable, into a symbolic challenge to China's sovereignty and territorial integrity." He recommended that sales be limited to the same level as under Carter "so long as Peking pursues a peaceful Taiwan policy." All that having been laid out, Szulc wrote, the President was still determined to proceed with the FX until the imposition of martial law in Poland in January. At that point, Reagan realized he needed to line up Beijing in a united front against the Soviet pressure on Eastern Europe. As Szulc put it: "In the end, Poland made the difference" ("The Reagan Administration's Push Toward China Came from Warsaw," *Los Angeles Times,* January 17, 1982, part IV, p. 9).

[31] "Chinese Comment on Arms Sales to Taiwan: USA 'Going Too Far,'" *BBC Summary of World Broadcasts,* January 15, 1982, reporting the full text of Mei Ping's *Xinhua* commentary, which first appeared on January 13, 1982.

Washington's response was to try to demonstrate some sensitivity to these sentiments. Upgrades to Taiwan's F-5Es had been considered in some parts of the administration in late summer 1981 as a way of fending off efforts by others in the administration to sell an FX (or to sell a "disguised" FX that would be deceptively marketed publicly as simply an "upgraded" F-5E).[32] But in the wake of the January decision to scuttle the FX for Taiwan, and although future upgrades were not foreclosed "as circumstances warrant[ed]...based on our assessments of Taiwan's real military needs," Taipei was discouraged from seeking any "further improvements" of the F-5E "at this time" lest the surfacing of the issue provoke a PRC reaction counterproductive to Taipei's interests.[33]

By early February 1982, although China refused to join the United States in criticizing the Soviet Union over Poland[34] and was even boosting its trade with Poland's military government by a reported 25-30 percent,[35] Beijing eased its criticism of the aircraft decision. "Mei Ping" once again issued a commentary. Ostensibly aiming at Senator Jesse Helms for his "two Chinas" stance, Mei Ping reiterated that selling arms to Taiwan—which, he asserted, the U.S. had "recognized" was part of China—infringed on Chinese sovereignty. But, noting that China was "mindful of larger interests," Mei said China was "willing to negotiate with the United States for an end to the sales within a time limit."[36] This implied call for a phase-out was, of course, consistent with Huang Hua's private demand the previous fall, but in light of the harsh public criticism only two weeks earlier, it came across to outside observers as having

---

[32] Rope, interview by author; see also Tyler, *A Great Wall,* pp. 311-321. Tyler calls this plan Haig's "Houdini act," in which he aimed to announce that the FX deal was dead, but then "modify" the F-5E so that, in the end, it turned out—as if by magic—to look just like the FX would have, including having a single engine instead of the F-5E's standard two.

[33] State 016643, "Replacement Aircraft for Taiwan," January 22, 1982, paras. 3-4, *FOIA.*

[34] Richard Halloran, "China Refuses to Criticize Soviets over Poland," *New York Times,* January 30, 1982, sec. 1, p. 13.

[35] William J. Holstein, "China Increases Trade with Poland Despite U.S. Appeals," *United Press International,* January 31, 1982.

[36] Mei Ping, "Who is Blackmailing," *Xinhua,* January 31, 1982, carried in "China Willing to Negotiate 'Time Limit' for US Arms Sales to Taiwan," *BBC Summary of World Broadcasts,* February 1, 1982.

"significantly softened" Beijing's terms for reconciliation with Washington.[37] Clearly the choice of the same commentator to reveal that shift was not by accident.

The U.S. side now hoped to reach a final agreement on a communiqué resolving this issue by the tenth anniversary of the Shanghai Communiqué at the end of February, but this proved impossible.[38]

Despite the alleged "softening," Foreign Minister Huang Hua, briefing European Community Ambassadors in early February, characterized Sino-American relations as being at a "delicate and explosive" stage, indeed in a "crisis." Huang focused on Taiwan arms sales, claiming that China did not have much "room for maneuver" on the Taiwan issue.[39]

The situation was further complicated by congressional notification in mid-April of the $60 million military spare parts package for Taiwan that had been announced—and caused a stir—in December.[40] The April notification led to the PRC cancellation of Defense Secretary Caspar Weinberger's first trip to China.[41]

---

[37] Michael Weisskopf, "Peking Acts to Bolster U.S. Ties; Article Softens Stance on Sales of Arms to Taiwan; China Suggests Time Limit on U.S. Arms Sales to Taiwan," *Washington Post,* February 1, 1982, A-1.

[38] A variety of other circumstances were believed to have come into play, including opposition to Deng over his reform program, forcing him to be firm on foreign policy issues, especially over U.S. policy toward Taiwan (Tokyo 00762, "Asssec [sic] Holdridge's Briefing for Japanese on US-PRC Talks," January 18, 1982, para. 6, *FOIA*).

[39] Beijing 01421, "Chinese Officials Comment on Taiwan," February 8, 1982, *FOIA*.

[40] In press reporting on an April 5th conversation between Secretary Haig and PRC Ambassador Chai Zemin about this sale, the outlines of a possible agreement began to emerge publicly. One report by Bernard Gwertzman of the *New York Times* noted that the U.S. had proposed to China "that the two sides issue a declaration in which Washington would pledge not to provide Taiwan with military equipment beyond the quantity and quality of its current arsenal" ("Haig Meets with Peking Officials to Discuss Arms Sales to Taiwan," April 6, 1982, A-1). Gwertzman's report was picked up by the Taiwan press shortly thereafter.

[41] Tyler, *A Great Wall,* p. 323.

How PRC domestic politics played into all of this is not entirely clear. There may well have been a need for Deng to play a tougher hand starting as far back as June 1981, when he moved to assume the chairmanship of the Central Military Commission and the post of General Secretary of the Party. But the U.S. position on arms sales against the background of Reagan's general inclination toward Taiwan certainly forced an increasingly sharp reaction through the fall, as we have seen.

Here again, in early 1982, as Deng prepared to consolidate his leadership at the 12th Party Congress set for September, it appears that he decided it was wise to allow more conservative Party "elders" a greater voice in foreign policy. Still, the U.S. Embassy in Beijing assessed that, while Deng had "allowed the Taiwan issue to drift in a manner which has exacerbated Sino-US tension for some time, presumably deliberately," there had been no diminution in Deng's ability to ultimately control and manipulate the main lines of domestic or foreign policy, including the difficult questions of Taiwan policy.[42]

Nonetheless, because of the deterioration in the spring, George H.W. Bush, now Vice President, was brought out of the bullpen once again to stabilize U.S.-PRC dealings over Taiwan. Bush added Beijing to the end of a scheduled trip to Asia in early May. In giving Taipei advance notification of the Vice President's planned stop in the PRC, care was taken to include the President's personal assurances to President Chiang Ching-kuo that the United States would make available to Taiwan "the equipment Taiwan needs for its defense." Chiang was further informed:

> As we have told you in the past, we will not accept a time certain limitation on arms sales to Taiwan; we will carry out the TRA; and we will exert no pressure on Taiwan to enter into negotiations with Beijing.[43]

The *China Times* also reported from Washington that State Department officials had said "the question of sovereignty over Taiwan is not negotiable at all."[44]

---

[42] Beijing 02685, "Taiwan Arms Issue," March 6, 1982, *FOIA*.

[43] State 111437, "Informing Taiwan of Vice President's Trip," April 26, 1982, *FOIA*.

[44] Taipei 02016, "Norman Fu's Commentary on US/PRC Talks," April 12, 1982, *FOIA*.

Bush's visit was preceded by a stream of extremely harsh rhetoric in Mainland and PRC-controlled Hong Kong media, including warnings in at least one case of a possible suspension of U.S.-PRC relations if the Taiwan arms sales time-bomb were not defused.[45] However, when the Vice President arrived in China, Deng and other senior leaders welcomed him as an "old friend."[46] This was no doubt helped by the fact that Bush carried with him a positive letter from President Reagan for Party Chairman Hu Yaobang. During the trip, the White House released not only that letter but also two other letters that Reagan had sent a month earlier to Deng Xiaoping and Premier Zhao Ziyang. All three letters included reference to the importance of a stable strategic relationship between the two countries. They also directly addressed Taiwan. To Hu, Reagan wrote:

> [T]he United States *will continue to adhere firmly* to the positions agreed upon in the joint communiqué in the establishment of diplomatic relations between the United States and the People's Republic of China. *Our policy will continue to be based on the principle that there is but one China.* We will not permit the unofficial relations between the American people and the Chinese people on Taiwan to weaken our commitment to this principle.[47]

To Zhao:

> We will welcome and support peaceful resolution of the Taiwan question. In this connection, we appreciate the policies which your government has followed to provide a peaceful settlement.

> As I told Vice Premier Huang [Hua] in Washington [in October 1981], we welcome your nine-point initiative.

---

[45] *Xinwan Bao* (Hong Kong), May 2, 1982, as reported in Hong Kong 06870, "Bush China Visit: Talking Tougher Yet Leaving Room," May 4, 1982, *FOIA.*

[46] Tyler, *A Great Wall,* pp. 323-324.

[47] "Letter From President Reagan to the Chairman of the Chinese Communist Party (Hu), May 3, 1982," in *American Foreign Policy Current Documents 1982* (Washington, D.C.: Government Printing Office, 1985), p. 1030. Emphasis added.

As I also told the Vice Premier, we expect that in the context of progress toward a peaceful solution, there would naturally be a decrease in the need for arms by Taiwan.[48]

And to Deng:

The United States firmly adheres to positions agreed upon in the Joint Communiqué on the Establishment of Diplomatic Relations between the United States and China. *There is only one China. We will not permit the unofficial relations between the American people and the Chinese people on Taiwan to weaken our commitment to this principle.*

I fully understand and respect the position of your government with regard to the question of arms sales to Taiwan. As you know, our position on this matter was stated in the process of normalization: the *United States has an abiding interest in the peaceful resolution of the Taiwan question.*

We *fully recognize the significance of the nine-point proposal* [of September 30, 1981].[49]

Taken together, this is a striking set of statements. The man who was speaking two years earlier of reestablishing official relations with Taiwan was now recommitting to the principles of the normalization communiqué, pledging to base his policies on the "principle of one China"—indeed, stating flatly that "there is only one China," explaining that the United States "fully understand[s] and respect[s]" the Chinese government position on Taiwan arms sales, noting that the U.S. "welcomed" the nine-point proposal and "fully recognized" its

---

[48] "Letter From President Reagan to Chinese Premier Zhao, April 5, 1982," in ibid., p. 1029. Emphasis added.

[49] "Letter From President Reagan to Vice Chairman of the Chinese Communist Party (Deng), April 5, 1982," in ibid., p. 1028. Emphasis added. There is at least one discrepancy between this officially released text and a version reported by a correspondent covering the Bush visit. According to the latter, after saying that the U.S. "fully recognize[s]" the significance of the nine-point proposal, the letter went on to say: "and the policy set forth by your Government as early as January 1, 1979" (Christopher S. Wren, "Bush Leaves China with New Ideas for Resolving Taiwan Arms Dispute," *New York Times*, May 10, 1982, A-3). As this phrase underscores that Reagan's key point was peaceful resolution, it is a curious omission, and may simply have been a printing error.

significance, and observing that there would "naturally" be a decrease in Taiwan's need for arms in the context of "progress" toward a peaceful solution.

Reagan restated the strong U.S. "abiding interest" in a peaceful resolution of cross-Strait issues and made clear the connection to Taiwan arms sales. But he went well beyond the Shanghai and normalization communiqué statements on "acknowledging the Chinese position" on "one China" and paid respect to the nine-point proposal that, for all of its emphasis on "peaceful reunification" and "a high degree of autonomy" for Taiwan, was based on an acceptance by Taiwan of the sovereign control of the "Central Government" in Beijing.

While Reagan obviously meant to focus on a peaceful process, Taipei's reaction was that the President had sold out Taiwan. The Foreign Ministry spokesman charged that the American leader had "ignored our national interests" in endorsing the nine-point proposal and said that, if that proposal were ever implemented, it would mean the communization of the island, since Beijing would not allow Taiwan to have its own social system and government, whatever its promises to the contrary.[50]

In their meeting, Bush reportedly told Deng that the U.S. refusal to accept a "date certain" for ending arms sales did not mean that anyone in the Administration saw such sales going on forever, and Deng seized on that statement to give new life to the negotiations.[51] This exchange was presumably at least in part what Vice Premier Wan Li had in mind when in his dinner toast he termed the visit "useful"; similarly for Bush when he told reporters on leaving Beijing that he had "some specific ideas" to bring back to Washington.[52] And on his return, it is evident that the Vice President became more active on this question, including gathering more information on the arms sales issue.[53]

But overall, with Bush's return to Washington, Alexander Haig recalls that six weeks of "silence and inaction" ensued on the American side, as Reagan came under criticism from conservative Republicans,

---

[50] "Taiwan Lashes out at Reagan," *United Press International,* May 12, 1982.

[51] Tyler, *A Great Wall,* p. 324.

[52] Michael Weisskopf, "Reagan Letters Seek to Reassure China on Arms Sales to Taiwan," *Washington Post,* May 10, 1982, A-21.

[53] See L. Paul Bremer, Memorandum for Ms. Nancy Bearg-Dyke, The White House, "Key Statements on Taiwan Arms Sales," op. cit.

with whom he, in fact, was sympathetic. Haig also recounts how, as he was preparing to resign in late June, he used that opportunity to press Reagan to make a compromise that would preserve the relationship with Beijing and American honor, as well as assuring the continued well-being of the people of Taiwan. Echoing his November 1981 memorandum, what he proposed was to reach an agreement with Beijing that permitted continued arms sales whose reduction in the future would be tied to progress on China's peaceful course of reunification. While it would include a statement looking forward to the "ultimate resolution" of this problem, no date certain for cessation of arms sales would be agreed.[54]

KEEPING FAITH WITH TAIWAN: THE "SIX ASSURANCES"

As negotiations with Beijing moved toward conclusion, Gaston Sigur, then Senior Director for Asia at the National Security Council, phoned Mark Mohr on the Taiwan desk at the State Department and asked him to draft something that would "ease the shock" of the communiqué on Taiwan, alleviating Taipei's feeling that it was being "sold out."[55] This exercise yielded the so-called "six assurances," transmitted to Taipei in mid-July 1982, only weeks before the issuance of the August 17 Communiqué.

As the U.S.-PRC communiqué was being issued, the Reagan Administration informed Foreign Minister Frederick Chien that Taipei could make public the following version of the "six assurances." They were to say that it was "their understanding" that the U.S.:

- Has not set a date for ending arms sales to Taiwan.

---

[54] Haig, *Caveat,* pp. 213-215.

[55] Mark Mohr, interview by author. The origin of the six assurances has been the subject of some controversy. John Holdridge, then-Assistant Secretary of State for East Asian and Pacific Affairs, wrote that he was given them by a Taiwan source (*Crossing the Divide,* pp. 231-232). Harvey J. Feldman, head of the ROC office at the time of normalization and a frequent writer on Taiwan issues, did some sleuthing on this question and concluded that Holdridge's memory misserved him, and that the six assurances indeed originated with the United States as Mohr states—not in Taiwan; see Feldman's "Taiwan, Arms Sales, and the Reagan Assurances, *American Asian Review* XIX, no. 3 (fall 2001), pp. 75-101.

- Has not agreed to consult with the PRC on arms sales to Taiwan.

- Will not play any mediation role between Taipei and Beijing.

- Has not agreed to revise the Taiwan Relations Act.

- Has not altered its position regarding sovereignty over Taiwan.[56]

- Will not exert pressure on Taiwan to enter into negotiations with the PRC.[57]

Not agreeing to a "date certain" for ending arms sales was central to the U.S. position. Declining to play a mediating role seemed as much a matter of self-protection as anything else, as American officials had warned for years about the pitfalls of any such involvement. But it was also consistent with the point about not pressuring Taipei to negotiate with Beijing. Moreover, the U.S. took the occasion to reiterate: "The U.S. does not take a position on the issue of reunification."[58] The assurance on the TRA reflected a rebuff of earlier PRC insistence that the Act be rescinded or at least amended in major ways.

---

[56] There is some difference of recollections about the origins of the assurance regarding sovereignty. David Dean, Chairman of AIT in 1982, happened to be in Mohr's office while Mohr was drafting the assurances, and Dean made inputs to the points. Dean had the impression that a senior foreign ministry official in Taipei might have played a role in the addition of the sovereignty point to five original points. Mohr's recollection is that he drafted all six. In any event, they agree that there was nothing very complicated or mysterious about the process; the points, many of which, as we have noted, had already surfaced in one way or another, were simply logical statements addressing the problematic aspects of the communiqué from Taipei's point of view. (All drawn from interviews by author.)

[57] State 3160, "Assurances for Taiwan," August 17, 1982, *FOIA*. Holdridge testified about the communiqué before Congress and, while not identifying them as "six assurances," made public their substance ("Opening Statement Made Before the House Foreign Affairs Committee, August 18, 1982," carried in full in State 243116, "Briefings and Press Guidance on US-PRC Communiqué," August 28, 1982, *FOIA*).

[58] State 230951, "Press Materials: US-China Joint Communiqué," August 18, 1982, conveying guidance prepared for John Holdridge's "background briefing" of the press the previous day.

Of the assurances, the two that have been most frequently the subject of later discussion are the ban on prior consultations with Beijing on arms sales to Taiwan and the statement of U.S. policy consistency on the question of sovereignty.

As to the "prior consultation" issue, while some have argued that this assurance strictly precluded *any* discussion with Beijing about arms sales to Taiwan, this appears to be an overreading. First of all, it was a statement that the United States *had not agreed* with Beijing to hold such consultations; it did not say there could never be such consultations. For years—before and after 1982—the United States made clear to Beijing that the nature of arms sales to Taiwan, including the quantity and the capabilities, was directly related to the "threat" the island faced. Logically, the point was not only that if the "threat" went up so, too, would arms sales, but, conversely, that if the threat were reduced, arms sales would follow suit. Reagan had, as we have seen, made that very point in his April letter to Zhao Ziyang.

What was more reasonably implied by the assurance was that the United States would not consult with Beijing on specific sales, nor would it allow Beijing to dictate which sales were "acceptable" and which were not. As the FX saga demonstrated, the United States was willing to take account of PRC views, but it would not negotiate with Beijing before taking decisions.

The assurance on sovereignty has been interpreted in a number of different ways. One interpretation is that the U.S. "would continue to regard Taiwan as part of China," but that the question of reunification was left to "the Chinese themselves" as long as it was peaceful.[59] More likely, and a view supported by the drafter of the assurances, is that, as in the Shanghai Communiqué, it skirted the issue of whether or not Taiwan was "part of China" and simply meant the United States would not force Taipei to accept the PRC position on sovereignty[60]—in a sense, a response to Taipei's criticism, noted earlier, that Reagan's "endorsement" of the PRC's nine-point proposal implied U.S. acceptance of ultimate unification on PRC terms. In the words of the message Lilley was asked to convey to Chiang Ching-kuo on the eve of its issuance, the communiqué

---

[59] Holdridge, *Crossing the Divide,* p. 232.

[60] Mark Mohr, interview by author.

...will not refer, either through language or by implication, to a U.S. position with regard to sovereignty over Taiwan. We take no position on that matter.[61]

THE COMMUNIQUÉ—DEFINED AND REDEFINED

Culminating months of negotiation, the communiqué was finally issued on August 17, 1982. After a brief review of the history of normalization, a reiteration of the principles of the Shanghai and normalization communiqués, and an explanation that the Taiwan arms sales issue had not been settled, there came a paragraph that voiced the PRC position on Taiwan. It stated that the Taiwan issue was an internal affair, although China had a "fundamental policy of striving for peaceful reunification."[62] In this context, then, came the key U.S. statements:

The United States Government attaches great importance to its relations with China, and reiterates that it has no intention of infringing on Chinese sovereignty and territorial integrity, or interfering in China's internal affairs, or pursuing a policy of "two Chinas" or "one China, one Taiwan." The United States Government understands and appreciates the Chinese policy of striving for a peaceful resolution of the Taiwan question as indicated in China's Message to Compatriots in Taiwan issued on January 1, 1979 and the Nine-Point Proposal put forward by China on September 30, 1981. The new situation which has emerged with regard to the Taiwan question[63] also provides favorable conditions for the settlement of United States-China

---

[61] State 228830, "Message to Chiang Ching-kuo," August 15, 1982, *FOIA*. Foreign Minister Frederick Chien felt that it was particularly important that this assurance be made public in light of the misunderstanding that could otherwise be generated by the communiqué statement that the U.S. and PRC respected each other's sovereignty and territorial integrity (Taipei 04476, "Message to Chiang Ching-kuo," August 16, 1982, *FOIA*).

[62] It is unclear why the reference to the "unchanging" nature of the policy did not make it into the final communiqué, but in explaining the language to all and sundry, including Chiang Ching-kuo, the U.S. took pains to state that the Chinese term used to express "fundamental policy" "connoted great authority and constancy" (State 228830, "Message to Chiang Ching-kuo").

[63] Amplified elsewhere to mean "Beijing's fundamental policy of a peaceful approach" (ibid.).

differences over the question of United States arms sales to Taiwan.

Having in mind the foregoing statements of both sides, the United States Government states that it does not seek to carry out a long-term policy of arms sales to Taiwan, that its arms sales to Taiwan will not exceed, either in qualitative or in quantitative terms, the level of those supplied in recent years since the establishment of diplomatic relations between the United States and China, and that it intends to reduce gradually its sales of arms to Taiwan, leading over a period of time to a final resolution. In so stating, the United States acknowledges China's consistent position regarding the thorough settlement of this issue.

In order to bring about, over a period of time, a final settlement of the question of United States arms sales to Taiwan, which is an issue rooted in history, the two governments will make every effort to adopt measures and create conditions conducive to the thorough settlement of this issue.[64]

The communiqué marked an important step, if not in resolving, then at least in setting aside a dispute that threatened the entire U.S.-PRC relationship. Some saw the communiqué as a way—without harming Taiwan's equities—to solve a practical issue that had originated largely out of the 1980 presidential campaign, and thus to save the relationship with Beijing for the sake of Washington's bilateral, regional and global strategic interests.[65] Others saw it has having a larger, overarching purpose, to shape the environment of cross-Strait relations away from militarization and toward economic and cultural exchanges, getting the

---

[64] "Joint Communiqué Issued by the Governments of the United States and the People's Republic of China, Washington and Beijing, August 17, 1982" in *American Foreign Policy Current Documents 1982*, p. 1038. The full text appears in the appendix.

[65] William Rope, Alexander Haig and Mark Mohr, interviews by author. While it can be argued that the dispute was a natural consequence of the unresolved differences over arms sales at the time of normalization, the record suggests that if the FX decision had been made earlier, perhaps in the summer of 1981, tensions would not have risen to the level they did. That is Rope's belief. That said, given the evolution of the political situation in Taiwan starting at the end of the 1980's—and the PRC reaction—an eventual problem was probably unavoidable.

U.S. out of the middle, so that both Chinese parties—but especially Taiwan—would see it in their own interest to pursue direct political dialogue.[66]

Although Taiwan issued a statement condemning the communiqué, charging the United States with making a "serious mistake" in judging Beijing's intention, Taipei's overall reaction was, in the words of James Lilley, then senior U.S. representative on the island, "muted."[67] This probably was due, at least in part, to the "six assurances." But Chiang was also given other, more forceful assurances that were not publicized and that probably affected his response. In a message to him on August 16th, Lilley conveyed the following:

> President Reagan wants me to assure you that he remains firmly and deeply committed to the moral and legal obligations in the Taiwan Relations Act, and that the security of Taiwan and the well-being of its people are continuing, steadfast interests of the United States. United States policy to provide Taiwan with sufficient arms to enable Taiwan to maintain a sufficient self-defense capability is a solemn undertaking of the legislative and executive branches of the United States Government, and is broadly and firmly supported by the American people.

> I can assure you that our approach to the new arms sales guidelines set forth in the communiqué will be gradual and evolutionary. Moreover, this new policy will guide our decisions on arms sales to Taiwan only so long as Beijing continues its current peaceful attitude toward Taiwan.

> That of course involves a judgment as to the current and potential threat to Taiwan. To enable us constantly to make that judgment in a fully informed manner, we will continue to monitor carefully Beijing's military production and deployment, and to analyze all indicators of Beijing's intentions toward Taiwan. If any of those factors change, that will of course affect our judgment of Taiwan's defense needs.

> Consequently, the communiqué will not limit our ability to respond to Taiwan's defense needs. The entire understanding on

---

[66] Chas Freeman, who was deeply involved in the actual negotiations in Beijing, holds this view (interview by author).

[67] Interview by author.

our side is predicated on continuation of a peaceful policy on the part of the PRC.[68]

Consistent with these promises to Chiang, Reagan wrote a so-called "codicil" to the August 17 Communiqué in which he spelled out his interpretation of what it meant. Originally reported by James Mann,[69] the text of the codicil was published for the first time in April 2001. It said:

> The U.S. willingness to reduce its arms sales to Taiwan is conditioned absolutely upon the continued commitment of China to the peaceful solution of the Taiwan-PRC differences. And this is a permanent imperative of U.S. foreign policy. The quantity and quality of the arms provided Taiwan [will] be conditioned entirely on the threat posed by the PRC. Taiwan's defense capability relative to that of the PRC will be maintained.[70]

---

[68] State 228830, "Message to Chiang Ching-kuo," op. cit. The intention to "sell Taiwan what it needs" and to maintain the communiqué's approach only as long as China maintained its peaceful policy was made in all Hill briefings (see, for instance, John Holdridge, Action Memorandum to the Secretary, "Taiwan Arms Sales: Calls to Members of Congress and Former Secretaries of State," August 16, 1982, *FOIA*). It was also important in responding to complaints from such people as Senate Judiciary Committee Subcommittee on Separation of Powers Chairman John P. East (R-NC) that the communiqué's provisions on arms sales to Taiwan were "directly contrary" to the requirements of the TRA (see State Department Memorandum for William P. Clark, The White House, "United States/People's Republic of China – Joint Communiqué," September 13, 1982, *FOIA*). While the response in that particular case was geared to substantiating the President's authority to make the undertakings in the communiqué under the terms of the TRA, the substantive U.S. position then—and since—has been that the United States could continue to sell the arms needed without violating the communiqué or the TRA; see *Taiwan Communiqué and Separation of Powers: Hearings Before the Subcommittee on Separation of Powers of the Committee on the Judiciary, United States Senate*, 97th Cong., 2nd sess., September 27, 1982, pp. 95-115 (hereafter *Senate Judiciary Committee Hearings*).

[69] Mann, *About Face*, p. 127.

[70] Robert G. Kaiser, "What We Said, What They Said, What's Unsaid," *Washington Post*, April 15, 2001. Charles Hill, who was Executive Secretary of the State Department at the time, confirms that Reagan told Secretary of State George Shultz about the codicil. Although Reagan never gave Shultz a copy, the President indicated that his purpose was to be sure there was "no mistake about what we were doing," which was to solidify the existing emphasis on a

In fact, in early 1983, Reagan adopted an interpretation of his commitments in the communiqué that scaled them back even further. In an interview with *Human Events*, a conservative publication, he echoed what he had told Premier Zhao Ziyang almost a year earlier, that if the two sides of the Strait ever worked out a peaceful agreement on unification, "then there wouldn't be any need for arms sales to Taiwan." But his amplification took a rather different turn:

> And that's all that was meant in the communiqué. *Nothing was meant beyond that. We're not going to say, "Well, just as time goes by, we're going to reduce the arms to them."*...We will continue to address their capabilities and their needs dependent on the situation in the region.[71]

Over the next several months—indeed in a pattern that has continued all the way up to the present—the Chinese complained about the evolving American explanations and interpretations of the August 17 Communiqué as well as about Washington's performance under its terms. Moreover, Beijing rejected any suggestion that in the communiqué it had "committed" to peaceful resolution of cross-Strait relations and dismissed any suggestion that how those relations were resolved was in any way related to the question of U.S. arms sales.[72] And as time went on, although relations moved pragmatically forward, the shrillness of the rhetoric escalated.

Less than two months after the communiqué came out, even before the *Human Events* interview, *People's Daily* groused:

> Reagan has completely violated the spirit of the joint communiqué issued by the Chinese and U.S. Governments on 17 August by treating a peaceful solution of the Taiwan problem by China as a precondition for halting U.S. arms sales to Taiwan,

---

peaceful solution and the importance of maintaining the cross-Strait military balance for that purpose. A goal of writing down these "clarifications," Hill recalls, was to reassure conservative Republicans such as Senator Jesse Helms (R-NC) that Taiwan was not being disadvantaged by the terms of the communiqué, and thus gain their acquiescence to it (correspondence with author).

[71] "Exclusive Interview: Reagan Responds to Conservative Criticism," *Human Events* XLIII, no. 9 (February 26, 1983), p. 19. Emphasis added.

[72] Voiced in a *Xinhua* article of August 20, 1982, cited in *Senate Judiciary Committee Hearings*, p. 122.

and this also conflicts with President Reagan's words about genuinely and sincerely improving relations with the PRC.

The joint communiqué of the Chinese and U.S. Governments stipulated the principle of a phased and eventually complete solution to the issue of U.S. arms sales to Taiwan, that is, the United States must gradually reduce its arms sales to Taiwan and completely halt them after a time. There cannot and should not be any preconditions on this point.[73]

Taipei's moderate reaction to the August 17 Communiqué was helped not just by U.S. pledges, but also by a pattern of continuing military sales. The F-5E co-production line was extended (formal notification went to Congress within days of the communiqué's issuance), a substantial arms sales package was agreed over the next several months (reportedly about $500 million, encompassing several "big-ticket" items, including Standard missiles), and the arms sales relationship continued to develop in robust fashion over the years following.[74] This was facilitated by a position taken during negotiations—and identified in press briefings at the time—that the calculation of "quantity and quality" would be subject to interpretation, taking into account a number of factors "including a variety of financial and quantitative considerations."[75]

From Beijing's perspective, there is another, frequently overlooked, feature of the August 17 Communiqué that was of great importance in connection with the sovereignty issue. For the first time in a public

---

[73] From a *Renmin Ribao* (*People's Daily*) article of October 10, 1982, cited in ibid., p. 124.

[74] Mohr, interview by author. Another report put the value of Taiwan arms sales at $530 million in 1983 and $1.085 billion in 1984; see Jonathan Marshall, Peter Dale Scott and Jane Hunter, "Growth of Reagan's Contra Commitment," online at http://www.thirdworldtraveler.com/Ronald/Reagan/ReaganContraCommit TICC.html. Rope recalls inflation-adjusted sales announced for FY83 at somewhat over $800 million and a roughly similar figure in 1984. Despite these differences, all agree that the numbers were significant.

[75] See State 230951, "Press Materials: US-China Joint Communiqué," op. cit. A set of talking points drafted a decade later for use with PRC officials averred: "[W]e made it quite clear during our [1982] Communiqué discussions that, when looking at the overall trend of US arms sales to Taiwan, inflation must be taken into account" ("Talking Points: Taiwan Arms Sales," April 22, 1992, *FRDC*).

statement, the United States committed itself to not pursuing a "one China, one Taiwan" or "two Chinas" policy. As the record amply demonstrates, this was not a new policy, dating back all the way to Henry Kissinger's July 1971 conversations in Beijing, but it had not appeared in either of the two previous U.S.-PRC joint communiqués nor, as far as we can tell, in any other official U.S. Government statement.

The pledge was apparently inserted by the U.S. into an early draft, intended not as a departure from policy but rather as a reflection of a long-standing position.[76] Its importance is especially clear when seen in the context of the "six assurances." The "assurances" against forcing Taipei into negotiations and denying any change in U.S. policy toward Taiwan's sovereignty clearly were meant as a rejection of any PRC attempt to force reunification on the island. This pledge against "two Chinas," in effect, placed a bracket on the other side of the equation by rejecting any U.S. support for a separatist solution.

IMPLICATIONS OF THE CRISIS

The August 17 Communiqué succeeded in setting the arms sales issue aside, but it did not resolve it for the long term, much less dispose of the underlying issue of sovereignty. Rather, it stood as the "cap" to the first of a number of post-normalization, Taiwan-centered crises where Washington and Beijing had to manage the fallout from the inherent incompleteness of normalization.

In this instance, the crisis was not primarily due to any misunderstanding of the deal struck in normalization. Rather, it was because Ronald Reagan simply did not care for the deal. What he may have misunderstood, or at least miscalculated, was the price Beijing was willing to pay to enforce its terms.

The PRC believed that, despite the unresolved arms sales issue, it had an understanding that the United States, at the very least, would not directly challenge or seek to undermine the PRC claim to Taiwan. However, first, the passage of the TRA and, then, Ronald Reagan's position on "officiality" raised serious questions about the viability of that understanding. In the process, among other consequences, Deng was rendered vulnerable to criticism from the CCP's conservative elders just when he was approaching a crucial juncture in his efforts to consolidate his leadership. The prospect of an advanced fighter aircraft

---

[76] Mohr and Hallford, interviews by author.

for Taiwan in that setting added importantly to his problem. But as we have seen, the issue was deeper, and even after the decision against sale of the FX, it took several more months for Washington and Beijing to come to terms.

The overarching strategic motivation for Beijing to develop better relations with the United States did not fundamentally change in this period. And Reagan and his aides apparently believed that both a sense of common purpose against Soviet expansionism and China's fears of Moscow would produce greater flexibility on Taiwan arms sales. But, just as Beijing had not allowed Nixon and Kissinger to use the Soviet card to leverage China into compromising on Taiwan principles, here again that proved to be the case.

Given the importance of the Soviet strategic challenge to the PRC, it should be instructive that Beijing would not buy into the "deal" implicitly being offered in mid-1981: weapons and high-tech, dual-use items for the Mainland as a trade-off for PRC acquiescence in continuing advanced weapons sales to Taiwan. The terms of the August 17 Communiqué did not differ all that much from what was in the air in June 1981—minus, of course, the FX. But by 1982, a "framework" was needed to put the controversy to bed.[77]

That being said, what this episode also demonstrated was that China remained open to matching firmness on "principle" with flexibility in practice when it judged that it had other important interests at stake. Despite initially insisting on a "phase-out" of U.S. arms sales to Taiwan, in the end it accepted a "phase-down" without an explicit American commitment to ending them. The PRC argued, including in its statement accompanying the communiqué, that "final resolution" logically only could mean ending the sales.[78] And in subsequent years, Chinese

---

[77] Moreover, Roger Sullivan points out that some misleading statements by Americans in the wake of normalization to the effect that the U.S. and China had "agreed to disagree" over arms sales—rather than what was the case, i.e., that they never resolved the arms sales issue but agreed to normalize relations, anyway—might have stimulated China's desire to reopen negotiations on this issue sooner rather than later. Despite the "incomplete" result represented by the August 17 Communiqué, Sullivan believes that the fact that Reagan was willing to negotiate on the issue and come to some set of rules in a sense "laid the issue to rest" for China. That is, it made clear that there had been no previous agreement on this question, not even an "agreement to disagree" (correspondence with author).

[78] Ironically, Senator East took the same position in attacking the communiqué.

officials tried to argue that the U.S. had agreed this was the case.[79] But Deng Xiaoping knew better, and so did everyone else familiar with the record.

Still, whatever words the United States had or had not agreed to in the communiqués, China was angry that Washington continued to challenge the most basic principle of sovereignty to which so many years of negotiation had been devoted.

Zhang Wenjin, now ambassador in Washington, told Vice President Bush in May 1983 that Beijing had resigned itself to a long and contentious diplomatic battle with the United States over Taiwan, and that, while that issue would inevitably be stormy, they needed to find other ways to build trust and confidence.[80]

BEIJING TO TAIPEI: STILL PROMOTING DIALOGUE

In early June 1983, Deng Yingchao, widow of Zhou Enlai and Chairperson of the Chinese People's Political Consultative Conference (CPPCC), gave what Deng Xiaoping later labeled an "important speech" opening the CPPCC's annual meeting. Citing both the January 1, 1979 Message to Compatriots and Ye Jianying's September 30, 1981 nine-point proposal, she said:

> We welcome these proposals heartily. We respect history and reality. We give full consideration to the wishes of people of all nationalities in Taiwan and the plight of the Kuomintang authorities in Taiwan. We think not only of the present but also of the future. After the reunification of the motherland, the CCP and the Kuomintang will co-operate, coexist, and supervise each other for a long time. After the reunification, Taiwan, as a

---

In response to the testimony of State Department Legal Adviser Davis R. Robinson that "final resolution of this question" did not necessarily mean termination of arms sales, East railed: "Well, if the English language means anything at all, final resolution means a terminal point...[We are being told that] '[f]inal resolution' does not mean final resolution. I do not know what it means. I do not think anyone could know. But it is quite clear, if you put it in the context of the whole, in the real world of politics and law, that it means a downgrading of the commitment to Taiwan" (*Senate Judiciary Committee Hearings*, pp. 103-107).

[79] Mohr, interview by author. Solomon also addresses this issue in *Chinese Political Negotiating Behavior,* pp. 128-129.

[80] Tyler, *A Great Wall,* p. 332.

special administrative district, may follow a system different from that on the Mainland so that the two may complement and support each other.[81]

Later that month, Deng Xiaoping met with American Professor L. Y. (Winston) Yang of Seton Hall University. Referring to—and building on—Deng Yingchao's statement, he laid out the basis for peaceful reunification under what came to be called "one country, two systems."[82] Promoting "talks" (*hui tan*) on an equal basis between the Communist and Nationalist Parties rather than "negotiations" (*tan pan*) between central and local authorities, Deng stated that, in the course of reunification, neither side would "swallow up" the other. At the same time, while Taiwan could retain its "independent nature," exercising "independent jurisdiction and the right of final judgement," "complete autonomy" for the island was impossible because that would mean "two Chinas." While the social system on Taiwan might be different from that on the mainland, he said, and Taiwan could keep its armed forces as long as they did not constitute a threat to the mainland, "only the People's Republic of China is entitled to represent China in the international arena."

Deng cautioned that "foreign interference absolutely will not be permitted." Specifically speaking of the U.S., he said relations had improved "somewhat" recently. However, he said:

> [P]eople in power in the U.S. have never given up "Two Chinas" or "One China and a half." The United States has lauded its system to the skies. But a president says one thing during the campaign, another when he takes office, another during the mid-

---

[81] "Session of the Sixth National CPPCC Committee Opens, Text of Opening Address by Deng Yingchao," *Xinhua*, June 4, 1983 in *BBC Summary of World Broadcasts*, June 7, 1983.

[82] "Deng Xiaoping on China's Reunification," *Xinhua*, July 29, 1983, transcribed by FBIS on August 1, 1983 (see p. 96, note 69). In the August 1993 "White Paper" on *The Taiwan Question and Reunification of China*, Deng Xiaoping is cited as having first come up with the "one country/two systems" formulation on January 11, 1982 (having already foreshadowed it as early as 1979 in the *Time* interview). The circumstances of this Deng statement are unclear, but what merits attention is that it was designed in the first place to apply to Taiwan and was only diverted to Hong Kong and Macao when it proved infeasible in the Taiwan context at that time. The full text of the "White Paper" is online at http://english.peopledaily.com.cn/whitepaper/7.html.

term election, and still another near the next general election. The United States has also said that China's policies are unstable, "but our policies are for more stable than those of the U.S.," he concluded.[83]

The American Embassy in Beijing, assessing PRC foreign policy five years after the establishment of U.S-PRC diplomatic relations, judged that Beijing was disappointed that normalization had not forced Taiwan into reunification negotiations. While China was frustrated that Washington had been less susceptible to Chinese pressure to curtail ties to the island than it had originally hoped, the Embassy believed that Beijing had come increasingly to the realization that it had to rely solely on its own dealings with Taipei—and could not count on help from Washington—to conclude the Chinese civil war. It also had been forced to realize that, contrary to its original expectations, the PRC would have to move ahead with Hong Kong reversion ahead of reunification with Taiwan.[84]

In preparing for his trip to China in April 1984, President Reagan issued a National Security Decision Directive that reaffirmed the U.S. intention to abide by the various joint communiqués with China, including specifically the August 17 Communiqué on arms sales. But he also reconfirmed America's "moral and legal commitment" to maintain unofficial relations with Taiwan, "including the continued sale of defensive arms." On the future of cross-Strait relations he once more underscored the central importance of China's "peaceful approach." He wrote:

> We believe the "resolution" of the Taiwan issue is a matter for the Chinese people to settle themselves, and our only concern is that it be done peacefully. A continued peaceful approach by Beijing to Taiwan is fundamental to our position on Taiwan arms sales and to the whole framework of our relations.[85]

---

[83] "Deng Xiaoping on China's Reunification," *Xinhua*, July 29, 1983, op. cit. An intriguing aspect of this report is that it was released more than a month after the original conversation took place.

[84] Beijing 19499, "China's Foreign Policy: A Five-Year Review," December 16, 1983, *FRDC*.

[85] Robert C. McFarlane, NSDD on the President's Visit to the People's Republic of China," April 21, 1984, enclosing National Security Decision Directive 140, online in Jeffrey T. Richelson, ed., *China and the United States: From Hostility*

The President rebuffed Beijing's urging to push Taiwan into talks,[86] and he continued to argue that it would be wrong to cast aside old friends (i.e., Taiwan) in order make new ones (i.e., the PRC). But during his visit to China, Reagan leaned forward a bit with Chinese interviewers on the question of whether the U.S. would "encourage" cross-Strait dialogue:

> [W]e will do anything we can to encourage the peaceful solution of this problem by the peoples [sic] of China.[87]

As it turned out, a fuller and more formal articulation of that stance came at a useful juncture nearly four years later, in Reagan's second term. On March 5, 1987, in a banquet toast in Shanghai, Secretary of State George Shultz offered the following:

> In the Shanghai [C]ommuniqué, as in the other two communiqués on which our relationship is based, the United States made clear that our policy is based on the principle that there is but one China. We have no intention of pursuing a policy of "two Chinas" or "one China, one Taiwan."

> In the Shanghai communiqué, the United States also reaffirmed its interest in a peaceful settlement of the Taiwan question by the Chinese themselves. We understand and appreciate that striving for a peaceful resolution of the Taiwan question is also a fundamental policy of the Chinese Government.

> These principles of one China and a peaceful resolution of the Taiwan question remain the core of our China policy. While our policy has been constant, the situation itself has not and cannot

---

to Engagement, 1960-1998, National Security Archive Electronic Briefing Book No. 18, http://www.gwu.edi/~nsarchiv/NSAEBB/NSAEBB19/08-01.htm

[86] See Tyler, A Great Wall, p. 334. Deng also complained of U.S. reluctance to get involved when speaking with an American journalist in September 1986. The Chinese leader argued that the U.S. was in a position to encourage and persuade Taiwan to start the process by agreeing to the "three links," but Washington clung to a position of "non-involvement"; see "New Development in Sino-U.S. Relations," in Han Nianlong, ed., Diplomacy of Contemporary China (Hong Kong: New Horizon Press, 1990), p. 422.

[87] "Interview with Representatives of Chinese Central Television in Beijing, China," April 28, 1984, online at http://www.reagan.utexas.edu/resource/speeches/1984/42884b.htm

remain static. We support a continuing evolutionary process toward a peaceful resolution of the Taiwan issue. The pace, however, will be determined by the Chinese on either side of the Taiwan Strait, free of outside pressure.

For our part, we have welcomed developments, including indirect trade and increasing human interchange, which have contributed to a relaxation of the tensions in the Taiwan Strait. *Our steadfast policy seeks to foster an environment in which such developments can continue to take place.*[88]

David Dean recalls that officials in Taipei were somewhat unnerved by the toast, worried about a subtle shift in policy away from earlier support for Taiwan.[89] Other former officials also recall that when he was briefed on the toast language ahead of time, Foreign Minister Frederick Chien had been particularly upset by the toast and had sought to have it toned down.[90] But Chiang Ching-kuo, who was fully briefed by Dean, did not interpose any objection and, in fact, had been considering a further opening to the Mainland before this; the Shultz toast gave him the opportunity to move that plan forward by a few months.[91]

Thus, despite specific problems and complaints of both sides, the U.S.-PRC relationship, including over the Taiwan issue, was in a largely stable and constructive period throughout the middle years of the 1980s. And as just noted, starting at the end of the decade, Taipei loosened its cross-Strait restrictions; consequently, those relations began to burgeon along many axes, including trade, travel, and investment. Even the tragic events at Tiananmen Square in June 1989 proved to have a more important impact on American perceptions of China—and the counterpoint those perceptions provided to an ever-more favorable image of a democratic, market-oriented Taiwan—and on other aspects of Sino-American relations than on U.S.-PRC interactions over Taiwan at the

---

[88] Full text reported in *Department of State Bulletin* (May 1987), p. 11. Emphasis added.

[89] Interview by author; see also David Dean, "U.S. Relations with Taiwan," in Hungdah Chiu, Hsing-wei Lee and Chih-yu T. Wu, eds., *Implementation of the Taiwan Relations Act: An Examination After Twenty Years*, Maryland Series in Contemporary Asian Studies, no. 2-2001 (163) (Baltimore: University of Maryland School of Law, 2001), p. 87.

[90] Charles Hill and Stapleton Roy, interviews by author.

[91] Roy, interview by author.

time.[92]   But as time went on, those contrasting images of "bad China" and "good Taiwan" combined with other factors to affect issues of great importance in Taiwan policy.

ADVANCED FIGHTER AIRCRAFT (II): F-16S

In 1992, President George H.W. Bush, strong supporter though he was of U.S.-PRC relations—and having taken considerable political knocks for that support in the wake of Tiananmen—was facing an uphill battle for re-election.   He needed Texas, where General Dynamics produced the advanced F-16 fighter that Taiwan had been seeking to buy for over a decade.

Determining how the decision over F-16s was made is analogous to the story of three blind men describing an elephant: there were numerous players, each with a somewhat different perspective and aware of a piece of the story. What seems clear, however, is that there was a conjunction of a heightened campaign by Taiwan for the sale, a sense in some (but not all) parts of the Administration of a genuine military requirement, and pressure from General Dynamics and Texas politicians who argued, implicitly and explicitly, that the thirty-two Texas electoral votes hung in the balance.

James Lilley, then Assistant Secretary of Defense for International Security Affairs, raised the F-16 issue with Defense Secretary Richard Cheney in May 1992 on a flight back from Australia, where they had attended a ceremony marking the 50th anniversary of the Battle of the Coral Sea. Lilley explained to Cheney that Taiwan's request had just been turned down once again, but that the PRC was purchasing Russian Su-27s, France was hotly marketing the Mirage 2000-5 that competed with the F-16, Taiwan's "Indigenous Defense Fighter" (IDF) was having developmental difficulties and did not have the necessary range and "loiter time," the F-5E had run its course, and another American plane added to Taiwan's inventory—the F-104—could not fill the gap. Lilley strongly urged Cheney to take another look at issue. The Secretary concurred and a memo went to the NSC, State and the White House calling for reconsideration of the decision. But it was greeted with silence until suddenly, as Lilley recalls, an instruction came down:

---

[92] Also noteworthy is that cross-Strait trade and investment continued to flourish with barely a hiccup, while the United States and, at least for awhile, Europe and Japan went through considerable soul-searching about their dealings with the Mainland.

"Form an interagency group to look at this." There followed a somewhat truncated interagency process that, Lilley judges, was more for show than anything else, since it appeared the decision had already been made. Consistent with this interpretation, this time, in sharp contrast with the FX case in 1981, no intelligence assessment of Taiwan's need for the plane was requested.[93]

As has been well reported, the political dimension of this issue was crucial,[94] the stakes underscored in late August by a broadside from Senator Lloyd Bentsen (D-TX), who argued that "hard-working Texas defense workers don't deserve to be penalized just because the [Bush Administration] insists on coddling Communist leaders in Beijing."[95]

In this heated political climate, and with the presidency seen as possibly in the balance, Bush announced on September 2, 1992 to cheering workers at the General Dynamics plant that the sale had been approved. But as opposed to the 80-100 planes that Lilley says he had in mind when urging reconsideration of the issue, the President approved all 150 that Taiwan had requested, representing an estimated $6 billion in sales.[96] Moreover, as then-Ambassador to China J. Stapleton Roy points out, the political motivation for the sale was clearly manifest in the decision to build new planes over a period of several years, rather than to immediately supply existing aircraft, even as a temporary measure, to fill

---

[93] Interview by author.

[94] See Don Oberdorfer, "1982 Arms Policy with China Victim of Bush Campaign, Texas Lobbying," *Washington Post,* September 4, 1992, A-31 and Tyler, *A Great Wall,* pp. 376-379.

[95] "Bentsen Urges OK of F-16 Jet Fighter Sales to Taiwan," Reuter report carried in *Los Angeles Times,* August 23, 1992, A-16. Even earlier, Texas' Democratic Governor Ann Richards had criticized Bush's reluctance to approve the sale (Robert G. Sutter and Wayne Morrison, *Taiwan: U.S. Advanced Fighter Aircraft Sales—Pro and Con,* Congressional Research Service report, September 1, 1992, p. 1, *NSA* 01550). General Dynamics estimated that an F-16 contract for Taiwan would save 3,000 of the 5,800 jobs the company had planned to cut by 1994 ("General Dynamics Says Taiwan F-16 Deal May Save 3,000 Jobs," *AFX News,* September 4, 1992).

[96] Interview by author. Lilley reported that, while Cheney favored the sale on substantive grounds, the Secretary later told him it would never have gone through without the Texas election issue. Cheney sought publicly to dispel criticism that this, as well as other weapons sales and defense outlays, were for political gain; cf. "Cheney Says Criticism of Arms Plans is Mistaken," *The Commercial Appeal* (Memphis), September 4, 1992, A-1.

any alleged "fighter gap." Ironically, however, though Beijing filed the expected protests, Roy concluded that the obvious domestic American political driver of the decision was ultimately somewhat reassuring to Beijing. China would have been far more irate, he believes, if Beijing had felt that, rather than merely seeking electoral support, the President was trying to bolster Taiwan's capability to resist a cross-Strait political settlement and promote independence.

The U.S. justified the sale publicly and privately as consistent with the TRA, insisting that it "advance[d] the central goal of the 1982 US-China communiqué on arms sales to Taiwan, promoting cross-strait peace and stability."[97] Washington also defended the sale by pointing to the F-16's "defensive nature." In this connection, it is interesting to note that, while Taiwan's Defense Minister hailed the sale as "a major breakthrough,"[98] the head of the Air Force in fact complained that, even though they were slated for a "mid-life upgrade," the F-16 models approved for sale to Taiwan were lower-capability models (so-called "As" and "Bs" rather than the more advanced "Cs" and "Ds").[99]

Beijing also took note of the specific models being sold[100] but, rather than expressing relief, predictably launched the "strongest protests" of "shock and outrage," characterizing the sales as "a flagrant obstruction and sabotage to China's peaceful reunification," threatening a "major retrogression" in Sino-American relations.[101] Nonetheless, although it continued to bluster for some time, Beijing swallowed the sale without downgrading relations, among other reasons, because it hoped Bush would win re-election and because it did not wish to cause problems for renewal of Most Favored Nation (MFN) tariff status, which was coming

---

[97] Department of State spokesman Joe Snyder, quoted in "US Defends Decision to Sell F-16s to Taiwan," *Central News Agency* (Taiwan), September 3, 1992.

[98] Cited in Lena H. Sun and Stuart Auerbach, "New Bush Policies Anger China, Trade Partners," *Washington Post,* September 4, 1992, A1.

[99] General Lin Wen-li complained that he was "not very satisfied," alleging that the "As" and "Bs" were inadequate given Taiwan's needs ("General Dynamics Says F-16 Deal May Save 3,000 Jobs," op. cit.).

[100] "China Reacts Angrily to US Decision to Sell Fighters to Taiwan," *BBC Summary of World Broadcasts*, September 4, 1992, carrying the full text of a *Xinhua* report of September 3, 1992 (1501 GMT).

[101] "China Reacts Angrily to US Decision to Sell Fighters to Taiwan," *BBC Summary of World Broadcasts*, September 4, 1992, carrying the full text of another *Xinhua* report of September 3, 1992 (1523 GMT).

up for a congressional vote.[102]   Thus, while there was considerable fallout from this sale on other significant issues—Beijing not only delayed important talks on missile, nuclear and other proliferation issues, but it reportedly soon shipped ballistic missiles to Pakistan and nuclear technology to Iran[103]—the F-16 sale had minimal immediate impact directly on the Taiwan front.

As it turned out, Bush did win Texas, though his victory there did not, of course, stave off his decisive defeat nationally at the hands of Bill Clinton. Perhaps for this, as well as for other reasons, Beijing apparently decided that it would never again tolerate any American step of such dimension that, whatever its motivation, bolstered Taiwan's ability to advance separatist tendencies.[104]

Lessons Learned

The F-16 episode emerged not so much from a misreading of previous understandings or disrespect for the terms of normalization. It came, rather, from a determination by the President that he had overriding considerations to which Beijing would have to accommodate. And he later indicated that he had hoped to be able to "make it up" to Beijing after the election.[105]   Still, the sale seemed to most people to be an obvious violation of the August 17 Communiqué.[106]   One result was that both sides lost a measure of confidence in the commitments previously made, the Chinese because they saw the U.S. treating the August 17 strictures with disdain, the Americans because they felt they could "get away with" such behavior since China "had little choice." This begged the question of what, other than outright support for

---

[102] Roy, interview by author.

[103] Steven Greenhouse, "Aides to Clinton Say He Will Defy Beijing and Issue Visa to Taiwan's President," *New York Times,* May 22, 1995, A6.

[104] Three weeks later, Beijing had an opportunity to threaten "serious consequences" over the U.S. sale of twelve anti-submarine helicopters. Since then, it has protested virtually every report of weapons sales, whether credible or the figment of a Taiwan reporter's imagination.

[105] Roy, interview by author.

[106] At the time, while anticipating a "rough patch" in the relationship, Acting Secretary of State Lawrence Eagleburger judged that "They have too much riding on the relationship with us in economic and political terms" to risk a rupture (Ruth Sinai, *Associated Press,* September 4, 1992, reporting an Eagleburger comment to CNN).

"Taiwan independence," Washington considered as a constraint on its behavior toward Taiwan. The fact that the U.S. Trade Representative, Ambassador Carla Hills, traveled to Taipei in December on an "unofficial" visit as the "guest of AIT" to attend a business meeting—but then called openly on virtually all senior ROC officials in their offices—compounded the difficulty of answering that question. She was the first American Cabinet-level official to visit Taiwan since 1979.

While upsetting to Beijing, all of this reminded the PRC once again that it could not depend on the United States to help solve its Taiwan problem.

7

Politics In Command

"From the outset, the Clinton Administration's policy was identical to that of the Nixon Administration and its successors: there was "one China," embracing mainland China and Taiwan. We would maintain full diplomatic relations with Beijing, the legitimate government of China, and unofficial relations with Taiwan. We also embraced the position that the ultimate status of Taiwan should be determined peacefully by China and Taiwan. In short, we planned business as usual..."

—Warren Christopher, *Chances of A Lifetime*

Bill Clinton rode to the White House in part on a platform criticizing the Bush Administration for "coddling" the "butchers of Beijing" and, early in his Administration, he adopted a policy of linking China's MFN trade status to improvement in its human rights practices. Although there was never any question that he intended to maintain the "one China" policy that had been embraced, enthusiastically or not, by each of his five predecessors, the new President had been to Taiwan four times as Governor of Arkansas and he seemed generally sympathetic to the plight of the people there.

BEIJING LAYS DOWN A MARKER: THE 1993 TAIWAN "WHITE PAPER"

Despite the important "unofficial" meeting between PRC and Taiwan "senior personages" Wang Daohan and Koo Chen-fu in Singapore in April 1993,[1] Taipei had begun to engage in an assertive "pragmatic diplomacy" campaign to increase its "international space" both in bilateral relations with other countries and in the broader international community. Senior Taiwan officials, including Lee Teng-hui, visited a number of countries "unofficially," where they not only played golf but met with top leaders. At this point, Taipei also engaged in a "bidding war" with Beijing, using aid to entice some smaller

---

[1] Later known as the Wang-Koo (or Koo-Wang) talks.

countries back into their diplomatic orbit. The PRC, angered by this diplomatic offensive and taken aback by its extension to a campaign for reentry into the United Nations in 1993, prepared a counter-offensive. Although Beijing's main complaints with the United States in this period focused on other issues, those differences contributed to a growing Chinese sense that the U.S. was the PRC's principal enemy.[2] This perspective factored importantly into the PRC's first Taiwan "White Paper," issued in August 1993.[3]

In large part, that policy paper was directed specifically at the political and governmental circles in Taiwan, cautioning against independence activity even as it laid out in fulsome terms the inducements Beijing had devised to promote peaceful reunification. But in reciting the history of "the Taiwan question," the paper also devoted considerable attention to the U.S. role, highlighting American culpability for delaying reunification:

> [A]t a time when relations across the Taiwan Straits are easing up, certain powers have seen fit to renege on their undertakings under international agreements and to flout the Chinese Government's repeated strong representations by making arms sales to Taiwan, thereby whipping up tension between the two sides of the Straits. This not only constitutes a serious threat to China's security and an obstacle to China's peaceful reunification, but also undermines peace and stability in Asia and the world at large.

> In September 1992 the U.S. Government even decided to sell 150 F-16 high-performance fighter aircraft to Taiwan. This action of the U.S. Government has added a new stumbling block in the way of the development of Sino-U.S. relations and settlement of the Taiwan question.

> It is clear from the foregoing that the U.S. Government is responsible for holding up the settlement of the Taiwan question.

There could be consequences if such "meddling" went too far:

---

[2] Kerry Dumbaugh, *China-U.S. Relations*, Congressional Research Service Issue Brief 94002, updated January 11, 1994, p. 8, *NSA* 01669.

[3] "The Taiwan Question and the Reunification of China," the full text of which is available online at http://english.peopledaily.com.cn/whitepaper/7.html.

Peaceful reunification is a set policy of the Chinese Government. However, any sovereign state is entitled to use any means it deems necessary, including military ones, to uphold its sovereignty and territorial integrity.

The White Paper emphasized that "sovereignty of each State is an integral whole which is indivisible and unsharable."[4] But practical compromises were permissible under certain carefully defined rules and conditions. Regional organizations such as the Asian Development Bank[5] and the Asia Pacific Economic Cooperation forum (APEC)[6] fell into this category. These were, however, to be seen as "ad hoc arrangements," and not as "models" applicable to other international organizations or inter-governmental gatherings.

Finally, in understanding the course of events over the next several years, it is noteworthy that the 1993 White Paper—in a departure from the 1979 and 1981 appeals—drew a distinction between "compatriots" in Taiwan, who had "contributed tremendously to the development of inter-Straits relations," and the authorities, who, while having "made [positive] readjustments in their policy regarding the mainland," were nonetheless guilty of a darker approach:

> [T]heir current policy *vis-a-vis* the mainland still seriously impedes the development of relations across the Straits as well as the reunification of the country. They talk about the necessity of a reunified China, but their deeds are always a far cry from the principle of one China. They try to prolong Taiwan's separation from the mainland and refuse to hold talks on peaceful reunification. They have even set up barriers to curb the further development of the interchanges across the Straits.

WASHINGTON ADJUSTS: THE TAIWAN POLICY REVIEW

Meanwhile, early on in his administration, reportedly under pressure from Congress,[7] Clinton had ordered a review of Taiwan policy. While

---

[4] Ibid., sec. V (2).

[5] Where Beijing had been forced in 1985 to accept Taiwan's continued membership as "Taipei, China."

[6] Where members had forged a deal bringing in the PRC, Hong Kong and Taiwan as a package in 1991, with Taiwan identified as "Chinese Taipei."

[7] Dean, "U.S. Relations with Taiwan," op. cit., p. 93.

maintaining the basic premises of the "one China" policy and the terms of the "unofficial" relationship with Taiwan, the review was designed to fine-tune the ground rules governing day-to-day dealings with Taipei including nomenclature of Taiwan's representative office, where and at what level meetings could take place, and the permissible parameters of travel by officials between Taiwan and the United States.

The State Department's first draft of the review was considered unsatisfactory by the NSC, some speculate because it did not ease the ground rules sufficiently. Moreover, as a former Clinton NSC official points out, more pressing priorities existed on the China front, including MFN renewal and nonproliferation.[8] As a result, the review lay gathering dust in various in-boxes from early fall 1993 until late spring 1994, when an imbroglio developed over a transit stop in Hawaii by Taiwan's president, Lee Teng-hui, bringing the question of how to best manage Taiwan relations back to the fore.[9]

The results of the study were finally announced in September 1994.[10] The most visible change was the name of the unofficial Taiwan representative office in the United States, which morphed from the "Coordination Council for North American Affairs" (CCNAA)—which many found incomprehensible and a challenge to find in any telephone

---

[8] Suettinger, *Beyond Tiananmen,* op. cit., p. 206.

[9] Lee requested an overnight rest stop and round of golf on the "Big Island" of Hawaii at a hotel owned by a Taiwanese friend. With Washington sensitive to the effects of Lee's recently-activated "vacation diplomacy," this was at first denied by the East Asia Bureau of the State Department (Dean, "U.S. Relations with Taiwan," p. 94). According to Stapleton Roy and Scott Hallford, the American Embassy in Beijing actually supported the transit, fearing—presciently, as it turned out—the consequences if it were denied (interviews by author). Subsequently, protests from Taipei and elsewhere led to a review of the decision, and Lee was then allowed a one-and-a-half hour refueling stop at Hickham Air Force base in Oahu (though not at the commercial airport, which was more accessible to the press). Although offered the opportunity to rest in the VIP lounge, Lee made a dramatic show of declining to disembark, an event that quickly transmogrified into a story that the United States had refused Lee permission to set foot on American soil.

[10] Except where otherwise indicated, the following discussion derives from "Taiwan Policy—New Practices," *NSA* 01907 and "Taiwan Policy—Elements Which Will Not Change," *NSA* 01908. (Although the National Security Archive dates both of these State Department documents to 1995, their content strongly suggests that they were actually drafted in 1994 in conjunction with the public announcement of the results of the review.)

directory[11]—to the more descriptive "Taipei Economic and Cultural Representative Office."[12]

Rules on economic exchanges were eased considerably. Sub-cabinet (i.e., Under Secretary-level) economic dialogue was proposed. High-level American economic and technical officials could visit Taiwan (although to be approved on a case-by-case basis), with visits by Cabinet officers in these areas "not ruled out."[13]

---

[11] But which had the virtue of not using the terms "Taiwan", "China" or "the United States," any one of which could have been misconstrued—or misused—to convey a sense of "officiality." For a discussion of the origins of this issue by one centrally involved, see the Oral History of Ambassador Charles W. Freeman, Jr., in Association for Diplomatic Studies and Training, *Foreign Affairs Oral History Project*, available on CD-ROM at Georgetown University's Lauinger Library.

[12] Which still avoided use of the word "Taiwan" and thus the questions about the standing of "Taiwan" as a sovereign entity.

[13] Assistant Secretary of State for East Asian and Pacific Affairs Winston Lord later testified that the Administration would even encourage such economic cabinet-level visits when it served U.S. purposes; see the *Federal News Service* transcript of his testimony in *Hearing of the East Asian and Pacific Affairs Subcommittee of the Senate Foreign Relations Committee on U.S. Policy Toward Taiwan*, 103rd Cong., 2nd sess., September 27, 1994 (hereafter *Senate Foreign Relations Committee on U.S. Policy Toward Taiwan*). Lord recalls, however, that criteria were established for approval of a cabinet-level visit. For example, such a visit would be approved in connection with an effort to promote agricultural exports; simply attending a conference was not sufficient justification to gain approval (interview by author).

J. Stapleton Roy feels that the Taiwan Policy Review got it exactly backward: instead of approving cabinet-level visits, they should have been banned, and instead of banning high-level political visits, it should have been recognized that they could not be resisted and efforts should have been made to shape such visits to U.S. interests, which, he believes, could have been done without great damage to U.S.-PRC relations (interview by author).

Hallford, on the other hand, then Roy's DCM in Beijing, saw the entire Review as stemming from domestic political pressures to enhance Taiwan ties and considered it unnecessary and simply buying trouble. Rather, he felt, if these policies and practices had been allowed to evolve in a natural way, the result would have been less disruptive to U.S. interests (interview by author).

As an historical footnote, when the first Bush Administration considered a similar easing on high-level economic visits to Taiwan, Beijing complained loudly and the idea was dropped (Mann, *About Face,* p. 272).

AIT staff were for the first time authorized access to the Ministry of Foreign Affairs in Taipei, and any authorized visitors to Taiwan were allowed to meet with any level of the Taiwan leadership "necessary to achieve their objectives." American Cabinet-level officials in non-national security areas were allowed to meet with Taiwan representatives and visitors in official settings in Washington. Office calls were still prohibited at the State Department, White House and Executive Office Building, and special rules were adopted for meetings at the Department of Defense below the level of the Secretary and, on the Taiwan side, below the rank of Chief of General Staff.

On the international front, the U.S. was to work "more actively" to support Taiwan's participation in international organizations—backing Taipei's membership where non-states were accepted as members, supporting "opportunities to have Taiwan's voice heard" where Taipei's membership was not possible.[14] More specifically on the last point, the U.S. would "withhold support for Taiwan's membership in organizations, such as the UN, which admit only states."

As for security-related matters, "[p]resent arms sales policy," based on requirements of the TRA and on adherence to the 1982 communiqué "as practiced," was to continue.

Finally, and critically for what followed, Taiwan's top leaders—understood to mean the President, Vice President, Premier and Vice Premier—were permitted "normal transits" of the United States—including overnight stopovers—"consistent with security, comfort and convenience" of the traveler,[15] "but no visits or public activities." Indeed, it was specified that the new rules "[f]orbid visits, as opposed to transits, by Taiwan's top leadership."

Taiwan was mildly discontented at what it considered the meager extent of the changes and, while Taipei's representative in Washington "welcomed" them, he noted that they had "not sufficiently addressed the needs arising from the close U.S.-Taiwan relationship."[16] Taiwan's American supporters, on the other hand, were far less restrained. Senator

---

[14] Lord recalls that the Administration worked on trying to put this approach into operation, but found that there were very few organizations that did not require statehood for membership. There was a handful of second-tier organizations, but "they did not amount to much" (interview by author).

[15] *Senate Foreign Relations Committee on U.S. Policy Toward Taiwan.*

[16] Donald M. Rothberg, "U.S. Expanding Ties with Taiwan—But No Recognition," *Associated Press,* September 7, 1994.

Hank Brown (R-CO) was among the harshest congressional critics, denouncing the results of the review as "treating one of our closest democratic allies in the Pacific worse that we treat North Korea, Cuba or Libya."[17] Senator Charles Robb (D-VA), Chairman of the Senate Foreign Relations Committee Subcommittee on East Asian and Pacific Affairs, was somewhat milder in his criticism, but even he said that, while "our relations with the Mainland are paramount," "I believe it serves us well to strengthen ties with Taipei, pressing the edge of the diplomatic envelope, if necessary." Robb concluded that "continuing to keep Taiwan at arm's length" made "little sense."[18]

Beijing predictably lodged strong protests, complaining that the steps taken went too far toward giving official U.S. recognition to Taiwan.[19]

In Hill testimony defending the results of the review, Assistant Secretary of State Winston Lord expressed the Clinton Administration's strong opposition to congressional attempts to legislate visits by "top leaders of the Republic of China" to the United States. He said that adoption of such legislation would create a situation that "China would undoubtedly perceive as officiality in our relations with Taiwan" and that would "derail this basic policy of several administrations." Such legislation, he argued, "would remove one of the most important elements which makes the relationship unofficial...revers[ing] commitments at the highest levels of the U.S. government over many administrations, reaffirmed time and time again." "If we do not observe our commitments," he asked, "what can we expect of others, including China, with respect to their commitments?"[20]

---

[17] Ibid.

[18] *Senate Foreign Relations Committee on U.S. Policy Toward Taiwan.*

[19] See Suettinger, *Beyond Tiananmen,* p. 207; James Mann, "U.S. Slightly Elevates Ties with Taiwan," *Los Angeles Times,* September 8, 1994, A4.

[20] *Senate Foreign Relations Committee on U.S. Policy Toward Taiwan.* A month later, Congress amended the Immigration and Nationality Act to provide that, whenever the "President of Taiwan" or other high official from Taiwan applied to visit the United States to discuss with "Federal or State" government officials trade, nuclear proliferation, threats to U.S. national security, environmental protection, protection of endangered species, or humanitarian disasters, the official "shall be admitted" to the United States unless otherwise excludable under U.S. immigration laws (PL103-416, enacted October 25, 1994).

Referring to the controversy over Lee Teng-hui's transit of Hawaii in May, Lord described Lee's refueling stop in Oahu, the first stop by a Taiwan president on American soil since relations had been broken in 1979, as "a step forward, not a step back." Specifically asked for the Administration's view if Lee were invited to receive an honorary degree at Cornell University where he had earned his PhD, Lord responded, "[W]e do not believe [non-transit] visits are appropriate or consistent with our unofficial relations with Taiwan."

But the horse was out of the barn. Apparently furious at the original turndown and what he considered humiliating treatment during his transit at Hickham, Lee was determined to overturn the Administration's position. He then orchestrated a broad-based, well-financed campaign not only in Congress but also throughout the United States to allow him to go to Cornell—a story that has been detailed quite well in a number of places.[21] The handling of that issue, discussed below, goes directly to our concern about whether the fundamental importance attached by Beijing to adhering to the basic principles and commitments of normalization—and the seriousness of any direct affront to China's concept of sovereignty—was really understood by the senior-most political and foreign policy leaders of the United States.

CROSS-STRAIT SPARRING: COMPETING PROPOSALS

As pressure grew in the U.S. to approve a Lee visit to Cornell, Beijing was active not only in opposing that visit or any other "separatist" activity but also in pressing its positive case for peaceful reunification. In a speech on the occasion of the Spring Festival in late January 1995, Jiang Zemin set forth what have come to be known as "Jiang's Eight Points."[22] In reviewing the stormy history of Taiwan-Mainland relations and the various proposals that Beijing had advanced over the years, Jiang warned of "the growing separatist tendency and the increasingly rampant activities of the forces working for the 'independence of Taiwan' on the island in recent years." In a cut at the United States reminiscent of the White Paper eighteen months earlier, he noted:

---

[21] See Tyler, *A Great Wall*, pp. 320-322 and Suettinger, *Beyond Tiananmen*, pp. 200-263.

[22] They can be found in "President Jiang's Speech on Reunification," *Xinhua*, January 30, 1995, carried in *BBC Summary of World Broadcasts*, January 31, 1995.

Certain foreign forces have further meddled in the issue of Taiwan, interfering in China's internal affairs. All this not only impedes the process of China's peaceful reunification but also threatens peace, stability and development in the Asia-Pacific region.

But the State President and General Secretary then turned to the positive side of the argument, listing eight points that would thereafter become part and parcel of the PRC's standard litany on Taiwan. Most of the points addressed promotion of cross-Strait trade and exchanges, building on a common cultural heritage, taking steps toward ending the state of hostilities, creating a mutually acceptable basis for reunification taking account of Taiwan's realities, and exchanging visits—including by leaders. In addition, Jiang addressed three points of direct relevance to U.S. policy:

- We should adhere to the "one China" principle. China's sovereignty and territory must never be allowed to be split.

- We have no objection to Taiwan's development of non-governmental economic and cultural relations with foreign countries. However, we oppose those activities to expand Taiwan's "international space" that are aimed at creating "two Chinas" or "one China, one Taiwan."

- We should strive for the [sic] peaceful reunification. Our not undertaking to give up the use of force is not directed against our compatriots in Taiwan but against the schemes of foreign forces to interfere with China's reunification and to bring about the "independence of Taiwan."

Two months later, on April 8th, Lee Teng-hui responded with a six-point proposal of his own in a speech to the National Unification Council, essentially rebuffing Jiang at all turns.[23] Lee, as Jiang, advocated increased trade and economic exchange, but Lee's proposal cast Taiwan as a mentor and the Mainland as a student. He called provocatively for "joint" maintenance of prosperity and democracy in Hong Kong and Macao, both due to revert to Chinese (PRC) sovereignty

---

[23] The following points draw on a translation of the full text of the speech as released by the Information Division of the Taipei Economic and Cultural Representative Office in the United States (TECRO).

shortly.[24] And while advocating peaceful resolution of disputes, Lee said this could only come when the Mainland was prepared to renounce the use of force against Taiwan.

Lee directly contradicted Jiang's concept of "one China" and the PRC's claim to be the single, legitimate representative of China in the international community. He said the two sides should:

- Pursue China's unification based on the reality that the two sides are governed respectively by two governments.

- Ensure that both sides join international organizations on an equal footing and the leaders of the two sides will meet each other in a natural way on such occasions.

It was against this background that, one month later, the U.S. House and Senate passed a concurrent resolution expressing the "sense of the Congress" that "the President should promptly indicate that the United States [would] welcome a private visit by President Lee Teng-hui to his alma mater, Cornell University".[25] Abandoning any sense of restraint on the sovereignty issue, and displaying no awareness of the minefield into which they were marching, Congress adopted preambular language that referred to "the Republic of China on Taiwan (known as Taiwan)" and stated that there existed "no legitimate grounds for excluding President Lee Teng-hui from paying private visits."

TAIWAN RESPONDS: THE LEE TENG-HUI VISIT

Despite Lord's testimony, which we have already reviewed, and assurances by Secretary of State Warren Christopher to PRC Foreign Minister Qian Qichen as recently as April that issuing a visa to Lee would not be consistent with the U.S. "one China policy," under the pressure of this resolution, and fearful that continued resistance would lead to a veto-proof binding resolution,[26] on May 22, 1995, the State

---

[24] Hong Kong reverted in 1997, Macao in 1999.

[25] H.Con.Res. 53, agreed to on May 9, 1995 with no dissenting votes in the House of Representatives (396-0) and only one negative vote in the Senate (97-1).

[26] Such a resolution, HR 1460, had been introduced in early April, forbidding the Secretary of State from barring any elected Taiwan official on the grounds of "adverse foreign policy consequences" (Suettinger, *Beyond Tiananmen*, p. 215).

Department announced that President Clinton had agreed to issue a visa to the Taiwan leader.[27]

Coming only eight months after the much-ballyhooed release of the results of the Taiwan Policy Review, according to which "visits" by Taiwan's senior leaders would be "forbidden," the justification was labored. Announcing that the decision followed "a revision of administration guidelines to permit occasional private visits by senior leaders of Taiwan, including President [Lee]," Spokesman Nicholas Burns asserted that Lee would visit the U.S. "in a strictly private capacity" and would not "undertake any official activities"; reading press guidance that turned the policy totally on its head, he said that this was thus "entirely consistent" with the "one China policy" and the maintenance of only unofficial relations with Taiwan.

When asked to explain why the Administration had shifted its stance on such a visit, the spokesman responded in rather understated fashion that, in addition to assuring itself that all activities during the visit would be private, and "having heard views" of China experts in the government, "[c]ertainly, the administration listened to the views of Congress."[28]

White House spokesman Michael McCurry cited the President's belief that issuance of the visa was "consistent with the values that we promote in this world as a democracy":

> We believe in freedom of speech, we believe in freedom of travel, and know that here in the United States those affiliated with academic institutions develop attachments to those institutions. And for a private, unofficial visit of this nature we

---

[27] Clinton actually approved the visa on May 19th, and it quickly became known through the Taiwan press. The following discussion of the State Department noon briefing comes from U.S. Department of State Daily Press Briefing, May 22, 1995, transcript by *Federal News Service*. For a textured discussion of the Lee visit, see Suettinger, *Beyond Tiananmen,* pp. 212-221.

[28] Other senior officials, speaking "on background," were more direct and attributed the decision to "intense pressure from the Republican-dominated Congress." One senior official claimed the non-binding resolution had forced the Administration's hand, since continuing to bar Lee would have given the impression that Clinton was bowing to Chinese pressure (Steven Greenhouse, "Aides to Clinton Say He Will Defy Beijing and Issue Visa to Taiwan's President," *New York Times,* op. cit.).

believe it very much warranted to allow President [Lee] the opportunity to visit his alma mater Cornell University.[29]

While the basic ground rules subsequently established between Washington and Taipei on Lee's itinerary were more or less followed, the Taiwan leader was cheered by supporters waving the ROC flag wherever he went, was greeted by Members of Congress, and delivered a speech at Cornell that was seen by the Administration in Washington— not to mention Beijing—as extremely provocative. Setting aside the almost thirty references to "Taiwan," which could have been either geographic or political, Lee plugged Taiwan's claim to separate sovereign status by referring to the "Republic of China" more than a half-dozen times, the "Republic of China on Taiwan" nine times, and his "country" or "nation" almost a dozen times. He touted "the Taiwan Experience" of promoting human rights, freedom and democracy as a model for the Mainland, whose leaders, he hoped, "are one day to be similarly guided" by the wishes of their people. As if anyone doubted it, except perhaps President Clinton, Lee made clear in other statements that the purpose of his trip was to "win international recognition of Taiwan as a political entity."[30]

Publicly, Beijing denounced the visit as "an act of perfidy,"[31] a "sheer betrayal" of the three joint communiqués,[32] and a "grave

---

[29] White House Daily Briefing, May 23, 1995, transcript by *Federal News Service*.

[30] Quoted in "Commentary: Where Does U.S. Want Relations with China to Go?," *Xinhua*, June 17, 1995. Warren Christopher has noted ruefully that "The calculation we had made was that, once in America, President Lee would not say or do anything that would ruffle China's sensibilities. That proved to be wrong" (*Chances of a Lifetime*, p. 243). Lord felt particularly betrayed. He had initially opposed the visit but did not object to the reversal in the face of congressional pressure, largely on the same understanding Christopher had that Lee would not engage in political activities. As he sees it: "Taiwan double-crossed us by lacing the speech with very provocative statements and formulations" (in *China Policy and the National Security Council*, an Oral History Roundtable convened by the Brookings-CISS National Security Council Project on November 4, 1999, online at http://www.puaf.umd.edu/CISSM/Projects/NSC/China.pdf). In both cases one can see the depth of misunderstanding at the time regarding Taipei's motives and the stakes for both Taiwan and the PRC.

[31] "Commentary: Where Does U.S. Want Relations with China to Go?," *Xinhua*, op. cit.

infringement" on China's sovereignty.[33] It warned that Washington was "playing with fire."[34] One commentator disparaged repeated U.S. government resort to the "pretext" that it had acted under congressional pressure:

> [A]nyone with some political common sense knows that it is the U.S. Government and not the Congress that formulates and implements the country's foreign policies, and that it is the government and not the Congress that carries out the international commitments of a state on its behalf. On the policy towards China, the government undoubtedly has the responsibility to abide by the three legally valid Sino-U.S. joint communiqués.[35]

Voicing, if perhaps in excessively strident terms, the view of many in China, the commentary went on:

> It must be pointed out that in the final analysis, the reason the U.S. Government has perfidiously and brazenly changed the 17-year-old policy pursued by previous governments of not allowing Taiwan leaders to visit the United States, is that it has never given up its policy of regarding Taiwan as its "unsinkable aircraft carrier," and its attempt to play the "Taiwan card" and to curb China's development, growth and unification. Connived at and aided by the United States, Lee Teng-hui and company are now very swollen with arrogance, creating tensions between the two sides of the Strait all of a sudden…The Chinese people attach importance to their relations with the United States and value their friendship with the U.S. people. *But they treasure more the independence and sovereignty which they have won through sustained struggle.*[36]

---

[32] *Guangming Daily* commentary, quoted in "Lee Teng-hui's Visit to U.S. and Sino-U.S. Relations, *Xinhua*, June 2, 1995.

[33] Foreign Ministry spokesman Chen Jian, quoted in "Lee's Visit to U.S. Damaging Sino-U.S. Relations, Spokesman Says," *Xinhua*, June 2, 1995.

[34] "United States is Playing with Fire," *Xinhua*, June 9, 1995.

[35] "Commentary: Where Does U.S. Want Relations with China to Go?," *Xinhua*, op. cit.

[36] Ibid. Emphasis added.

Unsurprisingly, Beijing's response went far beyond words. It immediately cut short the U.S. tour of its Air Force commander then under way, postponed its defense minister's visit to Washington scheduled for June, and, in a move whose scope was to broaden over time, cancelled bilateral talks on missile technology export controls and nuclear energy cooperation. After a few days, China recalled its ambassador as well.

Turning its attention across the Strait, Beijing cancelled a second round of talks between Wang Daohan and Koo Chen-fu scheduled for July as well as all other cross-Strait dialogues. Eventually, this expanded into a refusal to attend virtually any international meetings, even purely private scholarly meetings, where Taiwan representatives were in attendance.

In both July and August, the People's Liberation Army (PLA) conducted significant military exercises involving missile launches and live-fire tests in areas within one hundred miles of Taiwan, the first time it had fired its ballistic missiles far out into a sea zone "conspicuously adjacent to Taiwan."[37] And in mid-August, China conducted an underground nuclear test, its second in three months.[38]

In private, in a démarche on another subject in late June, the PRC Chargé d'Affaires in Washington seized the occasion to tell Winston Lord that the Lee visit had "shaken the very foundation" of the "one China policy."[39] In response, Lord asserted that the U.S. had not changed its "fundamental China policy," as the President, in a rare gesture, had explained personally to PRC Ambassador Li Daoyu. Lord characterized the PRC response as "not 'enlightened.'" Shortly thereafter, reflecting a new policy theme, "guidance" was provided for use by Embassy Beijing with Chinese interlocutors, arguing that "positive bilateral relations are as much in China's interests as ours."[40]

---

[37] Garver, *Face Off*, op. cit., p. 74.

[38] "Nuclear Notebook: Known Nuclear Tests Worldwide, 1945-1995," *Bulletin of the Atomic Scientists*, available online at http://www.thebulletin.org/issues/nukenotes/mj96nukenote.html#anchor255480. The other test had been on May 15th, six days after the joint resolution passed and four days before Lee's visa was approved.

[39] State 156528, "Second Demarche to Chinese Charge on AmCit Harry Wu's Detention in China," June 29, 1995, *NSA* 01855.

[40] State 159037, "Official-Informal," July 1, 1995, *FRDC*, online at http://foia.state.gov/documents/foiadocs/5408.PDF.

Not unexpectedly, China dismissed this argument, saying that it was the United States that that had caused the problem and that needed to "do something" to get the relationship back on track.[41]

In short order, the U.S. indeed did seek to steer relations back on track. In late July, on the eve of a trip to Asia, where he was to meet with PRC Foreign Minister Qian Qichen, Secretary of State Warren Christopher told the National Press Club that the United States "must not allow short-term calculations to divert us from pursuing our long-term interests" with China.[42] He described the Lee visit as "a special situation and a courtesy, consistent with American values and opinion." Christopher not only reaffirmed the "one China" policy in general, but he recited the entire mantra: support for the three communiqués, recognition of Beijing as the sole legal government of China, acknowledgment of the Chinese position that there is but one China and that Taiwan is a part of China, and reaffirmation that the United States had no intention of "advocating or supporting" a "two Chinas" or "one China, one Taiwan" policy.

Reflecting not only a certain impatience with Beijing for seeking to place all responsibility for improved relations on Washington's back, but also a growing anger at Taiwan's manipulation of the Lee visit— especially the political character of his Cornell speech, Christopher also spoke of the "shared responsibility" of the United States, PRC and Taiwan, upon whom it was incumbent to pursue policies that fostered continued stability in the region. The Secretary pushed back against those who might seek to disengage from China, contending that Washington's differences with Beijing were an argument for engagement, not for containment or isolation. Neither side, he said, had the luxury of walking away from its responsibility to manage their differences. Reiterating a long-standing position, Christopher said that a "strong stable, open and prosperous China can be a valuable partner for the United States and a responsible leader of the international community."

---

[41] Beijing 028695, "Independence Day Reception: Lee Visit Main Topic," July 3, 1995, *FRDC*, online at http://www.foia.state.gov/documents/foiadocs/541f.PDF.

[42] "America's Strategy for a Peaceful and Prosperous Asia-Pacific," Address to the National Press Club, Washington DC, July 28, 1995, in *U.S. Department of State Dispatch* 6, no. 31 (July 31, 1995), p. 592.

When he met with Qian in Brunei in early August, Christopher delivered a letter from President Clinton to President Jiang reaffirming the "one China policy." In that letter, Clinton called for maintenance of the framework, reached through "courageous political leadership and diplomatic skill," for managing differences, "especially over Taiwan." He went on:

> I know that your Government considers the recent private visit by Lee Teng-hui to Cornell University to be a very serious and sensitive matter. I respect your views but ask that you also respect mine. We permitted Mr. Lee to make a private visit to his alma mater for a personal purpose. We ensured there was no meeting between Mr. Lee and Administration officials. The visit was carefully managed to be unofficial in substance and, to the maximum degree within our control, in appearance. Most importantly, it did not represent any change in our policy of maintaining only unofficial ties with the people of Taiwan.[43]

The standard U.S. positions against supporting a "one China, one Taiwan" or "two China" policy, "Taiwan independence," or Taiwan's admission to the United Nations were also restated.[44]

Qian responded to Christopher that China attached importance to these statements but, citing a Chinese proverb—"promises must be kept, and action must be resolute"—indicated that China remained troubled by the U.S. unwillingness to promise that Lee would not be allowed to visit the United States again in the future. Such a visit by a sitting "president" of Taiwan would be tantamount, a PRC-controlled Hong Kong paper editorialized, to a "two Chinas" or "one China, one Taiwan" policy, however much it was billed as "private."[45]

Despite this bleat, it was clear that there would be no repeat of the Lee visit in the near future. Not only was the Administration disinclined to go through such trauma again, but various Members of Congress asserted that they had been taken aback by the strength of the PRC reaction and that they would not have voted for the concurrent resolution

---

[43] Excerpt from President Clinton's letter to Jiang Zemin, July 31, 1995, provided to author by former Clinton Administration official.

[44] "Key to Mending Sino-U.S. Ties Lies in Action," *Ta Kung Pao* (Hong Kong), August 3, 1995, A2, translated by FBIS (FBIS-CHI-95-162) on August 8, 1995.

[45] Ibid.

if they had understood the depth of PRC opposition.[46] Some months later, after his reelection, Lee himself poured cold water on the idea of a return visit, claiming he would be too busy for such travel.[47]

But, while no one actually anticipated being faced with another such dilemma soon, having gone through all that it had in connection with the Lee visa decision, the Administration was not prepared to accept the costs of ruling out any future visits "in principle." What it did do in the wake of this debacle, however, was to come up with an approach to "visits" by senior Taiwan leaders that said they would be considered case-by-case (i.e., Lee's visit was not to be taken as a precedent) and would be unofficial, rare and approved only for strictly private/personal purposes.

MILITARY SIGNALING: TENSIONS IN THE STRAIT

During August and September 1995, various trappings of a normal U.S.-PRC relationship resumed. The Chinese Ambassador returned to Washington, and Beijing granted agrément for a new American ambassador in Beijing.[48] High-level military exchanges were renewed. And Presidents Clinton and Jiang met on October 24th in New York.

The U.S. gushed over the Lincoln Center encounter between the two leaders, quoting President Clinton as rating it not only "positive" but the "best of the three meetings" he had held with Jiang thus far.[49] China also praised the meeting, though in somewhat more modest terms, as "candid, amicable, positive and useful," and said it was "conducive to the

---

[46] Some Members reported that the Administration had not made a serious effort to dissuade them (see Tyler, for example, who relates a claim by then-deputy Republican whip, Rep. Dennis Hastert (R-Ill), that "no one" in the White House, much less the President, had made a case against the resolution (*A Great Wall*, p. 416). Whether those Members known to be familiar with PRC views and in close touch with the PRC leadership could credibly cite White House inattention as a reason for misjudging—or ignoring—Beijing's likely reaction is perhaps a different matter.

[47] "Taiwan's Quiet Revolution," *Wall Street Journal,* March 27, 1996, A22.

[48] Shortly after Lee's visit to Cornell in June, J. Stapleton Roy had left Beijing quietly on a previously determined schedule to prepare for his next assignment as Ambassador to Indonesia.

[49] "Press Briefing by Winston Lord and NSC Director of Asian Affairs Robert Suettinger," October 24, 1995, *M2Presswire,* October 27, 1995.

improvement and development of the two countries' relations."[50] But whereas the U.S. characterized the discussion of Taiwan as "not a major part of the discussion"—taking only ten or fifteen minutes out of a total of two hours, consistent with the meeting's goal "to create a broad agenda"[51]—China focused more sharply on the handling of Taiwan. Speaking to the press afterward, Qian Qichen noted Clinton's reiteration of the U.S. "one China policy" and his commitment to abide by the three U.S.-PRC joint communiqués, which the Foreign Minister characterized as "earnest." He went on, however:

> This does not mean the Taiwan issue will not again be the main obstacle affecting Sino-US relations in the future…As the Taiwan issue has always been the most sensitive issue in Sino-US relations, it must be handled in accordance with the principles set in the three joint communiqués. It will be so in the future.[52]

This caution was backed up in Beijing by hard-line Premier Li Peng on the same day Jiang met Clinton in New York. Li laid out the inducements of Jiang's "eight-point proposal" of the previous January, but he also highlighted the PRC's refusal to renounce the use of force and castigated the efforts by Taiwan authorities to create "two Chinas" and the support given to those efforts by "international anti-China forces."[53]

Taking these themes a step further, a few days later, Vice Chairman of the Central Military Commission General Zhang Wannian minced no

---

[50] Foreign Ministry Spokesman Shen Guofang, cited in "Spokesman says Chinese, US Presidents' Meeting 'Positive and Useful,'" *Xinhua,* October 26, 1995, in *BBC Summary of World Broadcasts*, October 26, 1995.

[51] "Press Briefing by Winston Lord and NSC Director of Asian Affairs Robert Suettinger," October 24, 1995.

[52] Quoted in "Foreign Minister Qian Qichen on US, Taiwan, Hong Kong Issues," Xinhua, October 26, 1995, in *BBC Summary of World Broadcasts*, October 27, 1995 (hereafter "Qian briefing, October 24, 1995"). While verifying the positive and broad-gauged nature of the meeting, Robert Suettinger, who was the American note-taker, confirms that Jiang "focused on Taiwan in some detail" (*Beyond Tiananmen,* p. 242).

[53] "Speech at the Meeting of People of All Walks of Life in the Capital to Mark the 50th Anniversary of Taiwan's Retrocession," *Xinhua,* October 24, 1995, in *BBC Summary of World Broadcasts*, October 26, 1995.

words in stating that if Taiwan declared independence, or if foreign forces intervened to prevent unification with the Mainland, the PRC would "definitely use force." Furthermore, he blamed current cross-Strait tensions "solely" on the United States:

> Because the Taiwan authorities believe they have the support of the United States, they have gone further and further down the road of splitting China...Some people [in the United States] always hope to see China in chaos and collapse.[54]

Although few people thought that China really preferred a military solution to the Taiwan problem, an issue that percolates through assessments of this period concerns the signals that Beijing may have been getting from the United States about the American reaction to any threat or use of force. The U.S. position of "strategic ambiguity" had been in place for some time, avoiding a specific statement of what the United States would do in the event of cross-Strait hostilities. The ambiguous stance was meant to remind Beijing of the abiding American interest in a peaceful resolution of cross-Strait issues and caution the PRC not to assume that the U.S. *would not* intervene if it attacked Taiwan. At the same time, it was meant to warn Taipei not to assume that the U.S. *would* intervene if Taiwan provoked such an attack.

Some observers believe that the "measured" U.S. response to the PRC military exercises and missile tests in July and August 1995 conveyed a misleading message to Beijing that "strategic ambiguity" reflected an underlying "strategic ambivalence" regarding U.S. involvement in a Taiwan contingency, especially in the wake of the events of October 1993 when eighteen U.S. servicemen were killed in the streets of Mogadishu, Somalia, and U.S. forces were withdrawn over the next several months.[55] Of course, it was true that in this same time frame Washington cautioned that "U.S. policy, and adherence to the

---

[54] In Susan V. Lawrence and Tim Zimmerman, "A Political Test of When Guns Matter," *U.S. News and World Report*, October 30, 1995.

[55] See Garver, *Face Off*, pp. 74-88. Support for this assessment can also be found in remarks attributed to a senior State Department official who not only said "You don't really know what would happen until you get there," but went on to predict: "[But] we would not be in a position to react with force. We would not elect to do that I'm sure" (Lawrence and Zimmerman, "A Political Test of When Guns Matter").

three communiqués" depended on "peaceful resolution of the Taiwan issue,"[56] but the issue is whether this registered as a serious warning.

Whatever one's view about the adequacy of the signaling, U.S. concern was, in fact, growing that China might miscalculate the level of American resolve to maintain the peace. This was based in part on reports out of Beijing that some Chinese doubted U.S. determination to become involved, but it also arose from "an unprecedented demonstration of [Chinese] military capabilities" during exercises Beijing launched on the eve of Taiwan's legislative elections in December 1995.[57]

These exercises were backed up by tough rhetoric from the PLA. On the first anniversary of Jiang Zemin's eight-point proposal, the PLA paper, *Liberation Army Daily*, carried an editorial dutifully endorsing Jiang's positive message, but stressing the perfidy of Lee Teng-hui, who was "collud[ing] with foreign forces" to create "one China, one Taiwan." Warning that China's "peaceful way" to "terminate the nation's bitterness" did not mean that the process of peaceful reunification "can be delayed indefinitely," the editorial went on:

> The Chinese PLA is an army with high political consciousness and fighting capacity...[and will] never allow an inch of territory to be separated from the motherland's domain, and never allow any anti-China foreign forces to meddle in China's internal affairs.[58]

The concern was then exacerbated when Beijing sought to repeat its coercive tactics on the eve of the island's March 1996 presidential elections, carrying out "the largest multi-service exercise China [had] ever conducted in the Taiwan Strait area."[59] This time, it launched missiles into waters even closer to Taiwan's sea- and airport facilities at

---

[56] "Prepared Testimony by Kent Wiedemann, Deputy Assistant Secretary of State for East Asian and Pacific Affairs, Before the House International Relations Committee: Taiwan and the United Nations," *Federal News Service*, August 3, 1995.

[57] Office of Naval Intelligence (ONI), "Chinese Exercise Strait 961: 8-25 March 1996," p. 11.

[58] "Making Contributions to the Great Cause of the Motherland's Reunification," *Jiefangjun Bao* editorial carried by *Xinhua* on January 30, 1996 and translated by FBIS (OW3001142896) the following day.

[59] ONI, "Chinese Exercise Strait 961: 8-25 March 1996," p. 11.

the northern and southern tips of the island[60]—what Secretary of Defense William Perry called, in artilleryman's terms, "bracketing" the island.

In response, the U.S. dispatched two aircraft carrier battle groups to areas near Taiwan, not because Washington anticipated war, but in order to convey to Beijing the seriousness of the U.S. "abiding interest" in peaceful resolution of cross-Strait issues.[61]

Here we see that once again the unreconciled differences between Beijing and Washington over sovereignty issues gave rise to tensions, this time with a kind of military posturing that, in fact, has subsequently led both sides to make even more serious war preparations. The granting of the visa to Lee Teng-hui in 1995, against the advice of both China specialists and other senior advisers, reflected to a great extent the political dilemma the White House faced. But beyond that, it reflected a level of insensitivity, even unawareness, of what was at stake for both Beijing and Taipei. To both of them, this was a political issue of the most fundamental kind, rooted in their competing claims about sovereignty. To the American President, it was a question of freedom of travel, freedom of speech, and an old man who wanted to visit his alma mater. It is almost inexplicable that a person as politically astute as Bill Clinton should have allowed himself to be trapped in that fashion, or that he should not have more clearly understood the strategic stakes for the United States.[62]

---

[60] Ironically for Beijing, while the independence-minded opposition Democratic Progressive Party (DPP) fared poorly on this occasion, Lee is generally seen to have received a boost from the PRC's militancy, helping him win an outright majority.

[61] Suettinger describes the political, diplomatic and military dimensions of these events in vivid detail in *Beyond Tiananmen* (pp. 247-263). "Chinese Exercise Strait 961: 8-25 March 1996" also presents a highly detailed discussion of the PRC's exercises.

[62] One former senior official believes that Clinton was "not very well served" in this case. The advice the President got from his National Security Adviser, Anthony Lake, in particular, was strongly focused on not allowing the Chinese to bully the U.S. out of letting Lee make a "perfectly lawful" trip to the United States to exercise what were equivalent to "first amendment rights," a view with which Clinton was sympathetic. Although some of the President's advisers were quite strong in asserting that there would be a serious PRC reaction, the National Security Adviser, who had early in the Administration identified China as among reactionary "backlash states," felt they were overreacting to Chinese bluster and, as a consequence, did not clearly articulate to the President the potential adverse effects on the U.S.-PRC relationship (exchange with author).

In any event, the costs to U.S.-PRC relations were significant, as were the potential consequences for Taiwan's long-term security.

REINING IN AT THE BRINK OF THE PRECIPICE: REBALANCING THE RELATIONSHIP

After the election, Lee Teng-hui continued to speak in the language of "one China" even though his actions persuaded Beijing he was heading in another direction. Lee declared that strengthening cross-Strait relations was "one of our top priorities"[63] and pledged to strive for a "national consensus" by "the Chinese people on both sides of the Taiwan Strait" to promote a cross-Strait peace accord.[64] Aiming at the goal of "eventual unification," Lee proposed to take a "journey of peace to mainland China" to begin a process to terminate the state of hostility.[65] At the same time, he underscored the existence of two separate "jurisdictions" and argued that, "prior to reunification," Taipei would continue to press its bid to joint the UN.[66]

Predictably, these declarations changed nothing in the cross-Strait political dynamic, but trade and travel continued to flourish. In the meantime, on the American side, once again it was Secretary Christopher who used a public speech to try to refocus the issues in a more

---

(On "backlash states," see "From Engagement to Enlargement," a speech by Lake on September 21, 1993, online at http://www.mtholyoke.edu/acad/intrel/lakedoc.html .)

This was not Clinton's first—or last—misjudgment of China. In linking MFN to human rights improvements in 1993, the President set up a situation from which he inevitably had to retreat. And in April 1999, on political advice from senior members of his Administration, and over the objections of his policy team, he turned down an excellent WTO package brought to Washington by PRC Premier Zhu Rongji, which it took months to put back together. In all three cases, domestic politics and the role of Congress were of central importance and given priority over considerations of China policy. In all three cases, Clinton subsequently had to change course.

[63] Sofia Wu, "Lee Teng-hui Affirms Reunification Under 'Democracy'," *Central News Agency* (Taiwan), March 26, 1996, transcribed by FBIS (OW2603110796).

[64] "Taiwan's Quiet Revolution," *Wall Street Journal,* op. cit.

[65] Lee's May 20, 1996 inaugural address, text carried by *Central News Agency* (Taiwan) and translated by FBIS (OW2005032496).

[66] "Taiwan's Quiet Revolution," *Wall Street Journal.*

constructive way. Speaking to three of the premier American public policy groups dealing with U.S.-China relations, Christopher presented a comprehensive statement on China policy, including an explanation of the U.S. approach to the PRC, Taiwan and cross-Strait relations.[67]

There was no change in Washington's view that a weak China would not be in American interests. But in light of the recent events in the Strait, the formulation "strong, stable, prosperous and open" that the Secretary had used at the National Press Club the previous year seemed inappropriate. This time he said that the United States viewed China's development as a "secure, open, and successful nation that is taking its place as a world leader" as "profoundly in the interest of the United States." Once again rejecting notions of containment or isolation, and wanting to avoid any suggestion that he sought to undercut the PRC's modernization efforts or its stability, he argued that China's integration into the international system could best ensure that its development as a "strong and responsible member of the international community" took place in a way that promoted U.S. interests as well as its own.

Christopher reiterated the point made in the wake of Lee's visit in 1995: "We will do our part—but China, too, must do its part." While noting that the United States preferred dialogue and engagement as a way of managing differences with China, and with Taiwan at least partially in mind, Christopher said "we will not hesitate to take the action necessary to protect our interests." Specifically on cross-Strait issues, he reflected on the value of the "one China" policy for all concerned and spelled out what the U.S. had been saying privately to Beijing and Taipei in recent weeks:

> To the leadership in Beijing, we have reiterated our consistent position that the future relationship between Taiwan and the PRC must be resolved directly between them. But we have reaffirmed that we have a strong interest in the region's continued peace and stability—and that our "one China" policy is predicated on the PRC's pursuit of a peaceful resolution of the issues between Taipei and Beijing.

---

[67] The following draws on "American Interests and the U.S.-China Relationship," Address By Secretary of State Warren Christopher to the Asia Society, the Council on Foreign Relations and the National Committee on U.S.-China Relations, May 17, 1996, online at http://www.state.gov/www/current/debate/96517qa.html.

To the leadership in Taiwan, we have reiterated our commitment to robust unofficial relations, including helping Taiwan maintain a sufficient self-defense capacity under the terms of the Taiwan Relations Act. We have stressed that Taiwan has prospered under the "one China" policy. And we have made clear our view that as Taiwan seeks an international role, it should pursue that objective in a way that is consistent with a "one China" policy.

We have emphasized to both sides the importance of avoiding provocative actions or unilateral measures that would alter the status quo or pose a threat to peaceful resolution of outstanding issues. And we have strongly urged both sides to resume the cross-Strait dialogue that was interrupted last summer.

Christopher then made two specific proposals. First, he suggested "periodic cabinet-level consultations in our capitals" (as opposed to merely "on the margins" of international gatherings). And second, he said that the two nations' leaders should hold regular summit meetings.

China quickly seized on these suggestions, and working around political trials and tribulations in both countries, a diplomatic minuet began that led to the exchange of summit visits that brought Jiang Zemin to the United States in October 1997 and Bill Clinton to China in June 1998.[68]

In November 1996, as the efforts for improvement were beginning to take shape, and now at a slightly further remove from the events of March so that concern about the implications of a "strong" China for Taiwan's security had diminished somewhat, President Clinton returned to earlier formulations. He argued that "the emergence of a stable, an open, a prosperous China, a strong China confident of its place in the world and willing to assume its responsibilities as a great nation" was "in our deepest interest."[69] And he called for making China a "genuine partner."[70]

---

[68] Suettinger provides a detailed account of this period in *Beyond Tiananmen*, pp. 231-357.

[69] "The U.S. and Australia: Working Together to Meet New Challenges of the 21st Century," Address by President Clinton to the Australian Parliament, November 20, 1996 in *U.S. Department of State Dispatch* 7, no. 48 (November 25, 1996), p. 577.

[70] "Joint Press Conference with President Clinton and Australian Prime Minister John Howard, Canberra, Australia," November 20, 1996, *Federal News Service*

Over the course of the next several months, moving into Clinton's second term, senior officials began to speak out with increasing frequency on China policy in ways they had generally avoided doing in the first term, now trying to forge a public consensus behind a strategy of engagement. In making that case, they applied the lessons of the Lee visa experience and stressed the benefits of working within the terms of the "one China" policy for resolving U.S.-PRC differences.

Nonetheless, promoting Taiwan's security remained a priority, and Secretary of State Madeleine Albright reminded an audience at the U.S. Naval Academy that the U.S. would protect its own interests, citing the deployment of two American aircraft carriers to the region in spring 1996 to help lower the risk of miscalculation when tensions in the Taiwan Strait rose due to PRC military exercises.[71]

National Security Adviser Samuel R. Berger dedicated an entire speech to the subject of "Building a New Consensus on China,"[72] pressing the case that the direction China would take in the years ahead would be one of the most decisive factors determining whether the next century was to be one of conflict or cooperation. While China would define its own destiny, he said, American decisions would influence China's evolution.

Berger took on those who argued that the world had changed in ways that made existing China policy obsolete. Specifically on the issue of Taiwan—and the fact that Taiwan's democratic political evolution had begun to call into question the basis of the "one China" policy—Berger argued that the real question was not whether the U.S. supported democracy in Taiwan, but how best to sustain it. And there, he

---

transcript. Meanwhile, speaking in Shanghai the next day, within twenty-four hours of the President's remarks, Christopher also made a forward-looking speech about overall U.S.-China relations in which he reiterated the Taiwan-related points he had made in May, but, reflecting a certain lack of White House-State Department coordination, at the last minute decided to make his theme "cooperation" rather than "partnership"; for brief but focused accounts of the switch, see Christopher, *Chances of a Lifetime*, pp. 248-249 and Suettinger, *Beyond Tiananmen*, pp. 281-282.

[71] "Remarks Prepared for Delivery by U.S. Secretary of State Madeleine Albright: American Principle and Purpose in East Asia," 1997 Forrestal Lecture, April 15, 1997, *Federal News Service* transcript.

[72] See "Transcript of Berger Remarks to Council on Foreign Relations As Prepared for Delivery," June 6, 1997, carried by *U.S. Newswire* on the same date.

maintained, the "one China" policy provided the security and stability required for democratic development, economic prosperity, and burgeoning cross-Strait exchanges in which Chinese on both sides of the Strait could resolve their issues themselves—peacefully.

President Clinton echoed these themes in a speech on the eve of Jiang Zemin's arrival, and he told his audience that he would reaffirm the "one China" policy to Jiang. [73]

BEIJING'S POUND OF FLESH: THE "THREE NOES"

In the run-up to the Clinton-Jiang October 1997 summit, Beijing had pressed for a comprehensive statement of U.S. policy toward Taiwan, either in a "fourth communiqué" or at least in a joint statement to be issued at the conclusion of Jiang's visit. A "fourth communiqué" was rejected out of hand by the United States, in part because the very idea implied that the U.S. was changing policy at Taiwan's expense. Moreover, in light of the circumstances surrounding the Taiwan issue in 1995-1996, as well as the difficult political climate then prevailing in Washington over China policy, any "comprehensive" recital of U.S. Taiwan policy would have had to include some reference to the Taiwan Relations Act. That was clearly a non-starter for the PRC.

Still, given the recent tensions, it was not unreasonable to argue that the United States should lay out the totality of its approach to Taiwan in one form or another. The Joint Statement issued on October 29, 1997 contained only the barebones elements of U.S. policy toward Taiwan— reiteration of adherence to the "one China" policy and to the principles set forth in the three U.S.-China joint communiqués[74]—and even in various public remarks the President only supplemented this to the extent of emphasizing dialogue and peaceful resolution by the Chinese

---

[73] White House Office of the Press Secretary, "Remarks by the President in Address on China and the National Interest," October 24, 1997, online at http://clinton3.nara.gov/WH/New/html/19971024-3863.html.

[74] White House Office of the Press Secretary, "Joint U.S.-China Statement," October 29, 1997, online at http://www.usconsulate.org.hk/uscn/jiang97/1029f.htm It was also in the Joint Statement that Clinton and Jiang adopted a formulation that later proved politically charged in the United States: "The two Presidents are determined to build toward a constructive strategic partnership between the United States and China through increasing cooperation to meet international challenges and promote peace and development in the world." Excerpts are provided in the Appendix to this study.

themselves. But a more extensive statement was made privately to Jiang during the summit.

Vice Premier and Foreign Minister Qian Qichen hinted at this when he told a Washington press briefing the evening of the Clinton-Jiang meeting that:

> Since 1995 it has been stated that the US side will not support the independence of Taiwan, the United States will not support the so-called return of Taiwan to the United Nations, and the US side will not support "two Chinas" or "one China, one Taiwan."[75]

The PRC press immediately took it a step further, reporting—without attribution—that President Clinton had made these points to President Jiang.[76]

At his daily press briefing two days later, the State Department spokesman enumerated these positions and said that "we certainly made [them] clear to the Chinese."[77] This was the first time the United States had *publicly* and *officially* announced it did not support Taiwan independence, though it had been a privately articulated position for many years.[78]

But, as Jiang was about to leave the west coast for home, in apparent frustration that an American cabinet-level official had not made these points publicly, Qian Qichen, while still not citing Clinton by name, told a Los Angeles press conference that:

> Before *and during the Summit*, the US side said repeatedly it would not support Taiwan independence, "one China, one

---

[75] "Foreign Minister Faces the Press After Sino-US Summit," *Wen Wei Po* (Hong Kong), October 31, 1997, A4, in *BBC Summary of World Broadcasts*, November 1, 1997.

[76] See "Clinton Reiterates One China Policy," *Xinhua*, October 30, 1997.

[77] Department of State, Press Briefing by James Rubin, October 31, 1997, cited in Shirley A. Kan, *China/Taiwan: Evolution of the "One China" Policy—Key Statements from Washington, Beijing and Taipei*, Congressional Research Service study RL30341, updated October 16, 2002, p. 46.

[78] Dean, "U.S. Relations with Taiwan," op. cit., pp. 98-99.

Taiwan" or "two China's," and Taiwan's "reentry" into the United Nations.[79]

In light of the later furor over the "change in policy" and "tilt toward Beijing" allegedly represented by President Clinton's articulation of these so-called "three noes" while in China in June 1998, it is perhaps worth pausing to note not just that they were all laid out long before then, but how they were treated in Taiwan in October 1997. Although Qian Qichen had tried to be discreet in his October 29th press conference by casting these as long-standing positions, the Taiwan press immediately cited him as having attributed the remarks directly to Clinton.[80] In response, both DPP and New Party officials in charge of their parties' Mainland policy, though not necessarily approving of Clinton's stand, said they were "not surprised" by Qian's statement.

Similarly, the Foreign Ministry in Taipei, while making clear that it would closely watch future developments in U.S.-PRC relations, said that the U.S. position on Taiwan voiced during the summit "did not strike us as a surprising point of view."[81] Indeed, according to *CNA,* Taiwan's official news agency, the Ministry approvingly indicated that the United States had not departed from its long-standing position on the Taiwan issue and its commitments to Taipei.[82]

Although in late April Albright articulated the "three noes" in a Beijing press conference, that went virtually unnoticed, and as Clinton was preparing his visit to China, there was intense pressure from the Chinese for the President himself to state these points. They were not substantively new points and by now had been publicly voiced at various levels. But the PRC leadership obviously felt it imperative to get the U.S. on record at the highest level in order to limit future US. and Taiwan options.

---

[79] Han Hua, "Questions and Answers at Qian Qichen's Small-Scale Briefing," *Wen Wei Po* (Hong Kong), November 4, 1997, carried as part of "Text of Qian Qichen's LA News Conference," November 4, 1997, translated by FBIS (OW0411101097). Emphasis added.

[80] Flor Wang, "Analysts Discuss Clinton's 'One China' Principle," *Central News Agency* (Taiwan), October 30, 1997, translated in FBIS (OW3010160897). Interestingly enough, they were labeled the "three noes" even at that time.

[81] "Foreign Ministry Issues Statement on U.S.-China Summit," *Kyodo News,* October 30, 1997.

[82] H.C.M., "Taiwan Lauds US for Stance on Taiwan Issue," *Central News Agency* (Taiwan), October 30, 1997, translated by FBIS (OW3010135997).

In the run-up to the visit, Clinton once again offered a lengthy public rationale for the strategy of engagement. Repeating many of the points he had made in his speech on the eve of Jiang's visit to Washington the previous October, the President touched on everything from nonproliferation to Korea to international crime. Fireproofing himself against anticipated criticism that he was to be officially greeted in front of the Great Hall of the People on the edge of Tiananmen Square, and reflecting the salience of dissident issues at the time, Clinton also devoted considerable attention to human rights and religious freedom. About Taiwan, however, he said not one word.

That was all to change once he got to China. In a televised joint press conference following their formal meeting, Jiang and Clinton touched on Taiwan in concise, standard terms. But, later that day, in briefing the press on the leaders' meeting, National Security Adviser Samuel (Sandy) Berger said the President had restated the "basic" U.S. "one China" policy. He explained:

> It continues to be at the heart of our policy, based on the three communiqués. We don't support independence for Taiwan or one China, one Taiwan, or Taiwan's membership in organizations that require statehood; but that it is extraordinarily important to the United States that the issue between China and Taiwan be resolved peacefully.[83]

Berger noted that Secretary Albright had made the same points when she was in China, as had others. In essence confirming that Clinton had made these points to Jiang, Berger also allowed that it was "not inconceivable" that the President would publicly address Taiwan somewhat more specifically before leaving China. Pressed on when the United States started saying that it formally opposed independence for Taiwan, Berger said it had been part of U.S. policy for some time and was inherent in the three U.S.-PRC joint communiqués. "That goes back long before we got here," he noted.

When Clinton answered questions after his televised speech at Peking University on June 29th,[84] he did not go beyond observing that the

---

[83] White House Office of the Press Secretary, "Press Briefing by Mike McCurry, National Security Advisor Sandy Berger, and National Economic Advisor Gene Sperling," June 27, 1998, online at http://clinton6.nara.gov/ 1998/06/1998-06-27-press-briefing-by-mccurry-and-berger-and-sperling.html.

[84] White House Office of the Press Secretary, "Remarks by the President to

U.S. "one China" policy is embodied in the three joint communiqués and the Taiwan Relations Act. He rebutted the suggestion that U.S. policy was an obstacle to the peaceful reunification of Taiwan and the PRC. But in so doing, and in justifying defensive arms sales to Taiwan, he also repeated the assertion President Ford had made in 1975, an assertion that went beyond the actual facts:

> Now, when the United States and China reached agreement that we would have a one China policy, *we also reached agreement that the reunification would occur by peaceful means* and we have encouraged the cross-strait dialogue to achieve that.[85]

It was in an untelevised roundtable discussion at the Shanghai Library that Clinton uttered the "three noes" that produced major controversy. Creating a context for what he was planning to say by asking a Chinese roundtable participant to discuss Sino-American relations, Clinton then responded by noting that, in his Washington and Beijing conversations with Jiang, he had had a chance to reiterate U.S. Taiwan policy. He said that, in addition to the fact that "it has to be done peacefully," that policy was:

> [W]e don't support independence for Taiwan, or two Chinas, or one China-one Taiwan. And we don't believe that Taiwan should be a member in any organization for which statehood is a requirement.[86]

The Administration subsequently engaged in an intensive campaign to demonstrate that none of this represented any change in policy, having

---

Students and Community of Beijing University," June 29, 1998, online at http://clinton6.nara.gov/1998/06/1998-06-29-remarks-by-the-president-at-beijing-university.html.

[85] David M. Lampton notes that some in Taipei were upset by this statement, feeling it suggested the U.S. had moved away from support for a peaceful process to support for actual reunification (*Same Bed, Different Dreams: Managing U.S.-China Relations 1989-2000*, op. cit., pp. 102-103). However, two sentences later in his answer, Clinton caught this implication and corrected himself: "But we do believe it should occur—any reunification should occur peacefully."

[86] White House Office of the Press Secretary, "Remarks by the President and the First Lady in Discussion on Shaping China for the 21st Century," June 30, 1998, available online at http://clinton6.nara.gov/1998/06/1998-06-30-remarks-by-president-and-first-lady-at-shanghai-library.html.

been advanced publicly at various times—as long ago as the Nixon Administration and as recently as three days before by National Security Adviser Berger in Beijing.[87]   But the fact that it was stated publicly by the President, in China, in a formulation that had a decidedly "Chinese flavor" to it, on a trip when the President had declined to stop by traditional allies Japan and Korea, and with both the PRC and Taiwan playing it up—and that it was taking place in a heated American political atmosphere in which Clinton's overall credibility was under intense scrutiny—turned the "three noes" into a high-profile, politically charged issue in which it was alleged that the United States was tilting toward Beijing.

This may be one of those cases that underscores the wisdom of the old Chinese saying: Be careful what you wish for; you may get it. For, while Beijing got the President to utter the "three noes" in China, it is not hard to "connect the dots" between that event and the articulation a year later of the "two states theory" by Lee Teng-hui.

TAIPEI'S REJOINDER: THE "TWO STATES THEORY"

In the immediate aftermath of the Clinton statement, Lee Teng-hui issued a rebuttal to American audiences on the op-ed page of the *Wall Street Journal.*[88]   Echoing Taiwan's 1991 National Unification Guidelines[89] and building on the theme of "one divided China" with Taiwan and the Mainland "each being part of China," Lee argued: "[N]either has jurisdiction over the other, neither can represent the other, much less all of China."

Still, the two sides of the Strait were able to move ahead with an "informal" round of the Wang-Koo talks, the first time the two senior personages had gotten together since the abortive meeting that Beijing canceled in 1995 in the wake of Lee's Cornell visit. In October 1998, Koo Chen-fu traveled to Shanghai and Beijing, where he laid out Taiwan's position on the existence of two equal entities, while his host,

---

[87] White House Press Secretary Mike McCurry first made that assertion in Shanghai at a press briefing; see http://usinfo.state.gov/regional/ea/uschina/otrbrief.htm A "fact sheet" was later issued by the White House showing the origins of each of the points. Also see earlier discussion of Taiwan Policy Review.

[88] "U.S. Can't Ignore Taiwan," August 3, 1998, cited in Kan, *China/Taiwan: Evolution of the "One China" Policy*, p. 47.

[89] Text available at http://www.mac.gov.tw/english/index1-e.htm

Wang Daohan, countered that Taiwan's political status could be discussed "on an equal footing," but only under the "one China principle."[90] According to at least one source, Koo, who also was received by the top leaders in Beijing, told the press that he had informed Deputy Premier Qian Qichen that Taiwan would not consider unification until the Mainland was democratic and that any reunification proposal "must grant Taiwan a separate status from China."[91] Tang Shubei, Executive Vice Chairman of the Association for Relations Across the Taiwan Strait (ARATS), the PRC's quasi-official body for dealing with Taiwan, reportedly responded that this demand was "unacceptable."[92] Still, Koo and Wang Daohan agreed to hold further political and economic dialogue, carry out more exchanges between their organizations, and strengthen assistance in case of "incidents concerning the lives and property" of people from across the Strait. Most important, Wang accepted Koo's invitation to pay a return visit to Taiwan in the fall of 1999.[93]

The United States welcomed the beginnings of a renewed cross-Strait dialogue. Assistant Secretary of State Stanley Roth observed in March 1999 that, while it was "still nascent in substance," this renewed contact had the potential to contribute to the peaceful resolution of their difficult differences.[94] Taking care to say that the peaceful resolution of their differences was up to the two sides, themselves, Roth spoke of the "shelter of the TRA" that had fostered dramatic progress in Taiwan and facilitated the burgeoning of cross-Strait economic, political and other ties. And he noted that the dynamic equilibrium of the military forces on

---

[90] Drawn from a number of sources excerpted in Kan, *China/Taiwan: Evolution of the "One China" Policy*, p. 47.

[91] "Top Taiwanese Envoy Visits," *Facts on File World News Digest,* October 22, 1998, A1, p. 755.

[92] Ibid.

[93] Xue Bin and Zhou Xin, "Wang-Gu Meeting Reaches Four-Point Common Understanding," *Xinhua* (Hong Kong Service), October 15, 1998, translated by FBIS (SK1710055698).

[94] Assistant Secretary of State Stanley O. Roth, "The Taiwan Relations Act at Twenty—and Beyond," address to The Woodrow Wilson Center and The American Institute in Taiwan, March 24, 1999, online at http://usinfo.state.gov/regional/ea/uschina/rothtwn.htm.

the two sides of the Strait had "not changed dramatically over the last two decades."[95]

Roth also commented on the fact that military capability did not equate to security. While the United States would continue to guarantee that Taiwan did not lack the necessary defensive capability to counterbalance PRC military strength, another purpose of arms sales was to give Taipei the confidence to engage the Mainland. Roth harkened back to the theme sounded by George Shultz in 1987, saying that the United States would continue to contribute to an environment conducive to dialogue and the achievement of a lasting, mutually acceptable—and peaceful—resolution of differences across the Strait.

To Lee Teng-hui, statements like this, which presented an accurate picture of American attitudes, were doubtless disquieting. It was true that a generally sour tone had taken hold in U.S.-PRC relations over the months following the Beijing summit in June 1998—a souring fed by everything from allegations of Chinese money flowing into American election campaigns to charges of espionage and proliferation, suppression of unorthodox political forces in China, the failure to come to closure on a WTO agreement, and eventually the mistargeted bombing of the Chinese Embassy in Belgrade.[96] But though he might have taken heart from these problems between Washington and Beijing, Lee Teng-hui evidently still felt squeezed. Shortly after Clinton's trip to Beijing, Lee had established a small team to research ways to counter the "three noes." Now, a year later, concerned that Wang Daohan's forthcoming trip to Taiwan would lead to even greater pressure for negotiations within the "one China" framework, and that the U.S. might support that call, he decided to act.

Lee chose an interview with *Radio Deutsche Welle* in July 1999 to preemptively lay down a direct challenge to Beijing's version of "one China." He said that amendments to the ROC constitution in 1991[97] had transformed cross-Strait relations into a "state-to-state, or at least special state-to-state" relationship, not an internal relationship between a legitimate government and a renegade group or a domestic relationship between a central government and a local government within "one

---

[95] Ibid.

[96] See Suettinger, *Beyond Tiananmen*, pp. 351-380.

[97] While not yielding the ROC's formal claim to sovereignty over all of China, as noted earlier, the amendments limited the effective jurisdiction of the constitution to Taiwan, the Penghus and Jinmen and Matsu.

China."[98]   This "two states theory," as it quickly became known, predictably set off a hail of recriminations in China. Beijing offered a stern warning to "rein in at the brink of the precipice."[99]

Lee's statement also created consternation in the United States, and officials were quickly dispatched to both Beijing and Taipei to make clear Washington's unhappiness with—and non-support for—Lee's latest rhetorical excursion. A Defense Department team that had been scheduled to go to Taiwan to assess air defense needs was postponed, but there was no break in the overall arms sales relationship. And on July 21st, President Clinton addressed these questions in a White House press conference.

The President commented that one pillar of his China policy was pursuit of a peaceful approach, and he issued an indirect warning that the PRC should not react with military measures by reaffirming his adherence to the TRA, noting that any attempt to resolve differences by other than peaceful means would be a matter of the "gravest concern" to the United States. A second pillar was promotion of cross-Strait dialogue. And the third, which conveyed a blunt message to Lee Teng-hui, was adherence to the "one China" policy.

In September, Washington underscored its fidelity to the "one China" policy by speaking out in the UN against the motion to consider Taiwan's interest in joining the world body, the first time the U.S. had taken the initiative to actively join the debate in New York since similar measures had first been introduced several years earlier.

---

[98] Chinese language text provided by TECRO on July 10, 1999. Various translations are available online, one of which is found at http://www.taiwandc. org/nws-9926.htm

[99] See "Spokesman on Lee Teng-hui's Separatist Malice," July 11, 1999, Taiwan Work Office of the Chinese Communist Party Central Committee and the Taiwan Affairs Office of the State Council, available at http://www.china-embassy.org/eng/6918.html. In July 1999, one report of undetermined reliability stated that, at an enlarged Politburo on July 12th, Jiang Zemin warned that if Lee did not stop all independence activities, "we shall immediately announce moves to liberate Taiwan by military means and complete the great cause of national reunification"; see Lo Ping, "Political Bureau Studies New Strategy Against Taiwan," Cheng Ming, no. 262 (August 1999), pp. 9-11, online at http://www.globalsecurity.org/wmd/library/news/china/1999/fbis-chi-1999-0807.htm

Here it is instructive to consider that the firm American rebuff of Lee apparently had an important effect in constraining the PRC reaction. Beijing had frequently argued that, if it were not for U.S. support, Taiwan independence tendencies could not prosper. By making clear the U.S. did not support, and indeed rejected, the "two states theory," Washington provided Beijing with important political maneuvering room to handle this latest development in a more moderate fashion.

That said, the "two states theory" was a watershed in PRC views of Lee, whom it now saw as an unremitting Taiwan independence ideologue. Thus, the mollifying effect of the U.S. stance was not so great as to deter an apparent decision by Beijing to begin preparing the PLA in earnest to use force against Taiwan at some future time, if necessary. There is a range of views in the expert community about whether China's active military modernization program dates from this period or from the events of 1995/1996. In fact, relevant steps were probably taken at both times. For our purposes, the important common point to note is that, while PLA modernization would have proceeded in any event—and had been called for ever since the first Gulf War demonstrated the military gap with the United States, indeed even well before that—the developing concerns over Taiwan gave a sharp boost, and a focus, to the effort. Moreover, based on the U.S. aircraft carrier deployments in 1996, the United States now figured importantly as a likely participant in PLA planning for any Taiwan contingency.

At their meeting on the margins of the APEC leaders conference in Auckland, New Zealand that fall, Clinton commiserated with Jiang Zemin about Lee Teng-hui's role as "troublemaker," though the President also felt constrained to repeat his warning to Jiang not to ratchet up military pressure on Taiwan.[100] While Clinton did not have reason to seriously anticipate a military attack against Taiwan in 1999, an important long-term effect of the developments that we have been discussing is that the possibility of eventual major power war involving the United States and China has become increasingly real.

CHINA UPS THE ANTE: THE FEBRUARY 2000 TAIWAN WHITE PAPER

This danger was underscored in late February 2000 by the PRC's second Taiwan "White Paper." That treatise was in part a response—

---

[100] Kan, *China/Taiwan: Evolution of the "One China" Policy—Key Statements from Washington, Beijing and Taipei*, p. 51.

albeit long delayed—to Lee Teng-hui's *Deutsche Welle* interview and in part a caution to Taiwan voters on the eve of their presidential election. Beijing was concerned that in that election Lee was actually backing, not his own party's candidate, but Chen Shui-bian, the candidate of the Democratic Progressive Party (DPP), which had long advocated Taiwan independence.

The White Paper charged Lee with progressively betraying the "one China" principle, culminating in his "two states theory." It warned that if Taiwan denied the "one China" principle and tried to separate Taiwan from China, "the premise and basis for peaceful reunification will cease to exist."

It also rehearsed American culpability in this matter starting with the Korean War and called on the United States to fulfill "the series of promises" made in the three joint communiqués and elsewhere. "Acting otherwise will destroy the external conditions necessary for the Chinese government to strive for peaceful reunification."

Having issued these warnings, the paper then laid out what became known as the "three 'ifs'," the three conditions which, if realized, would require use of force against Taiwan. The last of these—the so-called "third 'if'"— incorporated into an official State document for the first time—and expanded on—Deng Xiaoping's warning twenty-one years before to Jimmy Carter about China's limited patience:

> [I]f a grave turn of events occurs leading to the separation of Taiwan from China in any name, or if Taiwan is invaded and occupied by foreign countries, or *if the Taiwan authorities refuse, sine die, the peaceful settlement of cross-Straits reunification through negotiations*, then the Chinese government will only be forced to adopt all drastic measures possible, including the use of force, to safeguard China's sovereignty and territorial integrity and fulfill the great cause of reunification.[101]

---

[101] *The One-China Principle and the Taiwan Issue*, released on February 21, 2000 by the Taiwan Affairs Office and Information Office of the State Council, online at http://www.china-embassy.org/eng/7128.html; emphasis added. The expansion came in the fact that Deng had spoken of the unacceptability of indefinite delay in *talking about* reunification; the White Paper made explicit what Deng had left implicit, that what was required was *agreement* on reunification. I am indebted to Richard Bush of the Brookings Institution for pointing out that the "first 'if'" contained a warning that, not just a formal declaration of independence, but, if taken far enough, *de facto* separatist

Reflecting the American perspective on the deal struck in normalization, Clinton responded a few days later, rejecting the use of force and making "absolutely clear" that cross-Strait issues must be resolved peacefully "and with the assent of the people of Taiwan."[102]

The grim reality of this situation, and resentment at efforts from both sides of the Strait to manipulate it, led the United States not just to caution Beijing once more about the use of force, but also to renew warnings to Taiwan about the risks to U.S. support if Taipei provoked a cross-Strait crisis.[103]

Even as a candidate for the Republican presidential nomination, while he expressed strong support for helping Taiwan defend itself under the TRA, George W. Bush also voiced his support for the "one China" policy, which he considered to be in the U.S. national interest. In the wake of the White Paper, Bush heightened his rhetoric—and reduced the level of ambiguity—regarding his intention to support Taiwan against any PRC military action. But, whether coincidental or not, one of the candidate's strongest statements underscoring the benefits *to Taiwan* of the "one China" policy also came only ten days after the White Paper was issued.[104]

---

measures short of that—i.e., separation "in any name"—could also trigger use of force.

[102] Kan, *China/Taiwan: Evolution of the "One China" Policy—Key Statements from Washington, Beijing and Taipei*, p. 53. This was the first time the "assent of the Taiwan people" was specifically mentioned. It may have been designed to reject a peaceful but coerced settlement, but the reality is that any kind of government-to-government deal over the heads of the Taiwan people had, in fact, been out of the question since at least the mid-1980s.

[103] Although the point was later given new emphasis, shortly before Lee's *Deutsche Welle* interview, Clinton had already made it: "We've maintained our strong, unofficial ties to a democratic Taiwan while upholding our one China policy. We've encouraged both sides to resolve their differences peacefully and to have increased contact. *We've made clear that neither can count on our acceptance if it violates these principles*" (White House Office of the Press Secretary, "Remarks by the President in Foreign Policy Speech," April 7, 1999, online at http://clinton6.nara.gov/1999/04/1999-04-07-remarks-by-the-president-in-foreign-policy-speech.html). Emphasis added.

[104] "Text: GOP Debate in Los Angeles," March 2, 2000, online at http://www.washingtonpost.com/wp-srv/politics/campaigns/wh2000/stories/text030200.htm

In March 2000, two days before Taiwan's presidential election, PRC Premier Zhu Rongji held a press conference at the conclusion of the National People's Congress. Responding to questions, he defended the recently-issued Taiwan White Paper in tough language, noting that without the "two states theory" there would not have been any need for a White Paper. He said that those Americans who criticized it—and especially (though he didn't use the term) the "third 'if'"—either had not read the paper or were unfriendly to the PRC and simply wanted to hang onto Taiwan as an unsinkable aircraft carrier to confront the Mainland.

When he turned to the Taiwan election, Zhu moved in short order from a hands-off approach:

> The election in Taiwan is a local election and, therefore, it is a matter of Taiwan people themselves and we won't interfere with it.

to a warning:

> Whoever stands for one China will get our support…Whoever continues Taiwan independence will not end up well.

an accusation:

> In the past few days, the Taiwan election campaign has been conducted with every possible treachery and scheme.

> There have been significant and dramatic changes with regard to the campaign. Every trick possible has been employed and used. However, the hidden intention (of these tricks) in my view is clear for anyone to see. It is clear that someone is trying to use the tricks to make the one who is for Taiwan independence to win the election.

and a threat:

> Now people of Taiwan are in a very critical and historical juncture and I advise all people in Taiwan not to act on their impulse since this juncture will decide the future of both sides across the Straits.

I am afraid you won't have another opportunity to regret…Please be vigilant![105]

On March 18th, Chen Shui-bian was narrowly elected over his divided opposition. China announced that it would listen to his words and watch his actions. In his inaugural address on May 20, 2000, Chen said:

> [A]s long as the CCP regime has no intention to use military force against Taiwan, I pledge that during my term in office, I will not declare independence, I will not change the national title, I will not push for the inclusion of the so-called "state-to-state" description in the Constitution, and I will not promote a referendum to change the status quo in regards to the question of independence or unification.[106]

The Clinton Administration appreciated this stand and, even more, that there had been a democratic and orderly transition of power—for the first time—from one party in Taiwan to another. Still, having gone through the trauma of the Lee Teng-hui visit and its aftermath, when Chen wanted to transit the United States in August of that year on his way to the Caribbean, the Administration insisted that he and his party follow strict ground rules, including no public events, no media reporting, and no meetings with Members of Congress. This caused a storm of protest, especially from Representative Dana Rohrabacher (R-CA), who managed to cause enough of a ruckus that Chen met quietly with him for a few minutes in his Los Angeles hotel.

This experience, and anger over a military incident off the coast of Hainan, would lead the Bush Administration to take a different approach.

---

[105] "Full Text of Premier Zhu's Press Conference," *People's Daily*, March 16, 2000, online at http://www.fas.org/news/china/2000/eng20000316N107.htm

[106] Taiwan Stands Up: Toward the Dawn of A Rising Era," online at http://www.taipei.org/chen/chen0520.htm.

8

Bush Takes Office:
A Changing Relationship in a Changing World

"...what the Chinese need to assume is that if they violate the one-China policy, the long-standing one-China policy which has clearly said that the United States expects there to be a peaceful resolution between China and Taiwan, if they decide to use force, the United States must help Taiwan defend itself. Now, the Chinese can figure out what that means, but that's going to mean a resolute stand on my part."

—George W. Bush, March 2000

Although Bush later denied any connection between the airplane incident over the South China Sea on April 1, 2001 and various decisions relating to Taiwan, it would seem that, at the very least, attitudes were affected. If there had, for example, been any inclination to apply restraint to the first Taiwan arms sales package in the Bush Administration,[1] it went out the window when pilot Wang Wei's PLA Navy F-8 collided with a lumbering U.S. Navy EP-3 reconnaissance aircraft in international airspace and the crew of the American plane, after successfully making an emergency landing at a Chinese air force base on Hainan island, was held for eleven days. While the mini-crisis over release of the crew—and later the plane—did not revolve specifically around Taiwan issues, the fact is that the reconnaissance missions were strongly related to a perceived acceleration of PLA acquisitions, deployments and training exercises directed against the island.

Moreover, beyond giving a brief rebirth to the description of China as a "strategic competitor,"[2] the fallout from the incident had important

---

[1] Recommendations for a robust arms sales package were already well advanced, as reported on the very day of the incident (Michael R. Gordon, "Secret U.S. Study Concludes Taiwan Needs New Arms," *New York Times,* April 1, 2001).

[2] The President himself had only used that phrase once in the election campaign,

implications for Taiwan and for U.S. policy, especially in the area of arms sales and other security relationships with the island.

At the conclusion of the incident, the President spoke of common interests between the United States and China, and urged:

> Both the United States and China must make a determined choice to have a productive relationship that will contribute to a more secure, more prosperous and more peaceful world.[3]

And in many important respects, he imposed that view on his administration, especially after the terrorist attacks of September 11th. But in the interim, Bush took a number of steps with respect to Taiwan that had significant reverberations.

On April 23rd, he decided on a major new arms package for Taiwan, offering several billions of dollars worth of equipment. The package included eight diesel-powered submarines[4] and four 1970s-era Kidd-class destroyers with upgraded radar systems, as well as anti-submarine aircraft, anti-ship missiles, minesweeping helicopters and various other items. It also included briefings on, but not sale of, PAC-3 missile defense weapons. Bush held off approval of state-of-the-art Aegis-equipped destroyers that Taiwan requested,[5] but said he would revisit the issue in a year or two "and would be inclined to approve such a sale if China continues to add to a 300-plus arsenal of ballistic missiles pointed

---

in a television interview in 1999, but it had somehow come to be picked up by the media as if it were his stock descriptor. Bush did use "competitor" quite frequently, but not "strategic competitor." Some of his senior advisers did occasionally use it, however.

[3] White House Office of the Press Secretary, "Remarks by the President Upon the Return from China of U.S. Service Members," April 12, 2001, online at http://usinfo.state.gov/regional/ea/uschina/crewrose.htm

[4] The submarines not only have not been delivered, but as of fall 2003 a supplier had not been identified. Moreover, Taiwan has been very slow to pick up on most of the other offers, creating some tension with U.S. officials who believe Taiwan must do much more for its own defense. Only in summer 2003 were there signs that Taipei would proceed with a number of the big-ticket items from the April 2001 package.

[5] These fleet air-defense systems were particularly neuralgic for Beijing due to their upgrade potential, which could conceivably permit the incorporation of certain ballistic missile defense capabilities. In the meantime, however, as cost factors have been scrutinized in Taiwan's legislature, Taipei's enthusiasm for Aegis has waned.

toward Taiwan."[6] Were he to do so—and the PRC's missile arsenal is still growing—it would likely set off a major row with Beijing.

PRC reaction to the overall offer—the largest single package with the exception of the F-16 sale in 1992—was swift and sharp. Vice Foreign Minister Li Zhaoxing protested to Ambassador Joseph Prueher that the sale was a "flagrant violation" of the three joint communiqués—especially the August 17 Communiqué—and "an open provocation to China's sovereignty and territorial integrity." In addition to emboldening Taiwan independence forces, Li charged, the move would "seriously impact" bilateral cooperation on nonproliferation.[7]

Li had hardly finished making his protest, however, when Charles Gibson of ABC-TV's *Good Morning America* asked Bush if the United States had an obligation to defend Taiwan if the island were attacked by the PRC. "Yes, we do," the President responded. With the full force of the American military? "Whatever it took to help Taiwan defend herself."[8]

Bush and his aides spent much of the rest of the day trying to reshape that answer to stress continuity with the policies of previous administrations. Speaking with John King of CNN, who asked about the *Good Morning America* remarks, the President started his response by citing the TRA and the "one China" policy, saying he strongly backed them both.

> [W]e expect any dispute to be resolved peacefully, and that's the message I really want people to hear.
>
> But as people have seen, that I'm willing to help Taiwan defend herself, and that nothing has really changed in policy, as far as

---

[6] John King, "U.S. Official: Taiwan Arms Sale Will Address Imbalance," *CNN*, April 23, 2001, online at http://edition.cnn.com/2001/ALLPOLITICS/04/23/bush.taiwan.04/index.html?s=1. In the intervening years, that force has grown to an estimated 450 missiles and is increasing at the rate of 75 per year.

[7] Embassy of the People's Republic of China in the United States, "China Strongly Protests U.S. Arms Sales to Taiwan (04/25/01)," press release online at http://www.china-embassy.org/eng/10040.html.

[8] "President Bush Discusses His First 100 Days in Office," *Good Morning America*, April 25, 2001 (transcript by *ABC News*).

I'm concerned. This is what other presidents have said, and I will continue to say so.[9]

Asked what his attitude would be if an attack grew out of a Taiwan declaration of independence, Bush drew on the formulation he had used in the Los Angeles debate a year earlier:

> I certainly hope Taiwan adheres to the one-China policy. And a declaration of independence is not the one-China policy, and we will work with Taiwan to make sure that that doesn't happen. We need a peaceful resolution of this issue.[10]

During the course of the day, in several other on-the-record and background interviews, the spinmeisters continued to underscore that there was nothing new intended, and while the President was serious in his concern about Taiwan's security, and use of American force was "certainly an option," Bush's emphasis was on peaceful resolution.[11]

The confusion about the bottom-line message was so great that, while some PRC media launched into tirades (the official *Guangming Daily* pulled out all the stops, including a call for Washington to "rein in at the precipice"[12]), the Party paper *People's Daily* focused in calmer fashion on Bush's later clarification that there was no change in policy.[13]

The good news for Beijing that week was that Taiwan's now-former president, Lee Teng-hui, postponed a planned trip to the United States.[14]

---

[9] "U.S. President George W. Bush's First 100 Days," *CNN International*, April 25, 2001 (transcript by *CNN*).

[10] Ibid.

[11] Ron Hutcheson, "Bush Would Do 'Whatever It Took' To Defend Taiwan Against China," *Knight Ridder/Tribune News Service,* April 26, 2001. In light of the subsequent scrambling, one official seemed to take defense of the President's words a little far in telling Knight-Ridder "Obviously, the president chose his words carefully."

[12] "China Warns US It Will Pay Any Price to Recover Taiwan," *Agence France Presse,* April 27, 2001.

[13] James Kynge, "China Adopts Muted Tone to Limit Row," *Financial Times* (London), April 27, 2001.

[14] Lee postponed his trip once again, from May to June, but he eventually made the trip to Cornell in late June, to a much more low-key reception than in 1995. Once he was out of office, the U.S. believed it had no basis to even consider denying him a visa.

The bad news was that it had to look forward to an extended transit of the U.S. by the current president, Chen Shui-bian, under much more liberal ground rules than had applied during his transit in August 2000 under the Clinton Administration. Chen would stop in New York City in late May for two or three days on his way to Latin America and in Houston in early June on his way home, in both cases engaging in highly visible "private" activities, including with Members of Congress. Beijing was having to adjust to the fact that the previous considerations of "safety, comfort and convenience" governing the transits of senior Taiwan travelers through the United States had been supplemented by the Bush Administration with one more criterion: "dignity."

The Chinese Foreign Ministry spokeswoman was doubtless speaking from the heart when she said, as had Li Zhaoxing in his protest to Prueher, that U.S-PRC relations had entered a "complicated and sensitive stage."[15] With Bush scheduled to attend the APEC leaders meeting in Shanghai in October and then move on to Beijing for a bilateral summit, PRC government officials and scholars were buttonholing every American they could to ask how to shape a successful Bush visit. Meanwhile, the English-language *China Daily*, having carried one of the more strident articles slamming the April 23rd arms sales decision,[16] now printed one of the most moderate articles about the Chen transit, pointing to its "private and unofficial" character, noting the prohibition on any "public or media events," and citing with obvious approval Colin Powell's reassuring words that this in no way modified, changed, or cast doubt on existing policy.[17]

Although China was able to roll with the Chen transit, the Lee visit, and the prospective arms sales, a series of issues that arose in this same period over U.S. missile defense, nuclear policy and long-range military planning suggested that, whether it clung to the term "strategic competitor" or not, the Bush Administration—or at least important parts of the national security team—viewed China as an inevitable, long-term strategic rival. And the most likely flashpoint, indeed the only one that

---

[15] Michael A. Lev, "Beijing Softens Anti-U.S. Rhetoric," *Chicago Tribune,* April 27, 2001.

[16] "Arms Sales to Taiwan Violate Agreements," *China Daily,* April 25, 2001, online at http://www.china.com.cn/english/11841.htm

[17] "US: Chen Shui-bian's Transit 'Private and Unofficial,'" *People's Daily*, May 15, 2001, online at http://fpeng.peopledaily.com.cn/200105/15/eng20010515_70014.html.

anyone could identify, was Taiwan. Thus, at least one foreign correspondent found Beijing in an anxious mood as summer approached.[18]

In the context of several visits by ranking State Department officials, U.S. Trade Representative Robert Zoellick's trip to Beijing in June, in particular, convinced many Chinese that the Bush Administration was serious about getting the relationship back on track,[19] and Colin Powell's visit to the PRC in late July took the recovery effort several steps further. Even before he got to China, Powell declared the EP-3 incident "behind us," and as he approached Beijing, certain high-profile human rights cases were moved toward resolution.[20] Still, although Taiwan was not particularly neuralgic in this period, Jiang Zemin felt obliged to reiterate to Powell the "principled stance" of the Chinese government on Taiwan, to which Powell responded with appropriate obeisance to the "one China" policy.[21]

IN THE WAKE OF 9-11:
ONCE MORE RESHAPING THE RELATIONSHIP

The world changed on September 11, 2001. Jiang was watching television when the images of the burning World Trade Center, and then the Pentagon, flashed on the screen. He instinctively grasped the importance of offering unstinting support to Bush at that moment of desperation, and his staff worked furiously on a condolence message as the clock neared midnight in Beijing so that it could be dated the 11th.[22] While it is too early even two years later to judge the ultimate impact of September 11th on Sino-American relations, it quite clearly provided a window of opportunity for both sides to move to greater cooperation in a way each had already determined was in its interest.

As the initial PRC verbal support for the war on terrorism began to assume substantive depth, and as China determined that it would not

---

[18] John Pomfret, "China Growing Uneasy About U.S. Relations; Bush's Comments Cited as Catalyst," *Washington Post,* June 23, 2001, A1.

[19] Report by an American scholar who was in China at the time.

[20] "Remarks Following Bilateral Meeting with Chinese Foreign Minister Tang," July 25, 2001, online at http://www.state.gov/secretary/rm/2001/4277pf.htm

[21] "Sino-US Ties Improving: President Jiang," *People's Daily,* July 28, 2001, online at http://fpeng.peopledaily.com.cn/200107/28/eng20010728_76007.html.

[22] From a Chinese official.

vigorously oppose the United States on any issue unless absolutely forced to,[23] Washington reciprocated. This did not lead to a switch of U.S. "allegiance" from Taiwan to the Mainland, as some in Taipei feared. But it did lower the threshold of American impatience with gamesmanship from Taipei.

Although George Bush cancelled the Beijing bilateral summit in fall 2001, eventually rescheduling it for early the next year, he decided to attend the October APEC leaders meeting in Shanghai as planned, where he focused on garnering support from his APEC partners on the war on terrorism. He also seized the opportunity for a bilateral meeting with Jiang Zemin.

The focus of their meeting was on other issues, but Jiang could not pass up the opportunity—twice—in their joint press conference to remind Bush of the importance of handling bilateral ties, "especially the question of Taiwan," in accordance with the three joint communiqués. Bush, on the other hand, confined himself to a brief comment: "I explained my views on Taiwan and preserving regional stability in East Asia."[24]

In a later background briefing by a senior American official, this was expanded slightly to explain that President Bush had reaffirmed "very strongly" his commitment to the Taiwan Relations Act and his belief that Taiwan should be treated with respect. But, implicitly addressing the concerns raised by events of the spring, Bush also made clear that American policy toward Taiwan remained unchanged.[25] That said, Chinese officials took note of the fact that there was no public American reference to the "one China" policy or the three communiqués.[26]

When President Bush returned to China in February 2002 for the rescheduled bilateral summit meeting, the two leaders gave somewhat

---

[23] In some cases, such as Korea, pro-active cooperation became the order of the day.

[24] White House Office of the Press Secretary, "U.S., China Stand Against Terrorism: Remarks by President Bush and President Jiang Zemin in Press Availability," October 19, 2001, online at http://www.whitehouse.gov/news/releases/2001/10/print/20011019-4.html.

[25] White House Office of the Press Secretary, "Background Briefing by a Senior Administration Official on President Bush's Meetings with Chinese President Jiang Zemin and South Korean President Kim Dae Jung," October 19, 2001, online at http://www.usconsulate.org.hk/uscn/wh/2001/101902.htm

[26] From private conversations with author.

different emphases in their press conference remarks. Jiang homed in on "proper handling" of the Taiwan question as "vital to stability and growth" of U.S.-PRC ties. He said that, in their private meeting, he had laid out the Chinese position on peaceful reunification and "one country, two systems" for resolving the Taiwan question. Jiang also reported that Bush had emphasized U.S. adherence to the "one China" policy and the three joint U.S.-PRC communiqués.

Bush reported that the U.S. position on Taiwan had "not changed over the years." America believed in peaceful settlement of the issue and urged no provocation. The President also voiced continuing fidelity to the TRA. He made no public mention of either the three communiqués or direct reference to the "one China" policy, although the Chinese briefer asserted, as had Jiang, that in the meeting Bush had reaffirmed his commitment to both.[27]

In her later briefing on the meeting, National Security Adviser Condoleezza Rice noted that the President's point on provocations was that there should be no provocation from either side of the Strait. She said that Bush had expressed hope that China would be cognizant of changes in the security environment, and "how that affects American obligations under the Taiwan Relations Act." When asked if Bush had mentioned the three communiqués, as Jiang told the press he had, Rice merely responded that the President had affirmed that American policy has remained consistent since the "'79 agreements."

Speaking at Tsinghua University the next day, after a speech about freedom and American dedication to the rule of law, the first question from the audience was about Taiwan—why the United States always spoke about "peaceful resolution" and not "peaceful reunification." Bush never quite answered the question, indeed ducked it twice, focusing his answer on the importance of "peaceful dialogue" and "peaceful settlement," which he said he hoped would come about in his lifetime or that of his university audience. Bush went on, however, to finally voice direct support for the "one China" policy.

Asked about the three communiqués and the "three noes," Bush responded indirectly: "[W]hen my country makes an agreement, we stick

---

[27] Foreign Ministry spokesman Zhu Bangzao, cited in "PRC FM Spokesman: Bush Reaffirms 'One China' Stand in Meeting with Jiang Zemin," *Zhongguo Tongxun She*, October 19, 2001, translated by FBIS (FBIS-CHI-2001-1019).

with it."[28] He then moved immediately again to the TRA—and the issue of provocation:

> And there is [what is] called the Taiwan Relations Act, and I honor that act, which says we will help Taiwan defend herself if provoked. But we've also sent the same message that there should be no provocation by either party for a peaceful dialogue.

The President's reluctance to actually speak the mantra—the commitment to the "one China" policy and the three communiqués—might have hidden some deeper reluctance to pursue a policy consistent with what had gone before. Especially with regard to Taiwan's security, it is obvious that Bush does not wish to be bound by an interpretation of the August 17 Communiqué that would consign Taiwan to a widening gap in capabilities.

Taken as a whole, however, while the early signs were troubling, it seems that Bush has in fact settled on an approach that is very much in line with the policies of the past quarter-century. He has stretched the limits in some respects—for example, on the ground rules for transits by senior Taiwan officia ls. And the arms package he approved in April 2001 exceeded both previous limits and what many military professionals deemed sensible (especially with regard to the submarines). But he has come down squarely against provocative actions from Taipei—his repeated warnings in Beijing on this subject seemed at least equally directed at the island as at the PRC. And he has enforced on his Administration a tone that speaks of China not as an enemy but as willing contributor and even as a partner in important respects. Although he would no doubt recoil from the notion, the reality is that President Bush's Taiwan policy has almost totally embraced that of President Clinton, including the "three noes," even though he would never mouth those words.

PERENNIAL ISSUES: ARMS SALES AND TAIWAN INDEPENDENCE

For the Bush Administration, the two most problematic points in dealing with Taiwan at present remain arms sales and Taiwan's "status." Both relate, of course, to the core issue of sovereignty.

---

[28] One presumes he was addressing this remark to the communiqués, not the "three noes."

On the former, the focus has shifted from meeting Taiwan's seemingly boundless requests to getting Taipei to follow through on what has been approved and to get its organizational and doctrinal house in order. A combination of budgetary constraints and what is seen—in some quarters, anyway—as a growing reliance on U.S. deterrence has produced pressure from Washington for Taipei to focus on its real needs, instead of seeking glitzy items that may symbolize U.S. backing but are expensive and hard to integrate into the island's military.

When Deputy Secretary of Defense Paul Wolfowitz and Assistant Secretary of State James Kelly met separately with Taiwan Defense Minister Tang Yiau-ming at a U.S.-Taiwan Business Council meeting in Florida in March 2002, Beijing's apoplexy was on full display. In addition to canceling U.S. Navy ship visits to Hong Kong for a brief period,[29] on March 16th Vice Foreign Minister Li Zhaoxing summoned U.S. Ambassador Clark T. Randt. Li cited the fact of Tang's visit and reports of a visit "by another military official of Taiwan," the conversations with Wolfowitz and Kelly, rumors of another visit by Lee Teng-hui, and a recently publicized Defense Department *Nuclear Posture Review* that allegedly said nuclear weapons "would be used" in the event of a military confrontation in the Taiwan Strait.[30] Noting that the Taiwan question, and the issue of China's sovereignty and territorial integrity, remains the most important and sensitive issue "at the heart of China-U.S. relations" and demanding that the U.S. honor the "explicit commitments" it made in three communiqués, Li went on in high dudgeon:

> People cannot but ask: to where does the U.S. side intend to lead China-US relations. You talked about hoping to see a peaceful settlement between the two sides of the Taiwan Straits. Is what you are doing promoting peace? You repeatedly said that the United States pursues a one-China policy and abides by the three

---

[29] They were resumed a month later (John Tkacik, Jr., *Stating America's Case to China's Hu Jintao: A Primer on U.S.—China— Taiwan Policy*, Heritage Foundation Report No. 1541, April 26, 2002).

[30] Actually, the excerpts of the Nuclear Posture Review that have become publicly available do not say the nuclear weapons "would be used" in a military confrontation over Taiwan but, rather, that military confrontation over the status of Taiwan is "among the contingencies for which the United States must be prepared" in determining U.S. nuclear force requirements. For the excerpts, see http://www.globalsecurity.org/wmd/library/policy/dod/npr.htm

Sino-U.S. Joint Communiqués. Is any part of your acts mentioned above consistent with these Joint Communiqués?[31]

When the text of Wolfowitz's address in Florida was subsequently released, Beijing probably also noted his reference to increasing PRC military deployments—especially the growing number of short-range missiles opposite Taiwan in a threatening posture as well as naval modernization—as indicators that, whatever Beijing's expressed preferences, peaceful resolution of cross-Strait issues could not be taken for granted. Citing the TRA, the Deputy Defense Secretary resurrected Bush's assertion from a year before that "the United States is committed to doing whatever it takes to help Taiwan defend itself."[32] He went on to comment on the underlying political issue:

> We don't support Taiwan independence, but we oppose the use of force. We believe that the PRC and Taiwan should engage directly in dialogue to resolve peacefully the issues that divide them.

He then hit the themes of Taiwan's military reform:

> Taiwan needs reform in its defense establishment to meet the challenges of the 21st century...This reform includes strengthening civilian oversight of the military...It includes rationalizing the military acquisition process...And it definitely includes enhancing jointness between Taiwan's three services...
>
> [W]e hope that the civilian and military leadership in Taiwan will look at these kinds of issues from a professional perspective...

And he cited American willingness to get involved:

---

[31] "China Summons US Ambassador to Make Representations," *People's Daily*, March 18, 2002, online at http://english.peopledaily.com.cn/200203/17/ eng20020317_92254.shtml.

[32] Wolfowitz repeated this line in remarks to an international audience at the so-called "Shangri-La Dialogue," an Asia Security Conference sponsored in Singapore by the International Institute for Strategic Studies (IISS) on June 1, 2002; see his address, entitled "The Gathering Storm: The Threat of Global Terror and Asia/Pacific Security," online at http://www.defenselink.mil/ speeches/2002/s20020601-depsecdef.html.

[W[e have had a lot of experience [with these challenges] over the years, and we are eager to help. Just as important as arms sales issues, these non-hardware or software exchanges serve very important purposes. They can help Taiwan to better integrate newly-acquired systems into its inventory…[and help define] requirements for defense modernization, to include professionalization, organizational issues, and training.

Moreover, these types of exchanges enhance Taiwan's ability to assess longer-term defense needs, and develop well-founded security policies. Such exchanges enhance Taiwan capacity for making operationally sound and cost effective acquisition decisions.[33]

What Wolfowitz did not say, and what remains an issue of contention within the United States, as well as in both Taipei and Beijing, is whether the U.S. seeks—or should seek—interoperability between American and Taiwan forces. The argument in favor is that, in a contingency, if the U.S. chose to become militarily involved, the two forces would be able to act in a coordinated fashion and, not unimportant, stay out of each other's way. The argument against is that it smacks of a reconstituted security alliance, in direct contravention of the terms of normalization, and would likely create serious strains in Sino-American ties and raise cross-Strait tensions.

When the PRC's then-vice president (now president), Hu Jintao, traveled to Washington in spring 2002, with both President Bush and other audiences, he handled the Taiwan question in low-key fashion, repeating the standard warnings about the need to manage the issue properly and noting that failure to do so could lead not just to stagnation

---

[33] "Remarks to U.S.-Taiwan Business Council," March 11, 2002, available online at http://www.defenselink.mil/pubs/foi/twn_us_council.pdf. A year later, Deputy Assistant Secretary of State for East Asian and Pacific Affairs, Randall Schriver, addressed the same group in San Antonio, Texas—and he made many of the same points about reform: modernization of the command and control architecture, jointness, prioritization of acquisition focusing on modern air and missile defense systems and anti-submarine warfare capabilities, and strengthened civilian control ("U.S.-Taiwan Relations: Remarks to the U.S.-Taiwan Business Council Defense Industry Conference," February 14, 2003, online at http://www.state.gov/p/eap/rls/rm/2003/17796pf.htm).

but even to retrogression in U.S.-PRC relations. But he avoided the more colorful rhetoric employed by Vice Minister Li in March.[34]

On Taiwan independence, the imprecision in the administration's articulation of its stance has created something of a muddle, and grist for endless press speculation. As we have seen, in Florida, Wolfowitz said that the United States "does not support" Taiwan independence, a formulation consistent with what has been said by policy officials for over thirty years. But on other occasions he has slipped, stating that the U.S. "opposes" Taiwan independence.[35] This may have been welcome in the ears of Beijing, but, if truly reflective of policy, would have inserted the United States back into the middle of the substantive issue from which it had assiduously sought to escape. Even more relevant, President Bush has been cited by PRC media as having told President Jiang Zemin on more than one occasion that the United States "opposes" Taiwan independence.[36]

Deputy Secretary of State Richard Armitage tried to explain the nuances at a Beijing press conference:

> The wording is important. By saying we do not support, it's one thing. It's different from saying we oppose it. If people on both sides of the Strait came to an agreeable solution, then the United States obviously wouldn't inject ourselves. Hence, we use the term we don't "support" it. But it's something to be resolved by the people on both sides of the question.[37]

---

[34] George Gedda, "China's President-in-Waiting Meets Bush, Stresses Need to Avoid Trouble on Taiwan," *Associated Press,* May 1, 2002. The text of Hu's remarks is available at "National Committee on U.S.-China Relations Remarks of Vice President Hu," *Federal News Service*, May 1, 2002.

[35] At a briefing at the Foreign Press Center in Washington, having earlier in the briefing repeated his Florida statement that the "we do not support independence for Taiwan," in answering the final question about the meaning of U.S. statements that it has no desire to separate Taiwan from the Mainland, Wolfowitz said: "I just think it's another [way] of saying we're opposed to Taiwan independence." See "Foreign Press Center 'Invitation Only' Briefing," *Federal News Service*, May 29, 2003.

[36] For example, see "US Policy Toward Taiwan Swings to the Middle," *People's Daily*, June 13, 2003, online at http://taiwansecurity.org/News/ 2003/PD-061303.htm

[37] "Transcript of Deputy Secretary of State Richard Armitage Press Conference—Conclusion of China Visit," August 26, 2002, online at

In fact, Armitage is right, but his explanation is only half the story. The other half is that the United States does *oppose* unilateral steps by Taiwan in the direction of independence that would upset the *status quo*. That is an important element in what President Bush meant when, echoing Secretary Christopher's line of some five years earlier, he said in Beijing in February 2002 that there should be no provocation from either side.

STEPPING OVER THE LINE: *YI BIAN, YI GUO*

Armitage's explanation came only weeks after Taipei had taken a step that the Administration did oppose. Having tolerated without comment a number of measures over the previous two years to remove words and symbols relating to "China" from government titles, logos, signs, and schoolbooks, replacing them with "Taiwan"—what Beijing called a "desinicization campaign"—on August 3, 2002, Chen Shui-bian exceeded even the Bush Administration's tolerance. In a telecast speech to the 29th Annual Meeting of the World Federation of Taiwanese Associations meeting in Tokyo, Chen made a series of statements that stepped over the line as far as the U.S. was concerned.

He said that there is "one country on either side" of the Taiwan Strait (*yi bian, yi guo*) and that Taiwan was neither a part, nor a province, of another country. He went on:

> Only Taiwan's 23 million people have the right to decide Taiwan's future or fate, or to change the status quo. And how can we make the decision if it becomes necessary? The answer is a public referendum, which is the goal and idea that we have been pursuing for a long time.

> I therefore sincerely appeal to and encourage all of us to consider the importance and urgency of passing a referendum law.[38]

Days before this threatened breach of his May 2000 presidential inaugural pledge not to seek a referendum on Taiwan's status, Chen had already thrown down the gauntlet, when in his inauguration speech as DPP Party Chairman on July 21st he had said that, unless Beijing responded to Taiwan's goodwill, Taiwan would have to seriously

---

http://usinfo.state.gov/regional/ea/uschina/armit826.htm

[38] Lin Chieh-yu, "Chen Raises Pitch of Anti-China Rhetoric," *Taipei Times,* August 4, 2002.

consider "going its own way."[39] He hardened that line ten days later when he said that, if China forsook its ambition to take Taiwan by force, *then* Taiwan would *not* change the *status quo*.[40]

In his August 3rd telecast, Chen tried to explain that Taiwan going its "own way" meant following a path of "democracy, freedom, human rights and peace."[41] But it is hard to square that explanation with the fact that he was raising that specter *if* China did not reciprocate Taiwan's goodwill and cease its threats. Was he saying that, if Beijing ceased its threats, Taiwan would *not* pursue democracy, freedom, human rights and peace? Whether he was serious or merely carried away by his own rhetoric is open to interpretation, but clearly in his original DPP inaugural statement, at least, he was raising a threat to move toward independence.

The reaction of the Bush Administration to *yi bian, yi guo* was not as openly critical of Taipei as had been the Clinton Administration's response to Lee Teng-hui's "two states theory." But the consternation was unmistakable.

Taipei hurriedly dispatched Mainland Affairs Council Chairperson Tsai Ing-wen to the United States to explain that Chen's statements were not a push for independence and that, in any case, the president's statements did not necessarily equate to policy. Both sides made an effort not to engage in a public spat. That said, the Administration's annoyance was on full display, and twice in his August 26 Beijing press conference, Armitage responded to questions about the U.S. reaction to *yi bian, yi guo* by stating that the United States did not support Taiwan independence, making clear what Washington thought it was all about.

Here was a case where the U.S. *opposed* an action that implied movement toward independence. But to avoid a public falling out, the Administration chose not to directly address Chen's statement itself, but

---

[39] Stephanie Low, "'Pan-Blue' Camp Asks Chen to Clarify Remarks," *Taipei Times*, July 23, 2002.

[40] Lin Mei-chun, "Chen Keeps the Pressure on Beijing," *Taipei Times*, July 31, 2002. Keep in mind the construction in his May 2000 inaugural address: "as long as the CCP regime has no intention to use military force against Taiwan" Chen pledged, he would not declare independence or push a referendum to change the status quo vis-à-vis independence or unification. In May 2000 his statement presumed no intention to use force yet existed; in July 2002 he was suggesting it did exist and, implicitly, that unless that changed, he would act.

[41] Lin, "Chen Raises Pitch of Anti-China Rhetoric."

rather to speak of the goal, and so it was sufficient to say that the United States "[did] not support" that goal.

The nuanced difference between "opposing" provocative actions and "not supporting" the end-state of independence has also been evident in the Administration's handling of the World Health Organization (WHO) membership issue. Taiwan has for seven years sought entry as an "observer" to the WHO's policymaking annual meeting, the World Health Assembly (WHA). The Bush Administration, like its predecessor, has supported this quest, though all agree it has no chance of succeeding as long as the PRC continues to object.

The U.S. position remains that granting Taiwan "observer" status at the WHA does not engage the question of statehood or sovereignty, both because Taiwan is not seeking formal membership and because, in recent years, Taipei has pressed its case as a "health entity" akin to its status in the World Trade Organization (WTO) as a "customs territory."

But in mid-2003, after the PRC once again blocked Taiwan's application for WHA observer status—this time in the context of the SARS scare that seemed to justify some different, closer tie to WHO—Chen Shui-bian decided to place a "referendum" before the people of Taiwan asking their views on this subject. This question was to join some other questions put in similar referendum form, such as whether to construct a fourth nuclear power plant or cut the size of the legislature in half. But there was a key difference: the other topics only affected developments within Taiwan; the WHO issue raised cross-Strait questions.

The PRC is opposed to referenda in Taiwan in general, fearing that once one, even innocuous subject were so decided, the door would be open to considering far more sensitive issues in the same way, including the most sensitive question of "unification vs. independence." Moreover, as we have just recalled, Chen raised the question of a referendum law on August 3rd *specifically* in connection with deciding Taiwan's status—not over a nuclear power plant or some other local concern.

There are indications that Beijing recognizes the likelihood, despite its objections, that all three referenda will be held, and that it is beginning to adopt a more nuanced approach. It seems to be heading in a direction where it will raise less heated objection to referenda on purely "local" topics, but will maintain its adamant opposition to any similar treatment of issues that touch on sovereignty and Taiwan's status, such as—as Beijing sees it—WHO.

Chen claims that, consistent with his May 2000 inaugural pledge, he has no intention of making the WHO referendum a test of sovereignty. But having had the PRC representative to the most recent WHA meeting voice disdainful dismissal of Taiwan's concerns in the middle of the SARS crisis—and having had a film clip of the delegate sarcastically snorting "Who cares about Taiwan?!" play endlessly on Taiwan television—Chen argues that he wants to demonstrate who cares: the twenty-three million people of Taiwan. The fact that this might enhance voter turnout of his supporters, especially if the referendum is held on the day of the presidential election in March 2004 is, Chen suggests, purely coincidental.

The Bush Administration does not want to be in a position of telling Taiwan it should not exercise its democratic rights by holding a referendum. At the same time, consistent with the stance that neither side should engage in provocation, Washington is obviously unhappy at having been placed in an uncomfortable position where it genuinely questions the wisdom of holding this particular referendum and yet has been confronted by Taipei with what is essentially a *fait accompli* and where objecting publicly would only make matters worse. It seems unlikely that this issue will lead to a serious rift with Taipei, at least if Chen's leading policy advisers are as careful in handling this issue as they privately insist they will be. And especially at a time when the PRC and the United States are fostering ever-deeper cooperation on the potentially explosive North Korea issue and groping toward agreement on international financial issues, Washington and Beijing will want to manage this issue carefully. Still, the potential for surprises in the heated atmosphere of Taiwan's presidential campaign cannot be altogether ruled out.

THE "SIX ASSURANCES" AGAIN

Early in the current Bush Administration, Secretary of State Colin L. Powell reaffirmed the validity of the "six assurances."[42] Senator Jesse Helms pressed Powell particularly on whether the new team planned to consult with Beijing on arms sales to Taiwan; he was assured it did not. That issue arose once again a year later when Assistant Secretary Kelly

---

[42] See his remarks to the Senate Committee on Foreign Relations in "U.S. Senator Jesse Helms (R-NC) Holds Hearing on U.S. Foreign Policy," *FDCH Political Transcripts*, March 8, 2001.

mentioned them in Florida at the March 2002 U.S.-Taiwan Business Council meeting.

As Kelly later explained, the "six assurances" have been part of the U.S. policy framework since 1982, and while perhaps not the subject of public speeches in the intervening years, they have frequently been mentioned in congressional testimony. Moreover, at the meeting in Florida he detected some apprehension that the United States might seek to come up with a "model" for a cross-Strait solution. He therefore wanted to make clear that, in accordance with the "six assurances," the United States had no intention of becoming a mediator or of trying to compel Taiwan to enter into talks.[43]

There are different views about whether the "six assurances" were meant to be a temporary fix to help Taiwan get past the trauma of the August 17 Communiqué, or whether they were intended as statements of policy that would guide U.S. actions for the indefinite future in the areas they covered. Most of them were drawn up as actions that the United States "had not" agreed to do; no reference was made to maintaining those positions indefinitely. Nonetheless, they reflected long-standing positions. And this writer's own practice when in government was, consistent with Kelly's view, to treat them as part of the body of policy documents that, taken together, defined U.S. China policy and its approach to handling cross-Strait issues.[44]

But they are no more engraved in stone than any other aspect of the policy, and they are subject to change if a President decides to change them. As with the other aspects of the policy, however, one needs to have in mind their history and the likely consequences of moving away from them. Part of any judgment about these matters must lie in determining the real effect. What would be the likely consequence, for example, if the United States sought to mediate cross-Strait relations? Or if Washington sought to pressure Taiwan into reunification negotiations? But another part of the assessment would have to do with the original

---

[43] "U.S. Policy Toward the East Asia Pacific Region," Briefing by James A. Kelly, Assistant Secretary of State for East Asian and Pacific Affairs at the Foreign Press Center, Washington, DC, March 14, 2002, *Federal News Service* transcript, online at http://fpc.state.gov/8787.htm.

[44] Stapleton Roy confirms that he treated them very much the same way, keeping them in his desk drawer along with the three communiqués, the TRA and other papers that constituted the framework of U.S. China/Taiwan policy (interview by author).

circumstances in which they were drawn up as an identifiable list and the fact that these provisions have been part of the policy for so long. As with the various elements of the three communiqués, the *very act* of making a change would have an impact, whatever the substitute concept.

In reality, however, there already has been a change of sorts. Whereas the "six assurances" speak of not amending the TRA, that Act now has in effect been amended, though not in a way that will trouble Taiwan and its congressional supporters.

On September 30, 2002, Congress enacted H.R. 1646, the Foreign Relations Authorization Act for fiscal year 2003.[45] That law contains several provisions affecting Taiwan, including one that grants Taiwan status of a "non-NATO ally." Although the wording is provocative—and the President took specific exception to it when he signed the bill[46]—it is a legislative device to make Taiwan eligible for transfer of certain kinds of defense services and articles, including dual-use items having both military and industrial applications, but not to accord it "alliance" status.

A little-noted provision, section 326, authorizes the Secretary of State to detail an active duty member of the Foreign Service—or any other career employee—to AIT and allows other agencies to do the same with the concurrence of the Secretary of State. This provision was sought by the Administration because of difficulty it was encountering in attracting sufficient qualified personnel for assignment to AIT under the stringent procedures requiring resignation from government upon assignment there and reemployment upon departure from AIT, and because of certain other hardships imposed on the staff by the present arrangement, including with respect to medical care. It has been estimated that the change has "significant implications" for the

---

[45] When the President signed the bill into law on September 30, 2002, it became PL 107-228.

[46] The President said: "Section 1206 could be misconstrued to imply a change in the 'one China' policy of the United States when, in fact, that U.S. policy remains unchanged. To the extent that this section could be read to purport to change United States policy, it impermissibly interferes with the President's constitutional authority to conduct the Nation's foreign affairs" (White House Office of the Press Secretary, "Statement by the President," September 30, 2002, online at http://www.whitehouse.gov/news/ releases/2002/09/print/20020930-8.html).

assignment of government officials to AIT, including active-duty military personnel.[47]

Not only was the pledge that unofficial relations with the people of Taiwan would be maintained "without official governmental representation" repeated in several sessions leading up to normalization,[48] but in answer to a specific question about who would staff the non-governmental representation on Taiwan, the answer the U.S. provided to China was:

> The permanent personnel of this American non-governmental organization would not be active government employees.[49]

As we have already noted, this same assurance was contained in a paper handed to the Chinese Ambassador by Deputy Secretary of State Warren Christopher in March 1979 when explaining that the TRA was consistent with the terms of normalization.[50]

The point is not that the basic understandings of normalization have been undermined by this change; the agency in Taiwan carrying out these functions remains an unofficial, non-governmental institution chartered under the laws of the District of Columbia. The new provisions for staffing do not change that but, rather, are similar to arrangements under which government personnel are frequently detailed to non-government institutions (e.g., universities) for periods of time.

But it is a departure from what was conveyed to Beijing in response to a specific question as the PRC was determining whether U.S. intentions met China's criteria on a question that had been a major stumbling block to normalization for several years. It is almost certain that, if the answer given to the question in 1978 and 1979 had been that the permanent personnel of this American non-governmental

---

[47] Shirley A. Kan, *Taiwan: Major U.S. Arms Sales Since 1990,* Congressional Research Service report RL30957, updated April 18, 2003, p. 15.

[48] For example, see WH81342, "Instructions for Woodcock's Fifth Round," October 19, 1978, op. cit., para. 7.

[49] WH 81517, "Sixth Round of Talks," November 14, 1978, Carter Library, conveying instructions used by Woodcock on December 4th with Han Nianlong (as confirmed by Peking 216, "Sixth Session: December 4 Meeting with Han Nien-lung," op. cit.).

[50] See p. 109: "The American Institute in Taiwan will not have any US Government employees..."

organization *would be* active government employees, it would have posed a major problem. Today, it should not. The record is sufficient to demonstrate that the United States has been generally careful to remain true to the bargain struck in this respect. Moreover, other exceptions made to the original procedures in the meantime, under the Taiwan Policy Review of 1993/94, for example, have far greater political importance than this one—even if they were not the subject of a specific question and response twenty-five years ago—and the relationship has survived.

Still, every time an adjustment to the understandings of normalization, however minor, comes up for consideration, responsible officials must be certain that, on balance, the benefits outweigh the costs. As Winston Lord put it in his testimony almost a decade ago, if one expects China to live up to its commitments, the United States must live up to its own.

CRAWFORD: HOME ON THE RANGE

President Bush welcomed President Jiang Zemin to his ranch at Crawford, Texas, on October 25, 2002. Given the way the President manages invitations to the ranch, this was a very positive signal regarding the state of the relationship. And Bush finally was willing in Jiang's presence to publicly cite the key commitments:

> On Taiwan, I emphasized to the President that our one China policy, based on the three communiqués in [sic] the Taiwan Relations Act, remains unchanged. I stressed the need for dialogue between China and Taiwan that leads to peaceful resolution of their differences.[51]

When asked how he intended to translate the commitment to the "one China" policy into reality, Bush responded:

> [O]ne China policy means that the issue ought to be resolved peacefully. We've got influence with some in the region; we intend to make sure that the issue is resolved peacefully—and

---

[51] White House Office of the Press Secretary, "Remarks by the President and Chinese President Jiang Zemin in Press Conference, Crawford, Texas, October 25, 2002," online at http://www.whitehouse.gov/news/releases/2002/10/20021025.html.

that includes making it clear that we do not support independence.

Publicly, Jiang responded with notably minimal rhetoric, merely labeling the Taiwan question a matter "of concern to the Chinese side." Moreover, in their talks, he also reportedly briefly mentioned the possibility of redeploying PRC missiles back from the coast opposite Taiwan if the U.S. were to curtail arms sales.[52] The proposal itself, as understood, was unbalanced, since missiles could easily be moved back toward the coast, while an interrupted arms supply relationship would take considerable time to restore. And engaging China in this way would seem to run counter to the "assurance" against discussing arms sales with Beijing. That being said, a number of observers thought they detected an important break with China's past refusal to acknowledge that its deployments had any causal relationship to arms sales, and they hoped that Beijing would find a way to raise this directly with Taipei.

LOOKING AHEAD

When Bush met newly-installed President Hu Jintao on the margins of the G-8 Summit in France in June 2003, the substance of their exchange on Taiwan was virtually the same as the exchange that Bush and Jiang had in Texas.[53] Once again the press was stirred up by the fact that, although the American briefer stated that Bush had said he did not support Taiwan independence, the Chinese briefer related that Bush said he "opposed" it.[54] Predictably, the Taiwan media went into a feeding frenzy. It was silly and unwarranted, no matter which term Bush used; given the President's penchant for unique verbal constructions, parsing his sentences is a feckless endeavor.

That does not mean, however, that each phrase uttered by the President and his senior advisers will not be scrutinized by analysts on both sides of the Strait. It will. And even if the Americans mean nothing

---

[52] John Pomfret, "China Suggests Missile Buildup Linked to Arms Sales to Taiwan," *Washington Post,* December 10, 2002, A-1.

[53] White House Office of the Press Secretary, "Background Press Briefing by a Senior Administration Official on the President's Meeting with Chinese President Hu," June 1, 2003, online at http://www.whitehouse.gov/news/releases/2003/06/20030601-4.html.

[54] "U.S. Policy Toward Taiwan Swings to the Middle," *People's Daily*, June 13, 2002, available online at http://taiwansecurity.org/News/2003/PD-061303.htm

by a loose use of words, it is important to realize that it is sometimes hard to distinguish between mere carelessness and something more meaningful. At times of sound U.S. relations with both Taipei and Beijing, such as exist in late 2003, there is a greater margin for imprecision. In times of trouble and tension, however, it is another matter altogether. But even when things are going well, it is not just the words, but the policies and actions that matter. And a failure in Washington to perceive the life-and-death quality for Chinese on each side of the Taiwan Strait of matters that may appear marginal—or "fudgeable"—to Americans can have serious consequences.

— 9 —

Conclusion

From the very outset of the diplomatic positioning in 1969 through the course of normalization and up until the present, China and the United States have recognized the importance of developing less contentious, more productive relations. Their common commitment to contain Soviet expansionism, which provided the initial impetus, has given way over time to a much broader and deeper set of relationships. Although no longer premised on the potential for confrontation with a military adversary, these ties are nonetheless still "strategic" in the meaningful sense that they engage the most fundamental interests of both nations across a vast spectrum of issues.

In the struggle to forge—and maintain—such relations, both countries understood the need to come to grips with the single issue that had consistently caused them the most grief since the 1940s: Taiwan. Through accidents of history and political dynamics in both countries, the island had grown in significance for each, albeit in different ways.

For Beijing it symbolized sovereignty, occupying a place at the very core of China's own sense of national identity and dignity. It stood as an issue of principle that permitted no compromise. As a result, while gaining American acceptance of the PRC claim to represent Taiwan was very important, even more so was obtaining American recognition that resolving the Taiwan question was a sovereign Chinese matter. Without that, the United States would assert a right to block—or at least shape—reunification, making normalization impossible.

The Taiwan issue was seriously burdened, especially in the early days, by the fact that it had emerged as a remnant of the Chinese civil war, a struggle between contending Chinese political forces that had not been brought to closure. Later, as politics on the island evolved and "independence" became a more salient question, the issue became even more entangled with the question of national unity, which stretched back over a century to the time when Taiwan was "stolen" from China by Japan and, in all justice, had to be returned.

There was a parallel evolution in PRC priorities away from actual realization of reunification toward the acceptance of the "one China principle" by Taiwan. Beijing's vision of a future Taiwan developed into that of a virtually totally autonomous region within "one China." But that day need not come any time soon; only if Taiwan refused to embrace the principle of "one China" and threatened to move in the opposite direction, toward formalized separate status, did Beijing see a need to force the issue.[1] And then it was only in part a question of reversing Taiwan's own tendencies; in important part, it was a matter of rebuffing outside support, without which such tendencies could not flourish in the first place.

For Washington, Taiwan evolved from a bastion—and symbol—of anti-Communism to a model of economic and political openness that reflected—and engaged—American interests and values. For reasons of politics, principle and national security, while they could accept any deal reached voluntarily between the two sides, Americans could not accept a coerced resolution of the cross-Strait relationship.

To the United States, the Taiwan question was a problem to be managed, worked around, put to the side. From the very first days after World War II, Americans were sensitive to the need to avoid creating an issue of irredentism in which the United States became the villain in Chinese eyes. But, except for that brief period in the first half of 1950 when the only alternative to acquiescence to Communist takeover seemed to be all-out war, the United States was unwilling to sit by and simply let the island be overrun by Communist forces. Although the American legal position on Taiwan's "undetermined" status remained unchanged, Truman's requirement for determining it—i.e., some international act—was for all practical purposes replaced by the 1960s with a willingness to see the issue resolved by the two parties directly involved. But there was no diminution in the insistence that any resolution be peaceful.

As to what was required for normalization, in China's mind all else followed naturally from its position on sovereignty. If the United States accepted the principle of Chinese sovereignty over Taiwan, then Washington logically could not have diplomatic relations with Taipei—

---

[1] Deng Xiaoping introduced a sense of deadline in the late 1970s, as did the Taiwan White Paper in February 2000. Jiang Zemin was reported to have talked of a limited time frame to resolve the issue as well. But for the most part, the issue of "principle" has far outweighed considerations of timing.

or any official dealings with it or official representation. It could not have a defense treaty, station forces, or sell arms to an island whose sovereignty it recognized as coming under Beijing.

The United States could manage most of that. Dispensing with the symbols of sovereignty—diplomatic relations, official representation, formal defense arrangements—was "doable" with time and proper political management. But, given that this was a "hot potato" in U.S. domestic politics, that others would be taking lessons about American credibility from how the U.S. handled this question, and—especially over time, but even in the 1940s—that the overwhelming majority of "Taiwanese" opposed subordination to Mainland rule, it was both politically and strategically antithetical to U.S. interests to acquiesce in terms that denied America the ability to forestall a forceful takeover, whether through arms sales or through retaining a basis for direct intervention, should it come to that.

And thus the dance of negotiation, with each side seeking to move the other as close as possible to accepting *its* position. And after normalization, the maneuvering to hold the other side to what were seen as the explicit and implicit terms of the bargain.

All of this was vastly complicated by the evolution of Taiwan politics. The specific twists and turns in this process have not always been predictable and sometimes have seemed to reflect the whim of some mischievous gods. Thus, for example, the victory of the DPP candidate in 2000, who was an effective campaigner but whose election was only possible because of his opponents' inability to field a unified slate. But even had the election gone the other way, the direction of Taiwan's political thinking was fully in motion toward a greater sense of Taiwanese identity and more outspoken refusal to accept even nominal affiliation with the Mainland if it carried any implication of subordination to Beijing.

That did not, and does not, mean that a "one China" solution is impossible, just that defining it—and getting there—is far more complicated and requires far more nuance and creativity than the leadership on either side of the Strait has envisaged or displayed so far.

The United States has become to some extent the victim of its own creation. Having fostered a strong, democratic society in Taiwan in the course of over fifty years of intimate association with the island, it now finds that the result has sometimes proven messy and uncontrollable, not to mention unpredictable, especially when that democracy has not totally matured and battles are in important part over who is "in" and who is "out" rather than whose ideas are necessarily in Taiwan's long-term interest. And where ideas do matter, they are sometimes put forward in unduly stark and provocative ways. This is not in any way to argue that, from the American point of view, Taiwan is not a far more attractive society and compatible partner today than it was during its authoritarian past. The values that Americans share with the people in Taiwan are not only objectively "good," but they constitute a far healthier basis for Taiwan's future stable and prosperous development and for working together with Americans for shared objectives. But that does not make it easy.

In understanding both the past and the future of American policy toward Taiwan, it is fundamentally important to understand the significance for American interests of normalized relations with the PRC and of maintaining strong U.S.-PRC ties. This does not mean that the United States has to embrace the PRC's claim to sovereignty over Taiwan today any more than it did in the past. But to gratuitously challenge that position is bound to lead to needless crises that harm U.S. interests.

"The Taiwan question" is essentially a political question, not a military one. Military might certainly plays a role for all parties involved. But there is, literally, no military solution. A failed attempt to force a solution through military means would set off reverberations for decades to come. Taiwan would never feel safe; it would never be safe. Similarly, a "successful" use of force would only generate deep hostility in Taiwan over future generations. In either case, tensions would be created between China and all of its major partners—most especially the United States—that would damage the interests of everyone for the foreseeable future.

Even so, given all of the sensitivities and imponderables, there could be a war, and that prospect lies behind repeated American statements about the importance of maintaining peace and the U.S. policy of arms sales in the face of an accelerating PRC military build-up opposite Taiwan. There is a vicious circle in play, here. The PRC perceives separatist tendencies on the island and enhances its military capabilities as a deterrent. The U.S. (along with Taiwan) sees that build-up and feels obliged to bolster the island's defensive capabilities to avoid an imbalance that invites coercive measures from the Mainland. Beijing sees that bolstering process as emboldening Taiwan independence forces to pursue their separatist tendencies and enhances its deterrent. And the cycle repeats itself.

Given this situation, what did normalization resolve, if anything? Not only did it theoretically remove the United States from the middle of the Chinese civil war—thus allowing the two sides to address their relationship in a less urgent way—but, through a lengthy process, it began to create a sense of reliable expectations that neither the U.S. nor the PRC would challenge the other's basic positions—expectations on the part of Americans that Beijing would not force a solution on Taiwan, and expectations on the part of the Chinese that the United States would not try to block eventual reunification and would neither facilitate nor support independence in the meantime. Important differences of both principle and practice remained unresolved with respect to the threat or use of force. But at least for a long time, those differences were successfully handled by constructive ambiguity in expression backed by clarity in thinking, both sides understanding that any fundamental violation of the ground rules would be fatal to the relationship.

Over time, however, that clarity in thinking became muddled and the sense of reliable expectations began to erode. On the Chinese side, one saw spikes in attention to military solutions and to the setting of deadlines, which raised red flags in Washington. To some extent, these arose out of strictly domestic PRC dynamics. But they were usually directly related to developments on the island or—of particular importance to this study—to perceived changes in U.S. policy in support of independence.

Ronald Reagan at first seemed unwilling to work with the delicate nuances of normalization. Indeed, while supportive of better U.S.-PRC relations, when it came to Taiwan, he opposed what had been done. As far as Reagan was concerned, Carter had sold out Taiwan and treated it with disrespect, and, while he would not reverse course with Beijing, he was going to fix that.

Eventually Reagan came around to "play the game," but not until significant damage had been done. The costs came not just in the form of tense relations during the period before the August 17 Communiqué, but in terms of a residual level of mutual mistrust that the United States and China harbored about each other's strategic intentions. Although, over time, Reagan did seem genuinely to come to the view that, handled deftly, the U.S.-PRC relationship could be strengthened without damaging Taiwan's well-being, at first, he was convinced to tone down his rhetoric primarily on the basis of straightforward political expediency in the 1980 election campaign. If he caused a blow-up with China, undermining a major success of another Republican Administration less than a decade earlier, he would pay at the polls. So, while his political beliefs made him a strong supporter of Taiwan, his political realism ultimately tempered his handling of the issue.

For George H.W. Bush it was almost the opposite. His strong proclivity was to preserve the normalization arrangements, seeing them as not harmful to Taiwan—indeed, even beneficial—but, in any event, absolutely critical to the strategic relationship with Beijing. In Bush's case, however, politics pushed him to approve the sale of F-16s to Taiwan at the end of his administration, an action that has reverberated unhelpfully in Sino-American relations over the years since. While the Chinese did not mistrust Bush's motives, and that helped temper their immediate reaction, they saw Taiwan playing a role in U.S. domestic affairs—and able to manipulate American political forces—in ways that challenged China's basic sovereignty; yet they were helpless to do much about it. If the first Gulf War taught China a lesson regarding its military backwardness vis-à-vis the United States, the F-16 sale sounded an alarm regarding Taiwan's own capabilities—and the U.S. role in strengthening them.

Bill Clinton seems to have been fully committed to the overall framework of the normalization agreements, but he appears either not to have understood how intensely important the underlying principles were to Beijing or not to have cared. In his first two years, Clinton tended to downplay, across the board, the importance of larger security questions. He not only focused on economic issues—"It's the economy stupid"—to the detriment of other dimensions of policy, but specifically in terms of China policy, an emphasis on domestic American political issues and promotion of American "values" overwhelmed any strategic perspective. Even though he began to adjust course in 1994, delinking MFN tariff treatment (for the most part) from human rights, Clinton's continuing emphasis on values—and his own political vulnerability—led him to cave in to congressional pressures on the question of a visit to the United States by Lee Teng-hui. This had the dual effect of sparking the military confrontation in the Taiwan Strait in spring 1996—which, in turn, played an important role in energizing the PLA's Taiwan-centered modernization drive—and of reinforcing and deepening PRC suspicions about the independence attitudes of the Taiwan leadership and U.S. complicity in fostering them.

While the matched pair of state visits between Jiang and Clinton in October 1997 and June 1998 went some way toward repairing the bilateral relationship, the momentum they generated was soon supplanted by mutual nattering over a variety of issues, culminating in, among other things, the issuance of Lee Teng-hui's "two states theory" in mid-1999, only two months after the U.S. bombing of the PRC embassy in Belgrade and three months after the U.S. had turned down Beijing's hard-won WTO offer. All of this underscored in Beijing's mind the view that any U.S. support for the government in Taipei was a challenge to the PRC's "one China" principle and a manifestation of a larger problem in the relationship. At the same time, however, Washington's quick refutation of the "two states theory" was important in tamping down the immediate fallout and provided a useful lesson for the future: if the United States not only distanced itself from Taiwan independence activities but was willing to stand up and clearly, even if politely, criticize them, then this could affect the overall framework of the PRC's approach and allow a more considered, less confrontational response from Beijing.

George W. Bush was an outspoken supporter of the "one China" policy from the time he was competing for the Republican Party nomination in 2000, but his overall critical attitude toward China's policies and practices, in addition to his outspoken support for Taiwan's security created a climate of suspicion in Beijing regarding his ultimate intentions on cross-Strait relations. This was reified in early 2001 by a series of developments including the EP-3 incident, the announcement of an enormous Taiwan arms sales package, Bush's statement on "whatever it took" to help Taiwan defend itself, and a very liberal set of ground rules applied during Taiwan President Chen Shui-bian's transit of the United States in May. All of this seemed to contradict Bush's verbal commitment to "one China." He seemed not to grasp the interaction between Taiwan policy, on the one hand, and his larger China policy, on the other. In fact, to some extent one sensed, especially after the EP-3 incident in early April, that though he absorbed the lesson about the need for stronger U.S.-PRC relations, Bush became even more determined to demonstrate that he would not "cater" to Beijing on security issues, starting with Taiwan.

Over the course of the first year of the Bush Administration, however, the relationship began to improve, and by the time of the September 11th terrorist attacks on New York and Washington, both sides were ready to recalibrate and to set relations on a more stable, productive course. The effect of this for Taiwan was that, albeit only over time, Bush came to publicly endorse the basic guideposts of the "one China" policy in effect since Nixon, to the point that he was willing to speak openly—as President, in China—about the need to avoid provocation "from either side." And after Chen Shui-bian stepped over the line of U.S. tolerance in August 2002 with his rhetoric about *yi bian, yi guo*, his advocacy of referenda, and the threat that Taiwan would "go its own way," Bush signaled that Taipei needed to rein in its provocative rhetoric.

Just as Chen, in a fundamental sense, reflects he independence aspirations of most people in Taiwan—albeit tempered, as in the Taiwan populace at large, by a pragmatic instinct for survival—Bush reflects very strong feelings in the United States about the well-being of the people in Taiwan and the unacceptability of a coerced resolution of cross-Strait issues. But while Beijing and Washington might still jangle each other's nerves over Taiwan, they have generally been able to manage this delicate issue with sufficient care so as not to threaten each other's vital interests. Nonetheless, there is still a sense of unease among many Chinese about the durability of the current state of good relations and of the Bush Administration's willingness to put limits on its support for Taiwan as well as on its preparation for some presumably inevitable, long-term strategic competition with the PRC.

MANAGING THE DIFFERENCES

As of this writing, another presidential season is hard upon Taiwan and the campaign is well under way. Already we can see the tugging and hauling on the most politically charged issues of independence and unification. The principal candidates are exercising restraint, knowing that extreme positions would lose support of the essential middle. Still, Chen Shui-bian is once again citing *yi bian, yi guo*, the KMT is issuing instructions regarding travel to the Mainland, and campaigns for use of local dialects are under way. Moreover, both sides of the Strait are maneuvering with regard to the "three links" and PRC visitors to the United States are cautioning American leaders to adhere to the terms of the three joint communiqués.

Thus, the United States must remain alert to undue manipulation by forces in either Taipei or Beijing and avoid being drawn into the vortex. To do that, not just during the current campaign but for the foreseeable future, it is necessary to understand the fine texture of the normalization bargain, and not simply to be familiar with its broad strokes—as has often been the case before.

"One China"

Take "one China" as an example. The PRC holds to the "one China principle," by which it means there is only one China in the world, Taiwan is a part of it, its sole legal government resides in Beijing, and that the latter represents all the people of China—including those in Taiwan—in the international community. That "one China principle" also provides space for an almost totally autonomous Taiwan "special administrative region" with rights and privileges going beyond those of any other Chinese territory, including even Hong Kong. But such autonomy would only come within "one China," not as an equal or separate sovereign entity. An essential conceptual element of the "one China principle" is that there *is* "one China" today and that, while it is not "reunified," its territory and sovereignty are not—and cannot be—divided.

The U.S. "one China policy" is rather different. Beyond "acknowledging" the Chinese position that there is "one China" of which Taiwan is a part, it largely consists of things that the United States will *not* do. The U.S. will *not* "challenge" the PRC position on "one China;" even though this statement in the Shanghai Communiqué was not repeated in the normalization or August 17 Communiqués, it remains part of the principled underpinning of U.S.-PRC relations. Moreover, the United States will *not* pursue a policy of—or support—"one China, one Taiwan," or "two Chinas" or any variant of that formulation, and will *not* support "Taiwan independence." To one degree or another the U.S. will also *oppose* unilateral steps that move toward separate status for Taiwan. It will *not* have "official" relations with Taiwan. And, while it supports Taiwan's struggle for an effective voice in the international community, it does *not* support any efforts that would entail or imply conveying statehood on the island.

Nonetheless, the U.S. "one China policy" allows for activities that Beijing finds contradictory to its own "one China principle." Beyond all the other issues raised by the Taiwan Relations Act, from the very beginning, the U.S. stressed the importance of "peaceful" resolution of cross-Strait relations. Kissinger on occasion left the impression that the U.S. was only looking for a "decent interval" between normalization and whatever else might happen, but emphasis on the short term has given way to a longer-term insistence on peaceful resolution. Moreover, as we have seen, Zhou Enlai was not buying into the "interval" proposition in any case; rather, he stressed that the U.S. had no "right" to have any say in the matter whatsoever. Even then, but especially after normalization in January 1979, Beijing stressed its preference for peaceful resolution. (Recall that the Politburo decision in May 1971 embraced that preference, as well.) All of that being said, Beijing would not commit to forego use of force if elements in Taiwan or from abroad sought to sever the island's tie with the Mainland. That remains the case today. So, when the United States has insisted under the terms of its "one China policy" on continuing to sell arms to Taiwan—having taken great care to preserve, by its own lights, the legal basis for involvement in Taiwan's security—this has been viewed by Beijing as in direct contravention of the "one China principle."

In this connection, it is worth pausing a moment to consider that various—indeed almost all—senior U.S. officials since 1971 (Presidents, Secretaries of State and National Security Advisers) have gone beyond the U.S. position of "acknowledgment" of Beijing's position and said at one time or another that the United States "accepts" the "one China principle" or "bases its policy" on the "one China principle." For most of them it did not mean that the U.S. embraced the PRC view of sovereignty, but simply that it did not support or seek to foster "two Chinas" or "one China, one Taiwan."[2] But it is a sloppy and sweeping misstatement of policy that is open to mischievous misuse in either Taiwan or the Mainland.

Another issue that could bring forth the difference between the PRC's "one China principle" and the American "one China policy" has to do with travel to or through the United States by senior Taiwan officials, especially the president. Chen Shui-bian's triumphal procession through his transit stops in New York and Houston in 2001 caused considerable heartburn in Beijing as an apparent encouragement of Chen's political agenda. But it now stands as a precedent from which the Administration is unlikely to retreat. That being said, if the Bush Administration is careful to maintain certain basic rules that applied during that transit (e.g., no Administration official met with Chen in 2001), keeping those same rules for the next transit, while irksome to the PRC, should keep the fallout manageable. Making those rules even more permissive, however, would raise questions about U.S. intentions.

---

[2] Samuel Berger, National Security Adviser in the second Clinton Administration, notes that while senior officials had ideas about how cross-Strait relations should evolve, and discussed them internally, advancing an "American solution" was not seen as feasible, and attention was therefore focused, not on what the future might look like, but on preventing coercion from the Mainland and provocation from Taiwan (correspondence with author).

Moreover, there continues to be pressure from various sources—some in Taiwan, some in the U.S.—for a Chen visit, and not just to anywhere in the United States, but to Washington, D.C. Setting aside the extreme and out-of-bounds steps advocated by some people—e.g., reconstituting the alliance or declaring support for Taiwan independence—it is hard to imagine anything within the realm of what people are seriously proposing that would be more harmful to U.S.-PRC relations, or more gratuitously so. It is my own conviction that this will not be even remotely entertained by the White House before the 2004 U.S. presidential elections. What happens after that remains to be seen. But this issue cannot be treated lightly.

Security

The security issue is another difficult question that revolves centrally around the nature of the U.S. role; there is no prospect that Taiwan will "outgun" the PRC on its own. Two questions remain open. One is whether continued provision of arms by the United States, rather than giving Taiwan the confidence to deal with Beijing, as Washington hopes, instead gives Taipei such a sense of invulnerability that it feels free of any responsibility to fashion a stable, long-term relationship across the Strait, as Beijing fears. The other is whether, through the nature of the equipment and technology supplied, training arrangements, and linkages to American intelligence and early warning systems, the Mutual Defense Treaty is being reconstituted in everything but name. There is also the looming issue of whether the United States would become militarily involved if hostilities broke out—the ultimate "insult" to the PRC's position on sovereignty. Of course, in the event of hostilities, unless Taiwan had provoked the attack, Beijing's sensibilities on this question would not be Washington's first consideration.

From the American point of view, a great deal of this can be managed if only the PRC would slow or halt its build-up of missiles and other systems obviously designed to confront Taiwan. But that takes us back to the vicious cycle of military action and reaction. Various Chinese interlocutors continue to point to Jiang Zemin's proposal at Crawford to consider redeploying the short-range missiles opposite Taiwan if the U.S. curtailed arms sales. However intriguing the *fact* of the proposal, if not its terms, it seems unlikely to lead anywhere unless first framed in a cross-Strait political context that creates a mutual sense of trust about the future.

THE TIES THAT BIND

Finally, there is the question of the "status" of the three joint communiqués on which so much of this policy is built. Are the commitments in those three statements "binding" on both sides or not?

As discussed earlier with respect to the August 17 Communiqué, it is the position of the U.S. Government that all three communiqués set forth "parallel and interrelated statements of policy" by the U.S. and China, not international agreements, and therefore impose "no obligations on either party under international law."[3] Even in the case of the normalization communiqué, although the establishment of diplomatic relations has an enduring character, one could say that the communiqué itself simply "announced" that decision rather than that it was the legal instrument that "carried it out."

Because of the U.S. Government's official legal position on this, it is important that each new President recommit to the three joint communiqués, and however painful for some to do so—if only because they have disagreed with parts of them or because it all seems too formulaic—they have all done so.

There is, however, a debate about this legal interpretation. Not only is there a theoretical argument that the joint communiqués constitute "international agreements," but there is a body of International Court of Justice (ICJ) opinions that suggests they may indeed have the character of binding international agreements.[4] Moreover, even the State Department Legal Adviser in the Carter Administration, Herbert J. Hansell, considers the three communiqués "binding and enforceable obligations of the United States" (and, reciprocally, of China).[5] While it is true that the communiqués do not override U.S. law, Hansell also notes that the international legal effects of the communiqués are not changed by the enactment of the TRA:

---

[3] Testimony of State Department Legal Adviser Davis Robinson, in *Senate Judiciary Committee Hearings,* op. cit., p. 95.

[4] See, for example, *Aegean Sea Continental Shelf Case (Greece v. Turkey),* in particular the Judgment of December 19, 1978, available online at http://www.icj-cij.org/icjwww/icases/igt/iGT_ijudgment/_igt_ijudgment_19781219.pdf. See also *Maritime Delimitation and Territorial Questions between Qatar and Bahrain (Qatar v. Bahrain),* in particular the Judgments of July 1, 1994 and March 16, 2001, both online at http://www.icj-cij.org/icjwww/idocket/iqb/iqbframe.htm

[5] Letter to author, January 8, 2003.

The Act is domestic legislation with legal effect internally within the U.S.; but vis-à-vis China, the Congress can't unilaterally take from China the rights it previously acquired, nor relieve the U.S. of the obligations to China it previously incurred, in the communiqués.

Hansell endorses arguments by Professor of Law Ruth Wedgwood, that "[a]n undertaking doesn't have to have wax seals or plenipotentiary ceremonies in order to be enforceable," a notion consistent with the ICJ's confirmation two decades ago that even "unilateral statements made in solemn circumstances can be binding."[6] Ultimately, Hansell concludes:

> The bottom line is that in the joint communiqués China acquired rights and the U.S. assumed obligations that were cognizable and enforceable under international law, and those rights and obligations haven't been extinguished.

Nevertheless, while the ability to cite a "legal obligation" might be helpful in some circumstances, there is no court to which the U.S. or China could effectively appeal. The operative issue, therefore, is whether each side feels politically bound by the statements and commitments in those documents. As the State Department itself has said, even if the documents are considered not to be international agreements, *per se,* they "may create reasonable expectations by each party" that the other side would "carry out" the policies stated in them.[7]

Whatever one's view of their legal standing, it is important that each new administration not only recommit to the undertakings in the three communiqués (along with the TRA) as the policy framework for approaching the Taiwan question, but that it understand what is being endorsed. We cannot rewrite history to see whether a deeper understanding would have resulted in different decisions since 1979. But what we can do is learn from these experiences.

---

[6] Ruth Wedgwood, "A Pirate is a Pirate," *Wall Street Journal,* December 16, 2002.

[7] "Answers to Questions Regarding Taiwan Arms Sales," in *Senate Judiciary Committee Hearings,* op. cit., pp. 146-147.

REVIEWING THE PAST, CONTEMPLATING THE FUTURE

Despite the relatively calm state of affairs at present, PRC President Hu Jintao felt constrained to recite the familiar "one China" mantra to former President Jimmy Carter in early September 2003.[8] PRC Foreign Minister Li Zhaoxing did the same when he called on President Bush in the White House later that month.[9] This pattern could have reflected concern about manipulation of the cross-Strait issue in the Taiwan presidential campaign and a caution that the United States should therefore handle the matter especially carefully. Or it might have meant nothing more than that—like their American counterparts—the Chinese fear that an omission of a standard line would convey a wrong signal that they "do not care" any more, and could lead the U.S. to seek to move the goalposts. In any event, it underscores the point made earlier: words matter—for both sides—and a failure to think clearly and speak clearly can have consequences, sometimes very serious ones.

It may be that over time, the nature of this issue will evolve. While one should not expect Beijing to abandon the "one China principle," there could eventually be an evolution in the PRC's definition of that concept. The rise to power—or at least influence—of individuals and groups on the Mainland who are willing to accommodate the basic aspiration of the people in Taiwan to remain free from subordination to anyone else—to have a choice about their future—could open the door to peaceful resolution. Even in the shorter term, while the Mainland need not accept a Taiwan vision of a future in which there are two equal entities within "one China," if it could agree not to rule that out, then it would give meaning to its frequent claim that "everything can be discussed" within the framework of "one China."

There could also be a change in Taipei's position, perhaps going back to the notion that accepting the "principle" of "one China" does not mean accepting Beijing's sovereignty; those would be issues to be left to the future.

Even in the medium term, while basic issues of "reunification" are not going to be resolved, the problem can be "bounded" by those sorts of

---

[8] "Chinese President Meets Former US President," *People's Daily Online*, September 9, 2003, available at http://english.peopledaily.com.cn/200309/09/eng20030909_123964.shtml.

[9] "Bush Says Sino-US Relationship Full of Vitality," *Xinhua*, September 23, 2003.

shifts. If that happened, it would facilitate the making of an American policy that neither abandoned Taiwan nor challenged the PRC. Looked at from the other side of the coin, continued sound U.S. relations with both parties would contribute to a level of confidence about the consistency of American policy that enhanced not only their respective relations with Washington, but also their ability to deal effectively with each other.

Managing these complex and interlinked relationships could become more complicated over time, as China becomes a more formidable military power and issues of relative influence come even more centrally into play both in the region, in general, and over Taiwan, specifically. But in thinking about such a future, all would do well to consider that Taiwan is probably the only issue over which the U.S. and the PRC could come to blows, and that if they are able to deal with each other constructively at the strategic level, this will likely have a major impact on their ability to handle the Taiwan question peacefully, through political rather than military means.

The basic decisions regarding cross-Strait relations rest in the hands of those most directly involved: Taipei and Beijing. But the U.S. role is crucial. And, while, as we said at the outset, any President has the right to change policy, he has an obligation to do so only in the light of a considered understanding of what it is he is changing and what the long-term effects are likely to be. In the case of policy toward Taiwan, and its impact on overall U.S. relations with the PRC, this requires a dedicated effort to grasp clearly not just the broad outlines of the normalization undertakings, but the detail and nuance—and the essential ambiguities—that give them effect. To do less would be irresponsible, and could take us all over the brink of the precipice.

Appendix

EXCERPTS FROM THE JOINT COMMUNIQUÉ OF THE PEOPLE'S REPUBLIC OF CHINA AND THE UNITED STATES OF AMERICA (FEBRUARY 27, 1972)[1]

President Richard Nixon of the United States of America visited the People's Republic of China at the invitation of Premier Chou En-lai of the People's Republic of China from February 21 to February 28, 1972...

President Nixon met with Chairman Mao Tse-tung of the Communist Party of China on February 21. The two leaders had a serious and frank exchange of views on Sino-U.S. relations and world affairs.

During the visit, extensive, earnest and frank discussions were held between President Nixon and Premier Chou En-lai on the normalization of relations between the United States of America and the People's Republic of China, as well as on other matters of interest to both sides...

The leaders of the People's Republic of China and the United States of America found it beneficial to have this opportunity, after so many years without contact, to present candidly to one another their views on a variety of issues. They reviewed the international situation in which important changes and great upheavals are taking place and expounded their respective positions and attitudes...

There are essential differences between China and the United States in their social systems and foreign policies. However, the two sides agreed that countries, regardless of their social systems, should conduct their relations on the principles of respect for the sovereignty and territorial integrity of all states, non-aggression against other states, non-interference in the internal affairs of other states, equality and mutual benefit, and peaceful coexistence. International disputes should be settled on this basis, without resorting to the use or threat of force. The United States and the

---

[1] More popularly known as the Shanghai Communiqué. Source: Department of State, *United States Foreign Policy 1972: A Report of the Secretary of State* (Washington, DC: Government Printing Office, 1973), p. 640.

People's Republic of China are prepared to apply these principles to their mutual relations...

The two sides reviewed the long-standing serious disputes between China and the United States. The Chinese side reaffirmed its position: The Taiwan question is the crucial question obstructing the normalization of relations between China and the United States; the Government of the People's Republic of China is the sole legal government of China; Taiwan is a province of China which has long been returned to the motherland; the liberation of Taiwan is China's internal affair in which no other country has the right to interfere; and all U.S. forces and military installations must be withdrawn from Taiwan. The Chinese Government firmly opposes any activities which aim at the creation of "one China, one Taiwan," "one China, two governments," "two Chinas," and "independent Taiwan" or advocate that "the status of Taiwan remains to be determined."

The U.S. side declared: The United States acknowledges that all Chinese on either side of the Taiwan Strait maintain there is but one China and that Taiwan is a part of China. The United States Government does not challenge that position. It reaffirms its interest in a peaceful settlement of the Taiwan question by the Chinese themselves. With this prospect in mind, it affirms the ultimate objective of the withdrawal of all U.S. forces and military installations from Taiwan. In the meantime, it will progressively reduce its forces and military installations on Taiwan as the tension in the area diminishes...

The two sides agreed that they will stay in contact through various channels, including the sending of a senior U.S. representative to Peking from time to time for concrete consultations to further the normalization of relations between the two countries and continue to exchange views on issues of common interest.

The two sides expressed the hope that the gains achieved during this visit would open up new prospects for the relations between the two countries. They believe that the normalization of relations between the two countries is not only in the interest of the Chinese and American peoples but also contributes to the relaxation of tension in Asia and the world...

EXCERPTS FROM THE COMMUNIQUÉ ISSUED BY
THE UNITED STATES AND THE PEOPLE'S REPUBLIC OF CHINA
AT THE CONCLUSION OF HENRY KISSINGER'S FEBRUARY 1973
VISIT TO THE PRC (FEBRUARY 22, 1973)[2]

Dr. Henry A. Kissinger, Assistant to the President for National Security Affairs, visited the People's Republic of China from February 15 to February 19, 1973…

Chairman Mao Tse-tung received Dr. Kissinger. Dr. Kissinger and members of his party held wide-ranging conversations with Premier Chou En-lai…

The two sides reviewed the development of relations between the two countries in the year that has passed since President Nixon's visit to the People's Republic of China and other issues of mutual concern. They reaffirmed the principles of the Joint Communiqué issued at Shanghai in February 1972 and their joint commitment to bring about a normalization of relations. They held that the progress that has been made during this period is beneficial to the people of their two countries.

The two sides agreed that the time was appropriate for accelerating the normalization of relations. To this end, they undertook to broaden their contacts in all fields…

To facilitate this process and to improve communications it was agreed that in the near future each side will establish a liaison office in the capital of the other. Details will be worked out through existing channels.

The two sides agreed that normalization of relations between the United States and the People's Republic of China will contribute to the relaxation of tension in Asia and in the world…

---

[2] Source: Richard P. Stebbins and Elaine P. Adam, eds., *American Foreign Relations 1973: A Documentary Record* (New York: New York University Press, 1976), p. 82.

EXCERPTS FROM THE COMMUNIQUÉ ISSUED BY
THE UNITED STATES AND THE PEOPLE'S REPUBLIC OF CHINA
AT THE CONCLUSION OF HENRY KISSINGER'S NOVEMBER 1973
VISIT TO THE PRC (NOVEMBER 14, 1973)[3]

Dr. Henry A. Kissinger, U.S. Secretary of State and Assistant to the President for National Security Affairs, visited the People's Republic of China from November 10 to November 14, 1973...

The two sides reviewed international developments since Dr. Kissinger's visit to the People's Republic of China in February, 1973. They noted that international relationships are in a period of intense change. They reaffirmed that they are committed to the principles established in the Shanghai Communiqué and that disputes between states should be settled without resorting to the use or threat of force, on the basis of the principles of respect for the sovereignty and territorial integrity of all states, non-aggression against other states, non-interference in the internal affairs of other states, equality and mutual benefit, and peaceful coexistence. In particular, they reiterated that neither should seek hegemony in the Asia-Pacific region or any other part of the world and that each is opposed to efforts by any other country or group of countries to establish such hegemony.

The two sides agreed that in present circumstances it is of particular importance to maintain frequent contact at authoritative levels in order to exchange views and, while not negotiating on behalf of third parties, to engage in concrete consultations on issues of mutual concern.

Both sides reviewed progress made during 1973 in their bilateral relations. The U.S. side reaffirmed: The United States acknowledges that all Chinese on either side of the Taiwan Strait maintain there is but one China and that Taiwan is a part of China; the United States Government does not challenge that position. The Chinese side reiterated that the normalization of relations between China and the United States can be realized only on the basis of confirming the principle of one China.

---

[3] Source: *Department of State Bulletin* LXIX, no. 1798 (December 10, 1973), p. 716

Both sides noted with satisfaction that the Liaison Offices in Peking and Washington are functioning smoothly. Both sides agreed that the scope of the functions of the Liaison Offices should continue to be expanded...

The two sides stated that they would continue their efforts to promote the normalization of relations between China and the United States on the basis of the Shanghai Communiqué...

JOINT COMMUNIQUÉ ON THE ESTABLISHMENT
OF DIPLOMATIC RELATIONS BETWEEN THE UNITED STATES
OF AMERICA AND THE PEOPLE'S REPUBLIC OF CHINA
(ISSUED ON DECEMBER 15, 1978)[4]

January 1, 1979

The United States of America and the People's Republic of China have agreed to recognize each other and to establish diplomatic relations as of January 1, 1979.

The United States of America recognizes the Government of the People's Republic of China as the sole legal Government of China. Within this context, the people of the United States will maintain cultural, commercial, and other unofficial relations with the people of Taiwan.

The United States of America and the People's Republic of China reaffirm the principles agreed on by the two sides in the Shanghai Communiqué and emphasize once again that:

—Both wish to reduce the danger of international military conflict.

—Neither should seek hegemony in the Asia-Pacific region or in any other region of the world and each is opposed to efforts by any other country or group of countries to establish such hegemony.

—Neither is prepared to negotiate on behalf of any third party or to enter into agreements or understandings with the other directed at other states.

—The Government of the United States of America acknowledges the Chinese position that there is but one China and Taiwan is part of China.

—Both believe that normalization of Sino-American relations is not only in the interest of the Chinese and American peoples but also contributes to the cause of peace in Asia and the world.

The United States of America and the People's Republic of China will exchange Ambassadors and establish Embassies on March 1, 1979.

---

[4] Source: Department of State, *American Foreign Policy Basic Documents 1977-1980* (Washington, DC: Government Printing Office, 1983), p. 967.

EXCERPTS FROM THE TAIWAN RELATIONS ACT
(ENACTED APRIL 10, 1979)[5]

An Act

To help maintain peace, security, and stability in the Western Pacific and to promote the foreign policy of the United States by authorizing the continuation of commercial, cultural, and other relations between the people of the United States and the people on Taiwan, and for other purpose.

FINDINGS AND DECLARATIONS OF POLICY

SEC. 2.(a) The President, having terminated governmental relations between the United States and the governing authorities on Taiwan recognized by the United States as the Republic of China prior to January 1, 1979, the Congress finds that the enactment of this Act is necessary—

(1) to help maintain peace, security, and stability in the Western Pacific; and

(2) to promote the foreign policy of the United States by authorizing the continuation of commercial, cultural, and other relations between the people of the United States and the people on Taiwan.

(b) It is the policy of the United States—

(1) to preserve and promote extensive, close, and friendly commercial, cultural, and other relations between the people of the United States and the people on Taiwan, as well as the people on the China mainland and all other peoples of the Western Pacific area;

(2) to declare that peace and stability in the area are in the political, security, and economic interests of the United States, and are matters of international concern;

(3) to make clear that the United States decision to establish diplomatic relations with the People's Republic of China rests upon the expectation that the future of Taiwan will be determined by peaceful means;

---

[5] Source: Public Law 96-8.

(4) to consider any effort to determine the future of Taiwan by other than peaceful means, including by boycotts or embargoes, a threat to the peace and security of the Western Pacific area and of grave concern to the United States;

(5) to provide Taiwan with arms of a defensive character; and

(6) to maintain the capacity of the United States to resist any resort to force or other forms of coercion that would jeopardize the security, or the social or economic system, of the people on Taiwan.

IMPLEMENTATION OF UNITED STATES POLICY WITH REGARD TO TAIWAN

SEC. 3. (a) In furtherance of the policy set forth in section 2 of this Act, the United States will make available to Taiwan such defense articles and defense services in such quantity as may be necessary to enable Taiwan to maintain a sufficient self-defense capability.

(b) The President and the Congress shall determine the nature and quantity of such defense articles and services based solely upon their judgment of the needs of Taiwan, in accordance with procedures established by law. Such determination of Taiwan's defense needs shall include review by United States military authorities in connection with recommendations to the President and the Congress.

(c) The President is directed to inform the Congress promptly of any threat to the security or the social or economic system of the people on Taiwan and any danger to the interests of the United States arising therefrom. The President and the Congress shall determine, in accordance with constitutional processes, appropriate action by the United States in response to any such danger.

APPLICATION OF LAWS; INTERNATIONAL AGREEMENTS

SEC. 4. (a) The absence of diplomatic relations or recognition shall not affect the application of the laws of the United States with respect to Taiwan, and the laws of the United States shall apply with respect to Taiwan in the manner that the laws of the United States applied with respect to Taiwan prior to January 1, 1979.

THE AMERICAN INSTITUTE IN TAIWAN

SEC. 6. (a) Programs, transactions, and other relations conducted or carried out by the President or any agency of the United States

Government with respect to Taiwan shall, in the manner and to the extent directed by the President, be conducted and carried out by or through—

> (1) The American Institute in Taiwan, a nonprofit corporation incorporated under the laws of the District of Columbia, or

> (2) such comparable successor nongovernmental entity as the President may designate, (hereafter in this Act referred to as the "Institute").

(b) Whenever he President or any agency of the United States Government is authorized or required by or pursuant to the laws of the United States to enter into, perform, enforce, or have in force an agreement or transaction relative to Taiwan, such agreement or transaction shall be entered into, performed, and enforced, in the manner and to the extent directed by the President, by or through the Institute.

SEPARATION OF GOVERNMENT PERSONNEL FOR EMPLOYMENT WITH THE INSTITUTE

SEC. 11. (a)(1) Under such terms and conditions as the President may direct, any agency of the United States Government may separate from Government service for a specified period any officer or employee of that agency who accepts employment with the Institute.

> (c) Employees of the Institute shall not be employees of the United States...

JOINT COMMUNIQUÉ ISSUED BY THE GOVERNMENTS OF
THE UNITED STATES AND THE PEOPLE'S REPUBLIC OF CHINA
(AUGUST 17, 1982)[6]

1. In the Joint Communiqué on the Establishment of Diplomatic Relations on January 1, 1979, issued by the Government of the United States of America and the Government of the People's Republic of China, the United States of America recognized the Government of the People's Republic of China as the sole legal government of China, and it acknowledged the Chinese position that there is but one China and Taiwan is part of China. Within that context, the two sides agreed that the people of the United States would continue to maintain cultural, commercial, and other unofficial relations with the people of Taiwan. On this basis, relations between the United States and China were normalized.

2. The question of United States arms sales to Taiwan was not settled in the course of negotiations between the two countries on establishing diplomatic relations. The two sides held differing positions, and the Chinese side stated that it would raise the issue again following normalization. Recognizing that this issue would seriously hamper the development of United States-China relations, they have held further discussions on it, during and since the meetings between President Ronald Reagan and Premier Zhao Ziyang and between Secretary of State Alexander M. Haig, Jr., and Vice Premier and Foreign Minister Huang Hua in October 1981.

3. Respect for each other's sovereignty and territorial integrity and noninterference in each other's internal affairs constitute the fundamental principles guiding United States-China relations. These principles were confirmed in the Shanghai Communiqué of February 28, 1972, and reaffirmed in the Joint Communiqué on the Establishment of Diplomatic Relations which came into effect on January 1, 1979. Both sides emphatically state that these principles continue to govern all aspects of their relations.

4. The Chinese Government reiterates that the question of Taiwan is China's internal affair. The Message to Compatriots in Taiwan issued by China on January 1, 1979, promulgated a fundamental policy of

---

[6] Source: Department of State, *American Foreign Policy Current Documents 1982* (Washington, DC: Government Printing Office, 1985), p. 1038.

striving for peaceful reunification of the Motherland. The Nine-Point Proposal put forward by China on September 30, 1981, represented a further major effort under this fundamental policy to strive for a peaceful solution to the Taiwan question.

5. The United States Government attaches great importance to its relations with China, and reiterates that it has no intention of infringing on Chinese sovereignty and territorial integrity, or interfering in China's internal affairs, or pursuing a policy of "two Chinas" or "one China, one Taiwan." The United States Government understands and appreciates the Chinese policy of striving for peaceful resolution of the Taiwan question as indicated in China's Message to Compatriots in Taiwan issued on January 1, 1979, and the Nine-Point Proposal put forward by China on September 30, 1981. The new situation which has emerged with regard to the Taiwan question also provides favorable conditions for the settlement of United States-China differences over the question of United States arms sales to Taiwan.

6. Having in mind the foregoing statements of both sides, the United States Government states that it does not seek to carry out a long-term policy of arms sales to Taiwan, that its arms sales to Taiwan will not exceed, either in qualitative or in quantitative terms, the level of those supplied in recent years since the establishment of diplomatic relations between the United States and China, and that it intends to reduce gradually its sales of arms to Taiwan, leading over a period of time to a final resolution. In so stating, the United States acknowledges China's consistent position regarding the thorough settlement of this issue.

7. In order to bring about, over a period of time, a final settlement of the question of United States arms sales to Taiwan, which is an issue rooted in history, the two governments will make every effort to adopt measures and create conditions conducive to the thorough settlement of this issue.

8. The development of United States-China relations is not only in the interests of the two peoples but also conducive to peace and stability in the world. The two sides are determined, on the principle of equality and mutual benefit, to strengthen their ties in the economic, cultural, educational, scientific, technological and other fields and make strong, joint efforts for the continued development of relations between the governments and peoples of the United States and China.

9. In order to bring about the healthy development of United States-China relations, maintain world peace and oppose aggression and expansion, the two governments reaffirm the principles agreed on by the two sides in the Shanghai Communiqué and the Joint Communiqué on

the Establishment of Diplomatic Relations. The two sides will maintain contact and hold appropriate consultations on bilateral and international issues of common interest.

EXCERPTS FROM THE JOINT U.S.-CHINA STATEMENT
(OCTOBER 29, 1997)[7]

At the invitation of President William J. Clinton of the United States of America, President Jiang Zemin of the People's Republic of China is paying a state visit to the United States from October 26 to November 3, 1997. This is the first state visit by the President of China to the United States in twelve years…

The two Presidents had an in-depth and productive exchange of views on the international situation, U.S.-China relations and the important opportunities and challenges facing the two countries. They agree that a sound and stable relationship between the United States and China serves the fundamental interests of both the American and Chinese peoples and is important to fulfilling their common responsibility to work for peace and prosperity in the 21st century.

They agree that while the United States and China have areas of both agreement and disagreement, they have a significant common interest and a firm common will to seize opportunities and meet challenges cooperatively, with candor and a determination to achieve concrete progress…

The two Presidents are determined to build toward a constructive strategic partnership between the United States and China through increasing cooperation to meet international challenges and promote peace and development in the world. To achieve this goal, they agree to approach U.S.-China relations from a long-term perspective on the basis of the principles of the three U.S.-China joint communiqués.

China stresses that the Taiwan question is the most important and sensitive central question in China-U.S. relations, and that the proper handling of this question in strict compliance with the principles set forth in the three China-U.S. joint communiqués holds the key to sound and stable growth of China-U.S. relations. The United States reiterates that it adheres to its "one China" policy and the principles set forth in the three U.S.-China joint communiqués…

---

[7] Source: http://www.usconsulate.org.hk/uscn/jiang97/1029f.htm.

About the Author

Alan D. Romberg is a Senior Associate and Director of the East Asia Program at the Henry L. Stimson Center. Prior to joining the staff in September 2000, he spent many years working on U.S. policy issues in East Asia, both in government and in the think-tank community. During the Clinton Administration, Mr. Romberg served as Principal Deputy Director of the State Department's Policy Planning Staff (1994-98), Senior Adviser and Director of the Washington Office of the U.S. Permanent Representative to the United Nations (1998-99) and Special Assistant to the Secretary of the Navy (1999-2000). Earlier, he was Director of Research and Studies at the United States Institute of Peace in 1994, following almost ten years as C.V. Starr Senior Fellow for Asian Studies at the Council on Foreign Relations (1985-1994). Mr. Romberg was a Foreign Service Officer from 1964 to 1985, serving in various capacities dealing with East Asia, including as Director of the State Department's Office of Japanese Affairs and as Staff Member responsible for China at the National Security Council. He was Principal Deputy Assistant Secretary of State and Deputy Spokesman of the Department from 1981-1985.

Mr. Romberg has written extensively on U.S. policy, focusing in particular on U.S. relations with the People's Republic of China, Taiwan, Korea and Japan. Among his most recent works, *China and Missile Defense: Managing U.S.-PRC Strategic Relations* was published by the Henry L. Stimson Center in February 2003.